Arthur Bowen Richards Myers

Life with the Hamran Arabs

Arthur Bowen Richards Myers

Life with the Hamran Arabs

ISBN/EAN: 9783744752343

Printed in Europe, USA, Canada, Australia, Japan

Cover: Foto ©ninafisch / pixelio.de

More available books at **www.hansebooks.com**

THE HAMRAN ARABS

LIFE WITH THE HAMRAN ARABS

AN ACCOUNT OF

A SPORTING TOUR OF SOME
OFFICERS OF THE GUARDS IN THE SOUDAN
DURING THE WINTER OF 1874-5

BY

ARTHUR B. R. MYERS

SURGEON, COLDSTREAM GUARDS

WITH PHOTOGRAPHS

LONDON
SMITH, ELDER, & CO., 15 WATERLOO PLACE
1876

[All rights reserved]

TO

MAJOR-GENERAL HIS SERENE HIGHNESS

PRINCE EDWARD OF SAXE WEIMAR, C.B.

THIS VOLUME IS

(BY PERMISSION)

𝔇𝔢𝔡𝔦𝔠𝔞𝔱𝔢𝔡

IN REMEMBRANCE OF HIS PAST KINDNESS

TO THE AUTHOR

PREFACE.

AT THE REQUEST of many of our friends, I have consented to publish the following account of our sporting tour in the Soudan, during the winter of 1874-75. But little alteration has been made in the daily entries of my journal, as I think that those who take a personal interest in our welfare will feel more in accord with us as they follow us through our novel experiences, our little trials and difficulties, and, finally, through that one great calamity which cast so dark a shadow over our joys, if I retain it in the simple form in which it was originally written; and to those who knew him whose bright life was at last sacrificed to his love for sport, I feel every confidence that at least a portion of these pages will produce more than a passing interest.

To the general public I should apologise for adding

one more to the ever-increasing list of similar publications, when it can but take a low rank amongst them.

In conclusion, I would ask all my readers, as they will have ample scope for severe criticism, to bear in mind that the period to which my diary refers is very short; that, owing to the necessarily great sameness in the daily routine of our lives, little matters were apt to attract undue notice; and that, as we went out purely for the purpose of sport, this is the subject to which the following pages have been chiefly devoted.

CONTENTS.

CHAPTER I.

Arrival at Cairo—Reception by the Khedive—Our Staff—The first disappointment—Final arrangements at Suez—Great addition to our party—Visit to the photographer—How we fared on Christmas-day—Among the coral reefs—A patent hammock—M. Marcopoli—Arrival at Souakim—First Sunday on land—An Arab's genuine dollar—We settle down for the night—Enemies of the night—Departure of Gondokoro party—A valuable present . . . . PAGE 1

CHAPTER II.

The desert journey is begun—Hunger *versus* religion—Coke's camel shows off his paces—Important result—The Arabs are our masters—One practical lesson—Hadendowa Arabs' special pride—Their costume and armour—The right man in the right place—A dying camel—Model kitchen range—Ariel and Gazelle—Our first desert visitor—Arab home-life—A practical dairyman—Water filtration—Religious scruples are satisfied—A desert sunset—Even camel riding has its charms—Sport more varied—Whirlwinds and mirage—A narrative from 'Baker'—Loss of a valuable companion—Demonstrative joy—Arrival outside the walls of Kassala 18

CHAPTER III.

Munsinger Pasha—One of the family?—Our reception by the Governor—Daily details of desert journeys—Kassala—Visit to 'a happy family'—Our house—Nights at Kassala—Examination of stores—We entertain Munsinger Pasha—He tells us about his people—Government of the

Soudan—Vaccination—Capable development of country—The river Gash—Albert in his element—We ride round the Town—A new cotton manufactory—Very mixed society—On abolition of slavery—Munsinger's prophecy—We leave Kassala—Parting words of advice . PAGE 40

CHAPTER IV.

The Kassala mountain—Asclepias—Our relations 'at home'—Albert and Bob see a cobra—A domestic disturbance—Villainous thorns—Arrival at the Hamran village—Hospitable reception—Novel telescope—We bathe in the Settite—Sheik Aghill—A good practical lesson—Choosing horses and engaging our hunters—A very intelligent Sheik—His neighbours—A modest request 58

CHAPTER V.

Gwayha—Departure from—Sheik Aghill learns our names—Arab rifles—Life of the Hamran sword-hunter—'Baker's' pictures—Our four hunters—Essafi is appointed the chief—We see elephant tracks—Hippopotami—Disposition of hunters—Heartless proceeding—Only stunned—Vivian among the elephants—Successful result—An unexpected moonlight meeting—Essafi's excitement—Waiting for a shot—Tracking a wounded elephant—The unlucky eight-bore—Native visitors—Preparation for a great feast—First shot at a lion—Acacias—Native scent 70

CHAPTER VI.

A native fruit tree—Vivian again to the front—The successful sportsman's return—Our tents—A place vacant at dinner—Surrounded by buffaloes—Additions to game list—A delicacy from the forest—Hamran entertainment—Eccentricities of Uncle Sam—Catching turtle—Successful hunt—The Maäriff and Méhédéhét—Special characteristics—Unwelcome guests 87

CHAPTER VII.

Our new encampment—Good sport with a buffalo—Study of tracks—A night alarm—Its practical lesson—Jali, the chief of the Hamran Sword-hunters—Ostriches—Their local value—The guinea fowl—Coke is unfortunate—Essafi on the track of rhinoceros—We disturb the morning nap—Silver's vulcanite pad—Backsheesh—Our protectors—The dying hippo—Disturbance over the spoil—Arab method of preserving meat—Great increase of temperature—Superstition about rhinoceros' horn—A sudden call to arms—Result of playing with edge-tools—Giraffes 'at home'—Voracious companions—An old friend . . . . PAGE 100

CHAPTER VIII.

Abdullah returns to his master—The African buffalo—Bringing home a lively companion—Lions abound here—The Kassala post—The smooth-bore does its duty—Unpleasant society—Uncle Sam's invitation is refused—Our hunters' superstitions—Ostriches' eggs—Sanitary measures—How to catch a rhinoceros—Plenty of game—Extraordinary flight of small birds—The dead hippo—Study of native habits—Essafi's delicate attention—Coke's first lion adventure—A narrow escape—Uncle Sam's idea of safety 121

CHAPTER IX.

Cumming is attacked by a maāriff—Is wounded in the thigh—Arabs try to entertain him—Arab method of wrestling—Emanuel to the front—Crocodiles' eggs—Cunning of the elephant—Great sympathy of our neighbours—Various birds—The Aboo Goumba—Marabou storks—Albert and Essafi have a row—Its cause and consequences—Albert receives a lecture—Respective merits of our staff—Uncle Sam gives proof of his courage—'Inshallah'—Soreness of horses' backs—The great separation is arranged—Hamet's idea of a handsome costume 138

CHAPTER X.

A sorrowful parting—Our immediate neighbours—Mek Nimmur—The Basé—How they live—The Arabs' fear of them—Essafi's idea of plenty of water—A giant tree—Home of the bees—How their honey is taken—Sentenced to death—The old soldier's donkey—My first lion—Two shots are heard—Essafi's alarm—The explanation—Native language—We enter Abyssinia—Our Arabs object to come with us—Essafi's encounter with a wounded maāriff—Music of the night—Waiting upon a lion—Albert and the Italian oculist—A lesson in surgery . . 156

CHAPTER XI.

A very unlucky day—An ostrich lost—Final smash of my pet gun—Jarrone decamps—Bad news for the Hamrans—Their opinion of Munsinger—An addition to our party—A popular dish—Fire-flies—Hadji Basheer's grief over the loss of Jarrone—Surrounded by enemies—A fatal shot—Essafi loses his charger—Sheik Aghill and the Abyssinian chiefs—Curious shot at a cobra—We lie in ambush—Vivian has exciting sport with a lion—Mohamed deserts his master—We set fire to the jungle—Watching and being watched—Albert's career as an oculist—Its unfortunate finale—Chasing a wounded giraffe . . PAGE 177

CHAPTER XII.

Return to the Settite—Face to face—Lion-shooting experience—Twice disappointed—Comfortable quarters—Essafi in disgrace—Drawbacks to perfect happiness—Ants and butterflies—A charitable conclusion—Hauling a hippo to land—Peaceful enjoyment—When animals drink—Diligence in prayer—Governor, two goose!—Is it Jarrone?—Unadulterated 'butter'—Guided by vultures—Attacked by the Basé—Hadji Basheer visits the Arab camp—His new pet—Troops of baboons—Arab teeth—How to make a koorbatch—Giraffe-hunting—Habits of rhinoceros—The well-known foot-print—Satisfactory hunt—Jali arrives—A crocodile bags my hyæna—Departure of Kassala post—Losing a 'right and left' at lions—A fine specimen—Arrival of birds of prey—Tracking a female slave—Her escape—The slave trade—A cheap offer 196

CHAPTER XIII.

The rhinoceros bird—A lucky shot—A doubtful friend—One week's sport—Night visit to an unknown camp—A 'peculiar' Arab left to die?—Return of the sick horse—We lie in wait for ostriches—Their nest—Experienced thieves—The *Séance* is disturbed—Midnight visitors—Water from a new skin—Thirst—Thoughts of the Basé—Sheik Aghill with us again—His little dodges—We entertain him—Arab vanity—A disappointing study—Success of a galvanic battery—Suggestive performance of Aghill—His liberal offer—His appeal—Essafi is the sufferer—Dying struggle of a lioness—Is it by sight or by scent?—Shot at last—A feast for a *Gourmet*—A malformed head—Cumming visits us—The heat becomes oppressive—Approach of the rains—A doubtful performance—Buffalo hunt at night—A deaf and dumb Arab—He kills a wounded buffalo—More about Albert's past life—He converses freely with the deaf and dumb Arab—Surprising news . . . . PAGE 221

CHAPTER XIV.

A great gathering—An unpleasant position—Report of the Massowah party—Arkwright attacked by Abyssinians—His narrow escape—Cumming is nursed by Emanuel—A trapped rhinoceros—No news from home!—Small-pox at Kassala—Mohamed and Ibrahim fight—Hadji Basheer is wounded—Coke is chased by a rhinoceros—We feel more respect for this animal—Coke recognises an old friend—Hippopotamus shooting—An unnecessary alarm—Our fishing experiments 247

CHAPTER XV.

Homeward bound—Arab cattle—The proof positive—Fine specimen of the Hamran Arab—Ibrahim's treat—Dethronement of Aghill—Great rejoicings—Sport on April 1—Watching by night for elephants—A comfortable bed—Harmless visitors—Bad news from Ranfurly—A fatiguing ride—A capital joke?—Ranfurly is ill with dysentery—Its cause—Cumming's first rhinoceros—Not dead yet!—Success of Arkwright and Ranfurly—Ranfurly is better—The wart hog—Pork *versus* Koran 261

CHAPTER XVI.

Ranfurly and Arkwright separate—Arab elephant trap—Essafi gives me an easy shot at a lion—Questionable night visitors—Ranfurly feels the heat greatly—An eventful day—A shot in the right place—The diary is neglected—I pay the penalty of exposure to the sun—Another grave case—An unpleasant occupation—Surprising result—Vivian kills a fine lion—Albert ignores the sun—Our sick list increases—Great sport of Arabs—Abyssinian customs—An Arab killed by a lion—Albert very ill—Great prostration of Ranfurly and myself—A favourite practice amongst Arabs—Rain at last—Highest temperature yet recorded . . . . PAGE 275

CHAPTER XVII.

Return to the Hamran village—Aghill no longer all-powerful—Ranfurly rapidly losing strength—Great thunderstorm—Our parting with the Hamrans—First halt on homeward desert journey—An anxious night with Albert—Is he dead?—Where are the others?—Once again together—Our troubles increase—Albert utterly collapses—Arrival at Kassala—Kind treatment of Greeks—Lorenzo joins us—All at Kassala—An important question—Albert's shock—Preparations for departure—Great sport of our friends—Mr. Cohen entertains us—Last night in Kassala 290

CHAPTER XVIII.

Departure from Kassala—Our faithful friends—Stranded in the desert—We send for relief—Killing time—On again minus some baggage—A sudden check—Ibrahim supplies the larder—An appeal for water—Our limited supply—Ranfurly's condition is more hopeful—A bath in the desert—Hadendowa Arabs again—A night hurricane—A grave complication—Vivian is injured—Ranfurly's state becomes critical—More Arabs desert—We seize camels—Our guide loses his way—Anxiety about Vivian—Painful desert travelling—Burning winds and blinding sandstorms—Vivian still absent . . . 305

CHAPTER XIX.

A grave question to decide—Our little stores—Ranfurly's great trials—We keep watch over our last Arab—Vivian is heard of—Are our troubles now to end?—Unpleasant misgivings as to food—A lucky shot—The last desert dinner—No water!—The desert journey is over—A meeting of friends—House of Ali Effendi—Vivian arrives—The last night on land—What comfort in that prayer!—Visit to the Governor—Souakim and its inhabitants—Young girls and women water-carriers—Liberality of our host—We go on board the 'Coffeet' 325

CHAPTER XX.

Postponement of departure—Ranfurly sleeps—His last moments—His burial—Alli Addeen Bey—A curious coincidence—Good-bye to Souakim—How to regain stolen property—Result of experiments—Blowing a gale—An unpleasant roll—The priest's dream—Arrival at Suez—Our expedition is at an end . . . . . PAGE 341

APPENDIX—Weather Report 351

LIST OF ILLUSTRATIONS.

MOUNTED RELICS . . . . *Frontispiece*

WATER BUCK (*Kobus ellipsyprymnus*) . . . *to face page* 97

RHINOCEROS (*R. Keitloa*) . . . . . . ,, 116

MALFORMED MAÃRIFF (*Hippotragus Bakerii*) . ,, 238

SOUDAN SOUVENIRS . . . . . . ,, 293

LIFE WITH THE HAMRAN ARABS.

CHAPTER I.

December 11.—At last our much-talked-of shooting expedition to the Nile tributaries of Abyssinia feels like a reality, for we have set foot in Cairo, and now whilst wandering about in the midst of the teeming population of an Eastern city, jostled by men of all nationalities in their characteristic costumes, it is no wonder that the fact is brought very plainly before our minds that our winter programme has really begun, and that we must set to work in earnest to complete our arrangements for it. Our most important stores, including rifles, guns, and ammunition, were despatched from England last October, and one dragoman has already been engaged; and as our steamer does not leave Suez for Souakim until the 22nd, we have ample time at our disposal. Our own party at present only numbers four—viz., Lord Coke, Sir W. Gordon Cumming, Captain Vivian and myself, and on the arrival by the next mail steamer of Lord Charles Ker it will be complete. Two other friends are waiting here for the departure of the Red Sea steamer on the 22nd—viz., the Earl of Ranfurly and Mr. Charles Arkwright, but they purpose landing at a port beyond Souakim, named Massowah, to hunt chiefly in the Bogos country.

Life in Cairo has been so often described and is now so well known, that it would be but repetition to record our daily doings here, so I shall for the present confine myself to such matters of detail as have immediate reference to our expedition.

Dec. 14.—We have accomplished one important business to-day in having been presented to the Khedive by the Consul-General, who explained to him in French the purport of our visit. With this the Khedive was evidently much amused, but he was greatly astonished at our undertaking so long a journey as to the Soudan merely for sport when there was so much to be obtained in our own country. He has promised us every assistance in his power, so far as granting us firmans to the governors of those districts under his rule through which we shall have to pass.

Afterwards I presented a letter of introduction to Nubar Pasha from Mr. W. H. Russell, and though he is now out of office he may prove of great service to us, for he has most kindly promised me letters both to his cousin Arekel Bey,[1] Governor of Massowah, and to the governors of Souakim and Kassala, who he states are his intimate friends.

Our Maltese dragoman, named Emanuel Vassalo, has been very busy all day making out lists of things that he thinks we shall require, but as he has had no experience of such an expedition as ours they will need very careful supervision. He at least enters very keenly into the spirit of the thing, and, judging by his testimonials, we ought to consider we have found that wonder of wonders, an honest dragoman.

He has brought with him from Malta a young friend whom, according to his wish, we have agreed to take to act as an assistant to him. His name is Achille Perotti, but by common consent he is to be known for the future as 'Bob.' He has a thoroughly good honest face, and, what is also of great importance, he looks a strong healthy fellow.

This certainly cannot be said of another young fellow, named Albert Bensilum, whom we have engaged to-day as a second dragoman in consequence of his excellent testimonials and of his having spent one winter in Kassala, and therefore knowing something of the country we are about to visit. Of very slight build and sallow complexion, he does not appear to be the man to

---

[1] Arekel Bey, with some Egyptian soldiers, has been recently killed in Abyssinia by native soldiers.

stand the rough life we expect to encounter, but he declares himself to be thoroughly strong and well, and his perfect knowledge of English and Arabic makes him a valuable addition to our party. He looks like an Italian, but we have not as yet found out his nationality. Still one more addition has been made to our number to-day by the engagement of a cook, recommended by Emanuel, named Mohamed. He at least is not likely to suffer from the heat in the Soudan, for he is a swarthy Nubian, and almost as black as a coal. Having picked up a few English words in Nile expeditions, he would fain have us believe he is master of the language, but this is a minor matter if his knowledge of his special art is a trifle less limited.

The additional stores we are collecting here are rapidly assuming a rather too imposing appearance, owing to sundry sacks of rice, biscuits, potatoes, camel saddles (which have been made for us), water barrels, and leather bottles; besides numerous articles of food in smaller quantities and sundry camp requisites, that Emanuel considers indispensable; among these are two huge traps, with massive chains, which, owing to the great strength required to set them, promise to be a source of far greater danger to ourselves than to any night visitor to our camp.

Dec. 18.—I arrived last evening at Alexandria, and to-day, after seeing our goods cleared at the Customs, returned to Cairo. Fortunately for us the Khedive telegraphed to the Custom House officials to pass them without loss of time, or we should certainly have lost our steamer.

Our first disappointment dates from to-day; for Ker, who arrived at Alexandria this morning, has received very urgent telegrams from England, which will necessitate his return by to-morrow's steamer.

Dec. 22.—All at Suez last night; but preceded by Coke by two days, as he went in advance with Mohamed to see to our interests there; for not only have we to find our own supplies on board the steamer, but also a cook and kitchen utensils. He experienced great difficulty in getting our ammunition put on board the steamer, and not without telegraphing to the Consul-General for his assistance, when the matter was promptly settled. Besides our own party and the two friends mentioned as going to Massowah, there are other passengers who will join our mess on board—viz., Captain Burnaby, Mr. J. Russell, and M. Marcopoli, who will land at Souakim, *en route* to Gondokoro, to join Colonel Gordon's expedition; and also the Earl of Mayo and Mr. Flower, who intend landing at Massowah on a distinctly separate shooting expedition to that of Ranfurly and Arkwright. We therefore number, with our ten servants, twenty-one in all, and we have entered into a contract with a general provision dealer here to supply us with provisions and live stock for the voyage, for 44*l*.

It is calculated that the steamer, named 'Dessouk,' will arrive at Souakim, a distance of about 750 miles, in four days, and Massowah, 200 miles farther, in less than six days from time of departure.

Mr. Levick, the English post-master here, has given us very useful assistance in the despatch of our goods and through him we learn that we should have been saved much trouble and expense if we had had them consigned to an agent at Suez instead of Alexandria, where the charge for landing and carriage to Suez amounted to nearly 60*l*.

Suez has not many attractions for a stranger, so we have occupied a good part of the morning in a visit to the barber, who carried out our orders to the letter according to our individual tastes, some allowing the razor to make a clean sweep of their faces, whilst others preferred the very closest application of the scissors to their heads. Thus so altered as to be hardly recognisable to one another, and more nearly resembling a party of convicts, we adjourned to the photographer, and if he does us justice it will prove a valuable and interesting group to send to our friends on our return. After luncheon we were taken on board the 'Dessouk' by a Government steam tug, as she was lying about three miles from Suez; and at 4 P.M. she got under weigh, a fresh breeze blowing at the time from the south-east, the sky overcast and the day therefore cool. Mohamed at Suez did his utmost to get into our good graces, and, fearing lest anything in his charge might be stolen, would guard our stores by night and by day. To-day Albert has come to the front in a critical moment during the transfer of our baggage to the 'Dessouk,' in consequence of Emanuel having drunk success to the expedition just once too often with his friends at Suez to be of any use at the time.

By universal consent we have decided that a light breakfast at 8 A.M., a more substantial one at 11.30 A.M., dinner at 5 P.M., and supper at 9 P.M., will be the best way to kill time on board ship compatible with health; and our cook, Mohamed, has been appointed *chef de cuisine*.

Dec. 25.—With the thermometer standing at 84° in the shade, it is difficult to realise that this is really Christmas-day, but we have not been without the means of bearing it in mind in a social sense, thanks to a present from Mr. Grace, our Alexandrian agent, of a plum-pudding of most perfect home manufacture, and to another from the Peninsular and Oriental Company of some ice by which we were able to conceal any slight deficiencies in the quality of Cairo champagne; nor have we lacked the musical element, for Mayo has a banjo, and is accompanied by an English engineer of the steamer on the fiddle. The wind, however, is continuing to blow very freshly from the south-east, and causing the steamer to roll greatly has somewhat damped our spirits. We are, nevertheless, a very jolly party, and the 'Dessouk' is very comfortably fitted up, especially one large cabin, which was originally intended for the ladies of the Hareem.

Dec. 26.—Yesterday the Captain, an old Egyptian, told us that we should arrive at Souakim this afternoon in all probability, but in consequence of his fearing during the night that he might run the steamer on the coral reefs which abound in this part of the Red Sea, he altered the course so much to the east that we have lost ground considerably, and cannot now arrive before to-morrow. Whilst the steamer was being brought back this morning to her proper course, we had the pleasant excitement of suddenly finding that we were running right on to a coral reef; only two small points of rock appeared above the surface, but stretching along for a great distance directly in front of us the unmistakable line of breakers denoted the impassable barrier, with on one side of it a sheet of perfectly smooth water.

The excitement of the crew and the rapid bearing round again to the east, showed us pretty plainly that this obstruction had neither been expected nor observed much too soon for the general safety. At 4 P.M. we anchored in a harbour named Sheik el Baghout, where we must remain till daybreak.

In the meantime we are not allowed to go on shore, owing to quarantine being in force for some parts of the coast. The nights are so warm that we have preferred sleeping on deck, and Ranfurly has had to set up a patent hammock, with which some of our party have also been supplied, and here it certainly answers admirably. Its chief points of fixture are two very strong iron pins made like a corkscrew, which are meant to be screwed into the earth, but now have been driven into the deck, though the Captain, curiously enough, did raise some slight objection to the proceeding. These screws are placed at a short distance beyond the hammock, to which they are fastened by ropes, and the hammock is thus raised about a foot from the ground and made taut by fixing a forked stick about midway beneath the connecting ropes at each end. They are certainly pretty, but I doubt their being good serviceable beds for travelling over varied soils, and they have one disadvantage in being very expensive, each, if I remember rightly, costing over 10*l*. M. Marcopoli has proved himself a most agreeable addition to our present circle, and it is he to whom Sir Samuel Baker refers so frequently in 'Ismalia' as Marco Polo. He is a Greek, and has so thoroughly mastered Arabic that he not only speaks the language, but also reads it with perfect facility.

Burnaby is the most industrious of our party, and may frequently be seen holding a conversation with one of the crew with the assistance of an Arabic vocabulary (Sacroug), and he is making rapid progress in their language. There is a party of French Roman Catholic missionaries, including a bishop, on board, bound for Massowah, and when not occupied with their meditations they take great interest in hearing all about our future respective plans, though they perhaps would agree with the Khedive that we are putting ourselves to a very great amount of trouble merely for sport.

M. Marcopoli has translated for our benefit our various firmans. One from the Khedive to the Governor of Souakim orders that every attention shall be paid to us, and that all our ammunition and stores shall be landed without examination. Another, to Munsinger Pasha, the chief representative of the Government in this portion of the Egyptian dominions, whose head-quarters are at Kassala, requests that all necessary protection shall be given us whilst in his district, and that our wants shall be supplied so far as possible.

Dec. 27.—We arrived this morning in the harbour of Souakim, and anchored about a quarter of a mile from the town. At this distance it has a somewhat imposing appearance, as the chief buildings, with a few minarets, are collected together on a small island only separated from the rest of the town by a narrow strip of water, and slightly elevated above the mainland, which extends for miles as a low flat plain, bounded in the distance by ranges of mountains that have been partially obscured from our view by a slight mist.

After seemingly endless confusion and excitement amongst the black-skinned local boatmen, we succeeded at last in getting our apparently enormous stores transferred to their cranky boats, and then, under the guidance of M. Marcopoli, we landed on the island and went to the house of the governor, and in his absence were received by his representatives, to whom we presented our firmans. He at once, after promising us every assistance in his power, proceeded to show us a piece of ground on the mainland for the storage of our goods until the necessary complement of camels could be obtained, and he gave us every hope of being able to start to-morrow, or next day at latest. The chosen ground is a small square space close to the landing stage, bounded on three sides by piles of iron tubing, marked with the name of an English firm, for telegraph wires, and on the far side by a mosque, which separates us from the ground allotted to the Gondokoro party. Their number has been increased, with their consent, by the addition of two Greek captains, who are on their way to the White Nile to take charge, for the first time, of some steamers running between Khartoum and Gondokoro, and for a payment of 20*l.* per month. M. Marcopoli tells us that two Englishmen originally accepted the contract, and came as far as Suez, believing they were to command steamers running between Souakim and Berber, but upon hearing that this was merely a desert, and that they would have to find their way to Khartoum before their work commenced, they refused to go any farther, and consequently these two Greeks were engaged at a moment's notice to replace them.

One would imagine that this was a questionable experiment, and judging by what Sir Samuel Baker says in 'Ismalia' of the climate in that part of the White Nile, it seems likely that these new arrivals will not require 20*l.* per month wages for long.

Ranfurly and Arkwright have landed on an island near the town to try to get some wildfowl, but we have had our hands much too full of work to attempt any sport to-day. Having collected our baggage, we set to work in good earnest to sort it, to open the huge cases merely made for the sea voyage, and to decide what should be left behind in consequence of the loss of one-third of our number by the return to England of Ker and his servant, whilst Mohamed and his staff were well occupied in preparing dinner. Just before sunset a bathing party to a small island close by was formed, and thus, with the sudden darkness, our labours terminated for the day. Whilst at dinner the evening call to prayers from the mosque at our side brought, perhaps for the first time, to the recollection of most of us that the necessarily busy day we had just ended was really Sunday. After dinner, our friends from the opposite side of the mosque paid us a visit, and Marcopoli, ever ready to give us useful information, explained to us how to know the only Maria Theresa dollar which the Arabs of this country will accept.

In consequence of some alleged forgeries perpetrated upon them, these dollars, before being accepted, are always examined very closely, and on the crown must be counted seven stars, though they are only just visible to the naked eye, and also nine, equally small, on a brooch over the right shoulder. If in either case more or less stars are found, the dollar will not be taken, so in the payment of natives there appears to be a prospect of an expenditure of much time and patience. There is also another point about which they are very particular— viz., to have their money, like Scotch or Irish 1*l.* bank-notes, decidedly dirty. No gold coin will pass here, and only two silver ones, a piastre of an old Egyptian currency of the same value, but three times the size of the modern coin, and very much thinner, and the Maria Theresa dollar. These dollars are a decided nuisance owing to their great weight and bulk, but divided into bags of 500 we have managed to stow them away in our tin boxes.

Sunday, like other days, must come to an end, and so has our first in this region; and now our beds are arranged side by side on the open ground and surrounded by our baggage with a guard of three soldiers.

Fixing the hammocks by candle-light proved by no means an easy matter, but after numerous failures it was accomplished, and we settled down for the night.

Dec. 28.—If we had good cause to remember our first day on land, the night was not likely to be soonest forgotten.

Hardly had the last good-night been said, when a sudden crack is heard, and, looking up, we find one patent hammock has collapsed, and the victim of misplaced confidence stretched on the ground. A little later, 'crack' again, and down has come another; these occasional interruptions to a night's rest, though producing shouts of laughter at the discomfiture of the occupant, become, after sundry repetitions, somewhat monotonous; so one after another the hammocks are discarded, and an opinion generally expressed that my simple folding-up camp bedstead, with cork mattress, has its advantages. For a few moments quietude is restored, and then is heard close to us that most charming of musical effects, a solo on a drum, probably a military tattoo, which draws from Coke the very apt observation that the practice here is identical with that of St. James's Palace Guard with regard to this high-class music. This tormentor of our peace having at last withdrawn, we again close our eyes, trusting that they may soon remain so of their own accord; but vain was the hope, for two cats appear on the scene, and with their hideous cries, enough almost to awake the dead, scamper in and out amongst the iron piles until driven away by the shouts of Emanuel, who, with the soldiers, is keeping watch over our stores. Now surely there will be a little peace we think. Bah! donkeys bray in chorus; children screech; fish, that from the splashing noise they make one would imagine must be the size of sharks, playfully amuse themselves by trying how high they can leap out of the water; and the short intervals are well filled up by the most musical of crickets, if judged by their power of producing sound.

Yet another disturber of the would-be sleeper's rest arrives unexpectedly, and a no less important one than the moon, which shines in our faces with an intensity that can only be fully appreciated in the East—and who could be expected to sleep! Some of our party, however, are above being affected by such, to them, trifles, as one by one they pass into that state in which sound and light remain unnoticed, and when nasal music on their own account proves that their minds are for the time at rest. But there is one left to observe the night give place to the day, and to have full warning of it by the crowing of innumerable cocks around him, and such is his unpleasant experience of a first night in Upper

Nubia. A general stir is made about 6 A.M.; coffee, and a bathe in the sea, sharks or no sharks; breakfast, and then to work again in good earnest.

The Gondokoro division, having obtained their camels (nineteen), started on their desert journey to Berber at 1 P.M. Each one had purchased here a native bedstead, or 'angarep,' for one and a half dollars, and though cumbrous they are not heavy, and camels carry them very well merely placed on top of their loads. They simply consist of a framework of wood, filled in with crossed strips of goat-skin, and supported on four short legs rudely made and badly fitted. We have had a sale to-day, and it was fortunate for our friends, both on shore and on board, that our stores were in excess of our present wants, for we were able to add some important items to their under-estimated supplies. Already we have found our pocket-filters very valuable, for with only two suspended in a water-skin since our arrival they have kept up a sufficient supply into a bucket beneath them to satisfy the almost constant demands of our visitors as well as ourselves, and we feel some pride in having been congratulated by such experienced travellers as the Gondokoro division upon the completeness of our arrangements. Our various parties have now said good-bye to one another, and with sincere regret, for one could not help feeling at the time that in all human probability some of us will never meet again.

Our camel-men, headed by their chief, came this afternoon, and having arranged our baggage so as to calculate the number of camels that would be required, we have agreed in the presence of the Governor to hire thirty-two at four and a quarter dollars per head for the entire journey to Kassala, and to pay for them in advance, this being the invariable custom at Souakim, though not elsewhere. The quarter-dollar is the claim of the chief of the camel-men. Before leaving us, the Governor made a special request for some *good* medicine, and though it was slightly indefinite, our stores were equal to the occasion of finding him some that will give him every reason to remember us whatever his complaint may be. Messrs. Savory and Moore have supplied us with a specially made medicine-chest, which contains, both in quantity and variety, all that we can well require to meet every emergency. We have felt the heat to-day decidedly oppressive, reaching 90° Fah. in the shade, as our allotted ground in which we have worked so busily is very much shut in from any light breeze; and, in order to ensure a better night's rest, two of us have agreed to sleep in the Governor's house on the island.

CHAPTER II.

Dec. 29.—It certainly was a great luxury passing the night on a comfortable couch in a darkened room, excepting the proof afforded to us by two Turks, if they may be taken as types of the race, that the art of snoring is thoroughly understood by them. At last we have commenced the desert journey, and have halted for the night about eight miles from Souakim on a vast sandy plain, freely studded with stunted mimosas, now merely a mass of dry thorny branches, with here and there the skeleton of a camel. As we arrived here our hearts were gladdened with the sight of two or three hundred gazelles that at once called forth the rifles, and having succeeded in bagging four, which were considered enough for the larder, we returned home. There was great excitement at the time amongst our camel-men at the prospect of a feast on raw gazelle, which with them is considered a luxury. But unfortunately we had not remembered their religious scruples about eating flesh killed by the heathen, and did not let them give the *coup de grace* the consequence of which was that some of their party (numbering eleven) objected at first to eat it. Hunger, however, must be a desperate tempter, especially when tickled by the sight of others gorging, and therefore it was not surprising that the religious scruples should soon be forgotten, and all found squatting round a mangled corpse and thoroughly enjoying the bloody feast.

The two tents we have pitched were supplied by Messrs. Edgington, of London Bridge, and chosen by Coke, and they seem particularly well adapted for our work. Supported on a central pole having four arms, which when in position project at right angles at some distance from its summit, each tent is made to cover a twelve-foot square, and only requires a few pegs to be driven in to keep two sides fixed, whilst the other two can be left open to allow of a free current of air.

Dec. 30.—Though all were up by 6 A.M., it was 9 A.M. before we could get our lazy camel-men to complete their work of lading. The camel-saddles made for us at Cairo are very imposing-looking, and even comfortable, considering the creatures we have to ride; for we have been obliged to hire for personal use the ordinary baggage camel, which differs as much from the better class camel or dromedary as a carthorse does from a racehorse, though it is not, as many people think, a distinct species. Coke has had an unpleasant experience to-day of their rough action, for his camel, taking fright at a white umbrella, bolted off. Away it galloped at an astonishing pace, and though its rider showed very considerable daylight he managed to keep on its back until in his efforts to turn the brute's head round, the cord acting as bridle suddenly snapped, and he was at once landed on his back on *terra firma*, with most fortunately no more serious injury than a deep cut of one thumb. The camel continued its mad career across the plain until almost out of sight, when it turned round and ultimately allowed itself to be caught. In the meantime all the things slung on to the saddle had been jerked off, but were afterwards found uninjured. Amongst them was an eight-bore smooth-bore of mine, made by Holland, upon which I had set my heart to astonish an elephant or any other big game that might cross my path; but it was evidently made on an evil day, for very soon after it had this narrow escape from being broken or lost, and whilst we were sitting down at luncheon, it was taken off the saddle by our very willing but much too officious young dragoman Albert and placed against a tree, and then, forgetting it was there, he backed a camel on to it, and broke the stock in half. So ends, I fear, all my fond hopes of testing its powers, though Vivian intends trying to mend it. With charges of powder varying from 6 to 8 drachms, and with hardened spherical ball, its penetration, tested at the Silvertown ranges up to forty yards, was immense; and to prevent the recoil of so large a charge of powder, Messrs. Silver and Co. had fixed to the stock one of their patent vulcanite pads, which I was glad to find answered its purpose very well there. Something approaching to a row has been going on between our dragomans and Arabs, as the latter object to starting in the morning before they have said their prayers at sunrise; but they have at last submitted to this arrangement, and we may therefore escape having to crawl along under a broiling sun during the heat of the day simply for their benefit.

Dec. 31.—Our early programme has been carried out, but the Arabs have scored one against us, for after a light repast of biscuit, and that most useful of camp supplies, cocoa milk, and leaving most of our servants behind to complete the packing, we made a start with the understanding that we should arrive at water about 9 A.M., when a temporary halt would have to be made to water the camels. It certainly was a great comfort to us to be able to arrive before the great heat of the day in a valley between two desert mountain ranges, and to lie down quietly under their shade to wait the arrival of our party. Here we found small holes in the sand close to the rock, into which welled up a very pleasant-tasting soft and clear water; and though we could afford to look upon it with suspicion, having our water-bottles filled with cold tea, our Arab guide and camels had good cause not to be so particular. Hour after hour passed without any sign of our party approaching, and at last we became a little anxious lest, as seemed probable, they had taken a different route; but in the course of the afternoon our minds were relieved by seeing our men driving the camels towards us, freed from their loads; and then we learnt that we had been brought two hours' ride away from our proper route unnecessarily, and that we must return. It was evening before we arrived at our camp and almost famished, but we had gained one practical lesson—viz., never to leave our baggage camels behind us in future. This has consequently been almost a lost day, for we are not above twelve miles distant from our last camp, calculating by the usual $2\frac{1}{2}$-mile rate per hour of the baggage camel.

January 1, 1875.—The commencement of the new year finds us still wending our way slowly along the dreary sandy desert, with nothing for the eye to rest upon beyond scattered mimosas, tufts of dry grass, and now and again a gazelle; and though we do not find the long swinging motion of the camel very fatiguing, it certainly is painfully monotonous, and would be very conducive to sleep were it not for our fear of tumbling off our perch.

Of course we are glad to pick up any information of the country through which we are passing from our Arab companions, and on coming to two little mounds of stone, we were informed that two Mussulmans were buried there, and that God had killed them. On another occasion, when a gazelle was shot dead, one of them exclaimed that if a man were to die that way he would be sure to go to heaven. These men belong to the Hadendowa Arabs, who occupy a large tract of country between the coast and Kassala. They are fine-looking well set-up fellows of good stature, with well-formed heads and regular features, though their skins are nearly black. Their hair is their great pride, and it certainly is a marvel of artistic skill. A parting being made round the head on a line with the eyes, and the temples being like the face shaven, the crown of the head is covered with a thick mass of short curly black hair, that looks exactly like a mop. Below the parting, the hair is allowed to grow to considerable length, and is generally kept twisted into innumerable plaits; and even then, owing to its thickness, forms a great mass; but when undone on certain occasions it looks like a huge chignon, and must certainly prove an immense protection against the direct heat of the sun on their necks. Though so thick, their hair is of such fine quality that it feels almost like silk. In this mass is always kept their representative of brush and comb, which consists of a thin long piece of hard wood or bone, and it is frequently in use as a disturber of the peace of the very numerous occupants that are supposed to dwell in Arab heads.

Round their neck is fastened a string of brown beads, and round the right arm above the elbow little wooden or leathern boxes containing portions of the Koran, and worn as charms to keep off sickness. A sheet, white or of various shades of brown, according to dirtiness, wound several times round the loins and having one end occasionally thrown over a shoulder, and a pair of sandals, complete their costume. Each carries a long spear and curved stick, and some also a shield of rhinoceros or other hide. Altogether their appearance is most picturesque.

Jan. 2.—From Souakim to Kassala there are two main routes well defined by the great camel traffic. Our path so far has continued close to the telegraph, from which even the desert of Africa cannot now escape; and to-day we have been passing through a wide valley, flanked on either side by a fine range of rugged mountains, and have arrived at water which, though not fit for us to drink, will do for cooking as well as for the camels.

We took good care to be well supplied with means for carrying water, and have padlocks on our four large barrels to prevent the Arabs robbing us of this precious store, when our pig-skins and leather bottles are emptied. We saw a great number of gazelle to-day, and killed six.

Jan. 3.—This morning we did not get off till after 8 A.M., though up as usual before 5 A.M. It is most trying to the temper to watch our men arranging and putting on their loads, and squabbling amongst one another as to whose camel shall have an addition of the veriest trifle. Emanuel is most industrious at this work, dragging off one man here and another there, speaking a word of encouragement to one, and giving a good slap on the back of another. Lazy hounds as they are, they never really lose their temper, and only laugh however much Emanuel may knock them about. Our bag of six gazelle produced a great effect upon their locks this morning, for they appeared as white as snow, so besmeared were they with the fat, or marrow, which is much preferred, and afterwards we had the pleasure of seeing it gradually melt and trickle down their backs.

In this kind of travelling the smallest novelty is refreshing, and therefore two or three dome palms near the dry bed of a mountain stream attracted much attention, but our great excitement to-day was passing three caravans of camels laden with gum, oil seeds, and skins from Abyssinia, the largest numbering over six hundred. These camels were very much bigger than our own, and some were almost black.

This being their twelfth day from Kassala, we hope to arrive there in ten days, as we travel at a little greater speed, or, I should rather say, not quite so slowly.

Jan. 4.—Last night, for the first time, we heard the wild cry of the hyæna mingling with that of the jackal, and this morning there were very ominous-looking clouds hanging over the mountains; but no rain fell, and later in the day the sun shone with its usual intensity. He has already played much havoc with our faces, and few of our friends would find it easy to recognise us now. We found to-day, lying close to our path, a poor dying camel, and eighteen splendid vultures keeping watch over it; and some of them, a little hasty, had already begun to pluck its eyes out. Cumming saved it a little misery by putting a bullet into its head. Afterwards we came to a thick shrubbery, and then crossed the dry bed of a river, bordered on each side by lovely green bushes; and though we could give them no name, it was indeed a treat to find something so refreshing for the eyes to rest upon for a short time. We have halted this evening within half an hour's reach of water, found near the mountains, and we are told that lions abound there. Just before dinner a herd of cattle passed our camp, and in exchange for a few biscuits we procured a jug of delicious milk, with which we mixed a portion of our day's allowance of soda-water. Claret and soda-water are luxuries that we have only brought for the desert journey and the Red Sea; and, after our arrival at Kassala, whisky will be the stimulant of daily consumption, and there is no fear of the supply running short. Considering all things, we live uncommonly well, and have three good meals per diem, luncheon being the feeblest one, as we only take out in a saddle-bag such things as slices of cold gazelle, potted or Australian meats, sardines, figs, raisins, and Lehman's captain biscuits; and it certainly is a movable feast; for it entirely depends upon finding near our path a mimosa offering the pretence at least of some shade. Mohamed's kitchen range consists of a narrow iron trough on short legs, and having placed in this a few sticks and set them alight, he is soon able to produce a dinner that many an English cook might well not be ashamed of.

Jan. 5.—Our departure this morning was greatly delayed in consequence of the camels having strayed to some distance amongst the mountains during the night in search of water. Our surprise is that they are ever collected, for directly we halt in the evening they are turned loose and are not sought for until the morning.

We have found the heat to-day particularly trying, owing to the total absence of cloud and to the great reflection of heat from the rocky ground we have passed over. Every day we see some antelope, but we do not now waste our cartridges upon them when not wanted for the larder. At present we have only shot two varieties, one the common gazelle, and the other the ariel, which it much resembles in colour and horns, though twice as large in both respects, and showing more white behind. Near Souakim we found the ariel so tame that we had no difficulty in getting within easy range of them, but now both begin to require careful stalking from bush to bush to get even within 150 or 200 yards of them. We keep their horns if they are good, with merely the front of the skull, and this is cleansed by being put daily into the sand when we halt. Our Arabs value the skins of both very much, as they are very soft though strong, and therefore make capital water-skins.

The flesh of the ariel is better for food than that of the gazelle, but even of this one must after a time get tired, so it was with no small pleasure that to-day, for the first time, eight sand-grouse were bagged for the pot.

At 3 P.M. we arrived at a few huts, made of the leaves of the dome palm, which are stated to be exactly half-way between Souakim and Kassala. No natives were to be seen here, not even a woman or child, but we found an excellent well, and having replenished our water supply we resumed our journey. The camel-men are tending daily to become more troublesome, and at 4 P.M., having stopped their camels, declared they would go no farther, and that we might shoot them if we liked. This is, however, not our intended means of punishing them, for we think that cutting off their supply of gazelle, which they dearly love, and having one or more flogged at Kassala, will probably prove quite as much to their taste.

Jan. 6.—Last night the minimum temperature was

only 55°, and as 65° has been the lowest on any previous night, it really felt quite cold. Coke, however, ignores a tent and sleeps in his hammock, *when* the screws will hold, on the open ground about twenty yards from our tent, and not even the kind suggestion of Vivian that he might be eaten by a lion will make him alter his present programme for the night. A jackal did visit our camp last night, and we found his track on a waterproof sheet directly outside the tent. Vultures are becoming more numerous, and it is wonderful to see how rapidly they come into view, as they soar about in the sky directly we shoot a gazelle. We left one to-day, only for a few minutes, in the camel track for our followers to pick up, but before their arrival a huge vulture had cleared out its interior through the bullet wound; it was, however, partly disappointed in its feast, for such a delicate morsel as the liver raw was not to be lost in that way by our friends. One of them is ill to-day, and rumour says from eating too much gazelle; but a hollow cough heard at night in the distance is suggestive of something less easily remedied. We have halted again near a very good well.

Jan. 8.—Very late starting this morning, owing to the camels having strayed a long way off. Emanuel now goes out daily in search of them, for the Arabs are getting lazier than ever, and are very loth to rise from their morning repast, consisting of a bowl of dhurra made into a mash with gazelle and some greasy material, called by Mohamed butter, and far prefer sucking off their fingers at their leisure any of the remaining fat.

We really are quite helpless as regards both camels and camel-drivers, for if either want to lie down or go on they simply do so, whatever we may wish. We passed to-day a piece of ground surrounded by dome palms, where we found considerable life and animation. In the centre was a well about 40 feet deep, into which young Arabs were busily throwing leather buckets, and after hauling them up when full, emptying them into circular mud basins, placed round the well for the cattle to drink from. Other Arabs were counting their goats, some were washing themselves, whilst the younger portion of the community were beating off the rind of the dome nut (with which the palms are now laden) preparatory to its being baked for food. These palms with their characteristic bifurcating branches are very fine here, and as there is a considerable amount of vegetation in this oasis we saw numerous kinds of small birds.

These for the present we have left undisturbed, but before returning we hope to collect some specimens, as well as beetles and other moving things. Gazelles are becoming very scarce, and although we sadly wanted one to-day for the table it was not forthcoming, and made one feel inclined to say, on seeing one scamper off in the distance—

> I never loved a dear gazelle
> But it were *sure* to die.

Slightly altered from the original.

Jan. 9.—There was heavy dew last night for the first time, and the thermometer went down to 44°, and it consequently felt extremely cold towards morning. As neither the offer of money nor of biscuits would induce the natives to give us any milk, our dragoman Albert adopted the next best means to obtain some by catching a goat and milking it, remarking that if a native objected he would flog him, this being the custom of the country. No objection, however, was raised by the owner, who looked on with perfect indifference, and we had to thank our new dairyman for a refreshing draught of milk. Our vulcanite water-bottles covered with flannel answer admirably, for, filled before our daily departure with cold tea (made the previous night), they keep it cold almost throughout the day, and this, besides quenching the thirst better than water, has the additional advantage of ensuring the water being boiled, a point of no small importance at the present time, for though we are assured that the water taken from the wells we pass is excellent, its taste and colour rather suggest the reverse, and what we had for our baths to-day was nearly black with mud. We are very particular also about filtration, and directly we arrive in camp, even before pitching the tent, we have a post with hooks driven into the ground, and a water-bucket with filters suspended from it, and by this means we have an ample supply by dinner time. Camel-riding now over the burning plain, when not the smallest clouds come to our relief, is more trying than at first, and the sun is playing considerable havoc with the skin of our faces; but we can at least relieve our eyes from the intense glare by smoked glass spectacles with gauze frames, and by white umbrellas. There was great excitement this afternoon amongst our camel-men when a wounded gazelle gave them the chance of running forward and despatching it by hacking at the throat in a horrible manner with their curved knives until they had nearly severed the head from the body. This was the first opportunity they had been given to satisfy their religious scruples, for our expanding bullets generally destroy life at once, and their joy was proportionate; though it was afterwards somewhat marred by our laying claim to the liver.

Beautiful as the sunsets have been, that of tonight seemed somehow to far surpass the others in grandeur. We were crossing at the time a vast sandy plain surrounded save to the west by mountains, and with no sign of vegetation upon it but here and there a solitary stunted mimosa or a dry tuft of grass. Southwards in the direction of our route towered up before us range beyond range of innumerable peaks of mountains, some of them so perfectly pyramidal in form that they appeared to have been chiselled out. Eastwards was a nearer range upon which the setting sun threw such strange shadows that one moment from their depth it seemed as if these bare rocks were covered with forests; whilst at another moment, from their varied shades of colour, one could imagine that each mountain had its own special ore. Past them wended their slow way our long string of baggage-camels, followed by our riding-camels, the latter adding somewhat to this perfect Eastern scene by the bright red colour of their trappings; and then the sun went down and gave place to the glorious after-glow, when objects for a few moments became more distinct, as sometimes in the last flicker of his life does the intellect of the dying man clear up, and then, as in a moment—night.

It was very late when we encamped, for our men were afraid of halting near a mountain the supposed haunt of wild beasts; but we finally arrived at a village named Gadama, according to Albert, who says it consists of five cottages, four dogs, and some cows.

We are obliged to accept Albert as an authority, because he went this desert journey twice with merchandise four years ago.

Jan. 10.—Our progress to-day was soon cut short

by arriving at a well containing some really excellent water, and here the desire for a halt was unanimous, not only to fill our casks, but also our indiarubber baths, and to make the most of so great a treat. The guns also had a turn to-day, in consequence of the presence of numerous doves. These gave us a pleasant novelty for dinner, for gazelle-eating, like camel-riding, or even desert sunsets, can after a time become slightly monotonous.

Now that the back has become accustomed to camel-riding, one finds a certain charm in it; and, as hour after hour passes, the mind relapses into a half-dreamy state of reverie, in which the pleasures and sorrows of the past year flit rapidly before it, mingling with thoughts of what is in store for us during the next few months.

Jan. 11.—We have in vain tried to be on friendly terms with our respective camels, and have named them according to special characteristics. Coke declares his camel does everything in its power to annoy him. Only to-day it made a playful attempt to bolt again, but was fortunately checked in time to prevent a repetition of the previous catastrophe. At midday we arrived at one of the wells that are now comparatively numerous, and though hundreds of goats and cows were there, no milk would be given us. We gained a point in receiving permission to get some if we could, and immediately started in pursuit, and having succeeded in catching two goats, Albert acted as milkman again most successfully.

On these occasions a little wooden barrel, with a padlock, intended for carrying water for personal use, proves a valuable companion, for it is used now for carrying whisky, than which nothing is better to give a little tone to new milk to prevent its disagreeing with the weary traveller. The sport has been very varied to-day—gazelles, jackals, hares, sand-grouse, plover, and doves being amongst the killed and wounded; and also a tiny species of antelope, hardly bigger than a hare, and probably not so heavy, named 'Dik-dik,' which was the first we had seen, and was killed with shot by Vivian.

Since our departure whirlwinds of sand have been more or less seen every day, but to-day the wind has been more gusty, and the whirlwinds more numerous, and particularly grand, travelling along at great speed, and ascending to such a height that their points became lost in space, as if they were *en route* to make new worlds.

The mirage also was more than usually observable, and so distinct were the reflections of the distant rocks that it seemed almost incredible that they were not surrounded by water. Baker (*vide* 'Nile Tributaries of Abyssinia') graphically records an interesting story with regard to the deceptive character of this mirage, which had best be repeated in his own words:—

'Many years ago, when the Egyptian troops first conquered Nubia, a regiment was destroyed by thirst in crossing this desert. The men, being upon a limited allowance of water, suffered from extreme thirst, and deceived by the appearance of a mirage that exactly resembled a beautiful lake, they insisted on being taken to its banks by the Arab guide. It was in vain that the guide assured them that the lake was unreal, and he refused to waste the precious time by wandering from his course. Words led to blows, and he was killed by the soldiers, whose lives depended upon his guidance. The whole regiment turned from the track, and rushed towards the welcome waters. Thirsty and faint, over the burning sands they hurried; heavier and heavier their footsteps became—hotter and hotter their breath, as deeper they pushed into the desert—farther and farther from the lost track, where the pilot lay in his blood; and still the mocking spirits of the desert, the afreets of the mirage, led them on, and the lake glistening in the sunshine tempted them to bathe in its cool waters, close to their eyes but never at their lips. At length the delusion vanished—the fatal lake had turned to burning sand! Raging thirst and horrible despair! The pathless desert and the murdered guide! lost! lost! all lost! Not a man ever left the desert, but they were subsequently discovered, parched and withered corpses, by the Arabs sent upon the search.'

Jan. 12.—The only important event of to-day has been discarding Coke's camel, and reducing it to the ignominious position of a baggage carrier in consequence of its conduct having at last become unbearable.

Jan. 13.—An eventful day, and one that for me began very badly, for whilst shooting in a wood close to our camp before starting I lost my belt, containing my watch and other articles of value to me.

In vain I retraced my footsteps until the last moment I could spare before joining my party, nowhere could I find it; but on telling Emanuel of my loss, he despatched an Arab in search of it, and expressed the greatest confidence in his success. However, he rejoined us two hours later when at luncheon, having given up the search; and then an Arab, who had recently joined us, volunteered a good hunt, provided I returned with him, and that if he found it I would give him two dollars. The general opinion being in favour of this, I agreed, hopeless as I thought it; and having snatched up what remained of our luncheon in case of any emergency, and filled my water-bottle, I mounted my camel and started off at a trot. On arriving at our camping ground innumerable vultures were fighting over the remnants we had left, and gazelle playfully skipped about within easy shot as if they knew that I had other occupation in hand than their massacre.

It was very interesting to watch how keenly the Arab hunted for my footprints, and when found how carefully he followed them up, and my hopes of success rose proportionately; but after a time all traces were lost in the soft sand, and then after he had made sundry fresh starts I saw that, so far as he was concerned, all chance was over, for he would persist in wandering farther and farther away from the proper direction. At this time a burnt tree caught my eye that I remembered to have passed, and finding my track there, I followed it up until belt and all were in my possession. One long shout and my black friend was with me, and his delight at my success took so demonstrative a form that he caught me up in his arms, kissed my shoulders over and over again, and then, not satisfied, took off my helmet, kissed it all over, and finally began dancing around me. I really believe his delight was partly genuine, though it was without doubt much increased by my giving him the two dollars. Then, for the first time, I had an opportunity of trying the effects of rapid camel-riding, for the Arab, having mounted behind me, with thumps and shouts kept the poor beast at a very rapid trot for two hours, excepting an occasional halt necessitated by my feeling as if all the breath had been jolted out of my body; and then, much to my relief as well as surprise, we caught up with our caravan. Throughout yesterday we could see in front of us an isolated mountain, and directly beyond it we were told lay Kassala, but, like a 'Will-of-the-wisp,' it seemed as if we never could approach it. To-day again hour after hour passed in the same disappointing way, until the afternoon, when the few minarets of Kassala coming into view denoted the delightful fact that the chief part of our desert journey had really drawn to a close.

CHAPTER III.

AFTER finding a piece of moderately clean ground outside the town for our camp, we were escorted by Albert through a crowd of natives to the palace of the Governor of the Soudan country, and most fortunately found him at home. His name is Munsinger Pasha, and, though a Swiss by birth, he has made this country his home; and it was he who, as British Consul at Massowah, did such good service to the English army during the Abyssinian expedition. He speaks English very well, which is a great comfort, as we shall be able to explain our wants without the aid of an interpreter. He received us in his office, a bare-looking room with a raised cushioned seat at one end and a writing table to represent the furniture; and whilst he read our firmans we amused ourselves watching the movements of a little black boy about five years old, who played about the room quite regardless of us, as if he were thoroughly accustomed to official life; but his entire costume consisted only of a tarboosh and earrings, and as he remained apparently unheeded by the Governor, it occurred to us as probable that there might be the closest relationship between them. Munsinger Pasha at once gave orders for our goods to be removed into a house, and promised us every assistance and an unlimited number of men to transport them to our new home. We then complained to him of the laziness of our Arab followers, and evidently with good reason, for he said we ought to have completed the journey in eleven or twelve days, instead of sixteen; but he added that we were unwise in not accepting the offer of some soldiers made to us at Souakim, not so much for protection, as we had imagined, as to ensure the good conduct of these men. He says that we can get very strong camels here at short notice, and probably also horses, the latter, if of the ordinary kind, costing 4*l.* to 6*l.*; and he has promised to call upon us to-morrow, after having made all necessary arrangements.

The following table is a record of our daily progress across the desert, calculated at the usual rate of the baggage camel—viz., 2½ miles per hour, the total distance being thus represented as 296 miles. This, according to Munsinger Pasha, is 16 miles in excess of the generally accepted distance—viz., 280 miles.

Date.	Departure.	Arrival.	Distance (time of halts deducted).	Total.
	A.M.	P.M.		
December 29, 1874	11	3.30	8½	8½
,, 30	9	3.30	16	24½
,, 31	8	2	15	39½
January 1, 1875	7.30	6	26	65½
,, 2	8.15	2.30	15	80½
,, 3	8.15	4.15	20	100½
,, 4	7.45	3.45	20	120½
,, 5	8.30	3.45	18	138½
,, 6	8.45	4.45	20	158½
,, 7	8.30	3.30	17½	176
,, 8	8.45	5	20¼	196¼
,, 9	8.15	6.45	26¼	222½
,, 10	8.45	2.45	15	237¾
,, 11	8.15	5.45	24¼	262
,, 12	9.15	4.15	17½	279½
,, 13	8.30	3.30	16½	296

The town of Kassala, though the capital of the Soudan country and the great military centre of this portion of the dominions of Egypt, can be described in a few words, for it almost entirely consists of low houses, made of bricks baked by the sun, or of dried mud for the richer community, and of dhurra-stalks or palm-leaves for the poorer, and is surrounded by a fortified wall made of sun-dried bricks, and outside this by a moat. After passing through the chief gate of entrance, which is guarded by soldiers, a wide street crowded with Arabs buying and selling at the minute stores, consisting chiefly of grain and calico fabrics of European manufacture, one soon arrives at an open space, round which are congregated the few buildings of any importance, such as the mosque, palace, and prison, as well as two or three shops kept by Greeks for the supply of goods to the few Europeans who reside in or visit this place; and here, under the shade of a clump of trees, two oxen may be seen perpetually walking round in a circle whilst turning a wheel with buckets attached to it, which brings up from a well the chief supply of water to the inhabitants. This water is excellent, and is obtained from the Gash, a river that flows from Abyssinia, and when near Kassala gets lost in the dry season beneath the sand, and thus at no great depth passes under the town.

Beyond the main thoroughfare numerous narrow by-ways are found winding about amongst the houses, so narrow that there is barely room for a camel to pass, and so dusty that one feels almost stifled in them.

Whilst our house was being put in order we paid a visit to the establishment of a gentleman of European celebrity, named Cohen, where may always be seen the best specimen of 'a happy family.' In the outer court were dromedaries, very fine black ostriches, and an eight-year-old elephant; passing into the inner court, we were introduced to four little elephants, about two years old, so tame that Mr. Cohen's child of the same age was allowed to play with them; various kinds of antelope were wandering about at large, but the pet of the family was evidently 'Sarah,' a young hyæna that allowed herself to be caught when wanted, and in the meantime amused herself in playfully chasing a gazelle amongst our seats, whilst the child found great pleasure in nursing a young leopard. We were shown here numerous other varieties of animals, from giraffes to monkeys, some of them having been only just brought in by the Arabs. Mr. Cohen supplies the various Zoological Societies of Europe with the animals found in this country. Our house, though far from being palatial, has ample accommodation, for there is room in the courtyard for our stores, and actually something resembling a staircase leading to a first-floor, which consists of an outer court and four rooms. The walls are made of mud baked in the sun, and therefore not very attractive in appearance; but as a protection from both the sun and the outer world it answers its purpose admirably, and there is no fear of our having a heavy bill for damages, as the furniture only consists of a few strips of matting and an angarep.

Jan. 14.—Of all noisy places at night Kassala would not be far from heading the list, for by no human ingenuity could it well be surpassed in this respect. Not a moment's quiet, for innumerable dogs keep up an incessant barking to keep off the hyænas, whose cry is continuously heard in the outskirts; drums are being beaten, sometimes for a wedding, at others for a death; women are screeching, and priests are calling the faithful to prayers, or the watchers of the night are shouting in response to one another; whilst our old friends, the cocks, more cruel than ever, begin their crowing soon after sunset.

We have been very busy to-day overhauling our stores, and deciding what are to be left here for the return journey across the desert, and also thoroughly cleaning our guns and rifles; for, notwithstanding all our care, the sand has got into them greatly. The *black* leather cases, in which some of them were packed, have much contracted by the heat, but beyond a slight trace of rust here and there on the barrels, from which Messrs. Rigby & Sons' were quite free, our various weapons did not suffer from their sea voyages. The post for Souakim having left to-day, we had but little time for correspondence. On Tuesday, December 2, 1874, the present Red Sea postal system was first brought into operation. The steamers that leave Suez every third Tuesday for Massowah call at Souakim on the return journey, the following Monday or Tuesday week, so we shall be able to calculate the time of departure from Souakim of the steamer by which we decide upon to return, provided the new system continues to hold good.

At 7 A.M. Munsinger Pasha called to see if we were comfortable, and told us that horses would be brought for our inspection in the course of the day, and that two of our camel-men had been sent to prison; and when we suggested that they should only be frightened, he promptly replied that the koorbatch (whip) would be more practical, and then changed the subject. These Hadendowa Arabs have the character of being very lazy and great thieves, so it is no use wasting much sympathy upon them. In the evening Munsinger Pasha dined with us, and we gave him all the delicacies available from our home supplies, as well as a tiny antelope (Dik-dik), which was roasted whole and stuffed with rice and raisins, and was as tender as a chicken. Iced champagne was also not forgotten to be ordered, but unfortunately the freezing machine, though it had proved a great success at Cairo in an experimental trial, refused to act in consequence of its rather rough treatment during the journey. However, we consoled ourselves with the thought that champagne, even without ice, was not to be obtained every day in Kassala.

He gave us much interesting information on various subjects connected with this country. Kassala, he says, has now a population of about 25,000 persons, excluding the villages in its neighbourhood. A large portion of it is very migratory, consisting of various tribes who stay only for a short time for barter. There are a great number of men of bad character here who are sent in banishment from Cairo, and they are allowed to be at large so long as they behave themselves properly. Crime, excepting theft, is not common here, and theft is scarcely regarded as a crime among them, on the plea that God or the Devil made them commit it. The prison has generally about sixty culprits in it, almost all under punishment for theft; a surprisingly small number, considering that this is the only prison for the whole of the country over which he rules, consisting of a population calculated at 2,000,000, and that every temptation to easy theft is given by the people, who leave their houses (many of them having neither doors nor windows) quite open all day in their absence.

'Supposing,' said Munsinger Pasha, 'this were your custom in England, what would be your list of thieves?' Capital punishment is very rarely carried out, and especially as, until the last few months, this has only been sanctioned by Mussulman law when the murderer confessed his crime. Now, however, this is altered, and a man suspected of murder is tried by a military tribunal, and, whether found guilty or not guilty, the final judgment rests with the Pasha. He, though from the absolute clearness of the evidence, in some cases, might be compelled to sign the death-warrant, is very much averse to doing so, preferring to punish the criminal with the utmost severity, short of depriving him of life.

When capital punishment is carried out, it is by hanging, not by beheading, according to the strict custom, as this is considered less likely to be attended with unnecessary torture.

In the open space in the centre of the town are fixed

two high poles with a cross-bar, to which men are strung up by the thumbs as a punishment for any great crime, and this exquisite torture is sometimes continued from fifteen to twenty minutes. We were therefore not surprised on hearing that this public spectacle acted as a good warning to would-be offenders. It is difficult to bring the laws of civilised nations to bear otherwise than slowly upon the very mixed and half-savage tribes collected here; but though Egypt has only acquired this territory since 1822, great improvements have been introduced, and there is something like order established. Statistics of life and death are quite impossible, for the people are very tenacious about inquiries into family life, fearing that it means the extortion of taxes. The death-rate of the army quartered in Kassala, numbering 1,800, averages sixty per annum, or 33·33 per 1,000, intermittent fever and dysentery being the chief causes of this high rate of mortality. As in Cairo, vaccination is adopted, though not with the same success, owing to the bad supply of vaccine; but the people have great faith in it, and, failing this protection, they adopt the next best expedient in being inoculated from a small-pox case. The laws of morality are not very strict, for young girls can lead immoral lives without losing caste amongst their sex.

The system of taxation has been much altered of

late years, and the priesthood and 'nobles' who were formerly exempted have now to pay their share.

These 'nobles' are found amongst all tribes, and they claim descent from a few men who lived three or four centuries ago, and they are recognised as such by their people. They have their laws of primogeniture, the eldest son inheriting his father's estate, and the youngest having the house of his mother. After the death of the father, the first-born son has to provide for the family, to support his brothers until they are old enough to be independent of him, and his sisters until they marry, when he has to find dowries for them. So their laws, if such be a fair example of the generality of them, have a good deal of common sense to recommend them for adoption otherwise than in Egypt.

Munsinger Pasha has a great idea that the country in the neighbourhood of the river Gash might be brought under cultivation, and he has now engineers surveying one portion, eighty miles by twenty in extent, with regard to its capability of being inundated. If, as he believes, this can be done, it will be covered in a short time with crops of cotton and indigo, both of which are found to thrive here, 2,000 acres having been already tested with them most successfully, and specimens sent only this autumn to Cairo. To-morrow he proposes to take us for a ride round the town, and to show us the prison.

Our original intention on leaving Kassala was to go one or two days' journey along the river Gash in search of elephants, but we have been deterred from doing so in consequence of the river being now quite dry. After the rains, the Gash flows for one hundred days, commencing slowly about the middle of July, but when it attains to its full force, at the rate of eight miles an hour. After this period it becomes perfectly dry, excepting some large pools; and as these also subside through the sand, elephants leave the neighbourhood for the more permanent tributaries of the Nile. We have therefore decided upon continuing our journey southwards to the country of the Hamran Arabs, and after halting at their chief village to look for horses, as it is stated that we can buy them better and cheaper there, to try what sport is to be had in the neighbourhood of a river named the Settite; and, failing there, to go still farther south to the Salaam river.

Vivian and Cumming have invested largely to-day in the personal ornaments and armaments of the natives, though at first with some difficulty, as they would not give them up until forced to do so by a soldier. When, however, it became generally known that they were paid for in genuine good silver dollars there was no lack of supplies, and a crowd soon collected, ready to sell everything they had upon them. The present is an excellent time to buy their silver trinkets, for next Monday is the Feast of Beiram, when all are expected to keep open house, and they will sell their heirlooms in order to have enough money to buy supplies for this festive occasion. These ornaments are of rude workmanship as a rule, and the bracelets, anklets, nose and ear-rings nearly all consist of a solid piece of silver, of various sizes, bent so as nearly to complete a circle, and having each end beaten out after some simple design; and they are sold weight for weight against the dollars, the value of this coin here being twenty-five of their large piastres.

The only stimulant these Arabs drink is a kind of beer made from dhurra, which Albert says is very good, but we have not as yet acted upon his recommendation. He is quite in his element here, and finds so much entertainment as well as occupation in the trinket purchases, and in looking up his old friends amongst the Greek community, that Emanuel and Bob do not have much assistance from him in their really hard work.

Jan. 15.—All our arrangements for an early start to-morrow are complete, and only depend on the arrival of the promised camels. Munsinger Pasha has given us two soldiers belonging to the Bashi-Bazouks as protectors, and we have engaged as one of our guides an Egyptian named Ibrahim, who was with Arkwright on a somewhat similar expedition last year. In the afternoon we went for our promised ride with Munsinger Pasha, who, dressed in a loose white suit, and wearing only a tarboosh on his head, was mounted on his favourite donkey, whilst two of us had horses, and two donkeys. Four soldiers marching in front and four behind, armed with Remington rifles, formed his guard, and so we went round the town.

Ten years ago there was a mutiny of the whole army here, numbering at the time four thousand men, and for two months they held one half of the town, but they were then dislodged by troops sent from Cairo and Khartoum, and all perished excepting four hundred. Some of these were sent to the White Nile, and others are now employed on the telegraph line across the Desert to Souakim. As we passed amongst the straw houses in the poorest districts, it was almost surprising to see with what very marked respect Munsinger Pasha was received by the various tribes, every man standing up and bowing low before him, whilst the women shouted in their own peculiar way from within their houses in order to do him honour. He first took us to a large cotton manufactory, in which he takes great interest, as he thinks it will prove a complete success. The machinery was made in England, but the chief engineer is a Frenchman. The building is made of bricks, baked in a kiln close by; but many failures took place before the proper amount of sand to mix with the clay could be decided upon to ensure a good brick. A large acacia-wood behind the Kassala mountains supplies the material for fuel, and now that the people understand their work bricks can be turned out in any number required. For a time the manufactory will be worked by the Government, but Munsinger Pasha hopes that it will ultimately pass into private hands. Our next visit was to the prison, a low range of buildings surrounding a courtyard, in which, on our approach, the prisoners were drawn up in line, all of them having heavy chains round their ankles excepting two, who turned out to be our victims. As usually happens, these were the least idle of our camelmen; and therefore, after a little special pleading on their behalf, we succeeded in obtaining their release. We walked down the line, and the chief gaoler explained the nature of each crime, and a very curious list it was. The first two were boys, who were convicted of selling a little girl as a slave; then came a man who had murdered another, and had confessed his guilt, but there having been extenuating circumstances, he has been sentenced to imprisonment for life. Next came a horrible-looking creature, who, besides having chains round the ankles, had his wrists fixed in a block of wood; he was known as an inveterate thief, and had committed, it was believed, many murders, though none could be proved against him. A little farther on stood the handsomest man of the Hadendowa Arabs we have seen, who stole some camels and murdered the owner, one of another tribe, his excuse being that this man had done the same to his father ten years ago. As we left, there was a general appeal to Munsinger Pasha to release them, all declaring that they were innocent.

Of female prisoners there are none, for no accusations of crime are brought against them; and should one be committed by them, it is kept quiet and settled amongst the male community of the tribe to which they may belong.

Selling slaves, Munsinger Pasha says, no doubt still continues to a small extent secretly, but the risk to the slave-dealers is now so great that the practice must in time die out of itself, for their value has increased in proportion to the risk incurred. A few get probably sent secretly to the coast, and transported in small boats to Jedda, for the price of slaves in Arabia is now very high. When slaves are captured by the Government, the boys are drafted into the army, and husbands are generally found for the girls.

The negro soldiers behave themselves very well, but they are not nearly so well educated as the Egyptian soldiers, for all of these can now read and write. A negro band is generally stationed here, and it is a curious fact that whilst these men prefer the light European airs, and play them very correctly, the Egyptians prefer their own music.

Most of the soldiers of Munsinger Pasha's guard fought in Mexico under Bazaine.

He believes that within three years there will be a war between Egypt and Abyssinia about the Bogos country, which partly divides them, for the Abyssinians are very jealous of Egypt obtaining power in any portion of this disputed territory, and they are now only waiting until they are better prepared to wrest it from her. Mr. Cohen paid us a visit this evening, and expressed a great wish to join us if we could only delay our departure one day, as he is about to visit the same country to buy animals, and he would have us believe that his knowledge of the country would be of much service to us.

In this respect he is without doubt right, but on the whole we prefer his room to his company, for the Governor tells us that there is a very good feeling amongst the various tribes we shall meet for the English; and though Mr. Cohen may be well known as a purchaser of their animals, we cannot tell whether he may not be better known than respected. Owing apparently to the absence of competitors, he has the entire command of the market, and as he can make his own terms, his profits ought to be large; but the risks must be very great, for even since our arrival two of the young elephants we saw have died through injuries received from the native hunters either to the ribs or liver. Three fine giraffes were brought to him to-day, and bought, according to Albert, for twenty dollars each. As an extra servant, we have engaged a slave whom Mr. Cohen bought for twenty dollars and liberated, and then retained at wages of four dollars a month. He does not appear now to care for his bargain, and has granted us the great privilege of allowing us to take him to England *if* we care to do so. He is a nice-looking intelligent young negro named Abdullah, and in this country he may prove a very useful addition to our gradually increasing establishment.

Though all were astir at 5 A.M. to ensure an early departure, it was 1.30 P.M. before it was accomplished, owing to the difficulty of loading our camels in the narrow lane in which our palace is situated, though we have been able to reduce their number to twenty-three in consequence of our diminished stores and the greater size of the animals. The change in them has also given us one great advantage in addition, for, unlike the others, they are free from horrid sores on the back and hips. At the last moment Mr. Cohen called to tell us that he thought he could leave after all this evening, and catch us up; we hope, however, he observed that the announcement received no cordial response, as it will save future complications. Munsinger Pasha also came to bid us farewell, adding that he would not wish us good luck, as this to sportsmen was apt to bring the reverse. He brought us a letter to the Sheik of the Hamran village, asking him to look after our interests, and gave us some friendly words of advice with regard to using great caution in shooting big game, especially the rhinoceros, an animal that he considered most dangerous ; and added that, if we found ourselves in any difficulty with the natives, we were to communicate with him at once.

Go where we may, we can never expect to meet again a man who will take such a sincere interest in our welfare as Munsinger Pasha has done ; his frank open manner has quite won our hearts, and one cannot be thrown in his society for even the short time we have been, without feeling confident that he is thoroughly in earnest in the difficult task he has in hand in his official life, and wishing, for the future welfare of Egypt, that the Khedive could number many such men amongst his high officers of State.[1]

[1] Munsinger Pasha has been recently waylaid and killed when on a tour of inspection.

CHAPTER IV.

THE Kassala Mountain, as it is called, looks particularly grand when approached from the town. It comprises, really, several of varied height. The centre one is the highest, consisting of granite, and has the form of a huge smooth dome. At first our direction was eastward to the foot of this range, and in passing through this portion of the country we not only were able to notice the results, in cultivation, of the industry of the natives, but also of the hyænas and vultures, for as scavengers they leave nothing to be desired of them in saving the people from illness.

When animals die here from disease, the Arabs merely take them to an open space and leave them unburied, and the countless skeletons now there tell of the great havoc that a recent epidemic has produced amongst them. We arrived after sunset at a village named Hel-el-Shereef, where we must stay till morning, as this is our only chance of getting water until our arrival at the Hamran village. So far the country south of Kassala appears to be freely wooded, where not cultivated with dhurra, cotton, indigo, tobacco, onions, and probably other crops that we did not notice. Dome palms and asclepias are very numerous, the latter being a tree that exudes, according to Sir Samuel Baker, a milky juice, poisonous to all animals but goats, and it certainly is surprising to see the quantity that will now exude from a broken branch or leaf. It is now in blossom, and has a pale purple but not pretty flower, and there are also suspended from it numerous huge thin green capsules, some of them as large as a cocoa-nut, and inside these there is a mass of seeds packed closely together, and having long silky filaments at one end. The fibre of the tree is valued by the natives for making fine and strong ropes. Passing by the side of the mountain, as we turned southwards we saw a family of dog-faced baboons, playing about amongst the loose rocks close to us, and taking much less heed of us than we naturally did of them. So far as we are concerned this species of animal will not suffer from our invasion of their territory, for we have no intention of adding them to our game list. A little later we saw in every direction hundreds of guinea-fowl, and they kindly allowed us to thin their numbers to the extent we required, without much labour in stalking.

On arriving at 'Hel-el-Shereef' we were received by the Sheik, and several angareps were at once brought from the houses for our use. They certainly make very comfortable bedsteads, but they have the great disadvantage of being easily broken when packed on camels, and Vivian has already had to buy three for personal use.

Jan. 17.—The entertainment last night was varied by a watchman howling the whole time when saying his prayers, we are told; and by another playing some lugubrious air on a reed. A new system has been adopted with our camels, for they were kept all night within our inclosure, and only allowed to feed after daylight, consequently our departure was delayed till after midday.

The Sheik brought us some milk as a present, but he would not smoke a pipe we have brought for state occasions, as it is a day of fasting previous to the great Feast of Beiram to-morrow. He asked, however, for some sugar to sweeten water, as a drink for his sick child. Albert and Bob came back from a ramble in the woods in a state of great excitement, declaring that they had seen a snake as thick as two fists and fifteen feet long, and that they were so frightened that they ran away as fast as their legs would carry them. Having now the benefit of the moon to light us on our way we continued our journey till nearly midnight, and then encamped near some Arabs, who our soldiers say belong to a tribe that keeps up secretly the slave trade. For some days we have seen that a storm was brewing between our two dragomans, owing to paltry jealousies as to relative rank, though we tried to guard against this before leaving Cairo by distinctly placing Albert under Emanuel whilst we are together, a position rather galling to him, as he considers himself very superior to Emanuel in the social scale. To-night the bubble burst, and after a great many angry words had passed between them threatening to end in blows, a little law was judiciously administered and peace established between them. The row originated in Albert accusing Emanuel of trying to starve him by feeding him only upon rice which he could not eat, whilst Emanuel declared that both he and Bob ate everything that came from our table, and therefore could not require much in 'the kitchen.' Their respective temperaments are now well shown, for whilst Emanuel has quite recovered his temper, Albert looks very crestfallen, having had a good cry to relieve his feelings. Emanuel has a staunch ally in Mohamed, who in the midst of the row appealed to us to know if it was necessary for him to take any orders from Albert. Bob, on the other hand, though Emanuel's ally by right, seems evidently inclined to take Albert's part, as they are constantly together attending upon us.

Jan. 18.—Our longest day on camels so far, for leaving our encampment at 9.30 A.M. we did not halt for the night until 9 P.M. The country through which we have passed has been most monotonous, consisting chiefly of one flat plain covered with a short dry grass without even a stunted mimosa to break the sea-like expanse. The soil is now no longer sand, but a fine dark earth that only awaits the husbandman to render it of incalculable value to Egypt. Several ariel were seen, but no amount of careful stalking would enable us to get within 300 yards of them; and as the guinea-fowl have been equally wary, we stand a chance of running short of our fresh meat supply. Albert 'very feeble' to-day, but we hope it is only due to his digestion having been upset by yesterday's ebullition of temper.

Jan. 19.—Off again before 9 A.M., and, after passing through a mimosa-wood in which guinea-fowl were found in hundreds and bagged in proportion to our wants, we came again upon an immense plain, but with this great difference, that it was in parts cultivated with dhurra, now in full ear, and here and there a solitary Arab could be seen plucking the heads off. Several new kinds of trees, and birds of beautiful and varied plumage, were also noticed. In the afternoon we entered an immense forest of bare stunted trees of various kinds, but having as the one general characteristic the most villanous thorns that the ingenuity of Nature could well devise; and though our clothes are of stout material, they occasionally gave us some practical experience of their fish-hook propensities. Here in every direction could be seen innumerable birds'-nests suspended as by a fine cord from the tips of the branches, and looking like little baskets swinging to and fro with the slightest breeze. Our daily programme has been to depart with the baggage camels, halt for luncheon for an hour or two, keeping Albert to attend to our wants and act as interpreter, and later in the day to catch up with the others, who continue the journey without interruption. We passed them this afternoon, and with one soldier acting as our guide we arrived at the chief Hamran village about 7.30 P.M., and were received by the Sheik and several of his followers, and taken to a piece of ground outside the village to encamp upon, where we found a straw mansion for the use of strangers. Angareps were brought and the customary talk commenced, unaccompanied, however, on this occasion by the social pipe, for the Sheik 'don't smoke.' He offered to kill a sheep and give us food, but we explained to him that the rest of our party would soon arrive with all we required, and in the meantime accepted an invitation to pay a visit to a dead horse close by, on the chance of a shot at a hyæna. Watching for hyænas by moonlight when very tired and hungry is not a very pleasant amusement, especially if you are near your bait, so we soon gave it up; and on our return heard to our dismay that our party had encamped some way from us, not knowing where we were. Our first idea was to rejoin them; but it had to be given up, for the Sheik said, 'No, you have come here, and are my guests, and must not leave again;' and, wishing not to annoy him, we agreed to send for some food and tell them to come on in the morning. Two more long hours had to be spent before the much desired supply arrived.

The Sheik paid us occasional visits, and found great amusement in looking at the moon through our little whisky-barrel (now empty) with glass ends, and afterwards through a telescope, whilst his followers were quite content with the whisky-barrel effect, which no doubt was greatly aided by sundry fly-specks on the outside of the glass, and gave great scope for the fertile imagination of the Arab.

Jan. 20.—At 3 A.M. Emanuel arrived, and stated that he had halted at another village, as he was told by its Sheik that it was the chief one. We find that there are numerous Hamran villages, but whichever may be the largest, we have now no doubt that our Sheik is the chief of the Hamran Arabs. His name is Aghil, and he is the son of the late Sheik Owatt, and this village, named Gwayha, is the one in which he lives during the dry season. The first business of the day was to bathe in the Bahr Settite, that flows at about half a mile distance past the village, as we were told there was a shallow place free from crocodiles after the sun had well risen.

As the sight of land to the sailor, so was the pleasure to us, after three weeks of desert-travelling without the sight of water excepting an occasional well, to look upon this fine river flowing silently but rapidly between two high banks covered with verdure; and then we had the additional satisfaction of being able to realise that the sport for which we had come so far was almost within our grasp. At this time of year the river is very low, and where we bathed about one hundred yards in width, and used as a regular ford.

Paying this place a second visit in the afternoon, and walking afterwards a short distance along the bank, we caught sight of our first crocodile basking himself in the sun; but he glided at once into the river, not feeling disposed apparently to allow us to test the accuracy and penetrating powers of our rifles upon him. Sheik Aghill breakfasted with us, and having carefully watched us use our knives and forks, essayed to do the same. Unfortunately, by turning the edge of the knife the wrong way, he only succeeded in cutting his own finger; but, having had this very practical lesson, he soon became quite an expert. He is a well-made man, about five feet ten inches in height, has a dark brown skin, very regular features, and in appearance and manner looks quite the gentleman amongst his followers, though only differing from them in costume in the extra whiteness of the robe in which they are entirely enveloped, and in wearing a tarboosh. After breakfast, Munsinger Pasha's letter was opened with a great display of importance, looked at, nodded at, turned upside down, and then, with

F

an expression of satisfaction, placed in the bosom. These performances ought to have been very gratifying to us, but their effect was a little spoilt on our learning later in the day that there was not an individual in the village, the Sheik included, who could read or write Arabic. The next performance was the purchase of horses, or rather ponies, and about twenty were brought for our inspection, and each put through his paces in turn with an excited Arab on his back. Our choice having fallen on one, the saddle was taken off for further inspection, and then were exposed to view two such horrible sores that it would have been kind to shoot the poor creature without loss of time. Hardly any of them were free from sores, but we managed to pick out five tolerably sound, and averaging about 5*l*. 10*s*. apiece.

Twenty camels had then to be engaged, and here arose a difficulty, for the Sheik demanded twelve dollars per month for each, whereas our Kassala men had previously offered to come for four dollars. The Sheik, however, is all-powerful here, and after seeing him they would come to no terms without his approval, and finally we reduced his demand to eight dollars. Baker, in his 'Nile Tributaries of Abyssinia,' mentions that the people at the time of his visit to them were glad to engage themselves with their camels at one and a half dollars per month; and when we told the Sheik this, he replied, 'Yes, that was twelve years ago, in my father's time, when Europeans had scarcely ever been seen in this country; but now a few come almost every year, and things are dearer.' This, translated by ourselves, means that, with an uncommonly keen eye to the main chance, he gets a higher percentage of the earnings of his people. The camel question being settled, that of hunters had to be discussed. We thought that men on foot who knew the country were all that we should require; but to this the Sheik was much opposed, and advised us to engage some of their mounted sword-hunters, as he said, and with good reason, that if we were to chase giraffe or wounded animals men on foot would not be able to follow us, and would therefore be of no practical use; and though we felt sure that he was guided in his opinion far more by the extra dollars he could thus extract from us than by thoughts of our welfare, we could not but agree with his line of argument, and after considerable discussion reduced his terms from thirty dollars per month for a man and horse to twenty, and then engaged four at that rate. Still he was not satisfied, and tried very hard to induce us to take a fifth, and offered a bribe to Emanuel privately if he would use his influence with us. This was an interesting bit of news to us, when coupled with the fact that Albert had heard this hunter a few minutes before telling the Sheik he would give him half his wages if he succeeded in getting him engaged, for it forms a very good guide of the heavy claims the Sheik makes upon his people. He says that all the villages along the Settite, besides others, belong to him, but that only a few of them, this included, are under the protection of Egypt and pay any taxes to her, and that none of them supply soldiers to the Egyptian army. The neighbouring tribes of Bazé and Magurda (?) are under no authority, are very bad people; and if it pleases God that they should fight with them, they do so. He evidently finds our mode of living a pleasant change, for he was very ready to accept our invitation to dinner, and presented us with a sheep. Amongst our small luxuries is a camp armchair, which he takes good care to let us see he considers himself especially entitled to occupy, whilst sundry stools, slightly the worse for their rough life, are quite good enough for us.

After dinner we brought out several nice presents, hoping he would admire them and express a wish to have them; but in vain, for he would only turn them over listlessly, and one after another lay them aside, without scarcely making any comment, good, bad, or indifferent. This was really provoking, and especially when not even an Adams's breech-loading revolver that we fired off six times in rapid succession would produce the slightest expression of admiration or surprise. At last we found out the cause of this indifference by his telling Albert he wanted to see our rifles, and that if he found one he particularly admired he felt sure we would let him have it, for he would give us half this village if we asked him for it. As, however, we neither wished to test his magnanimity so far, nor had any intention of granting so mild a request, we tried to make a compromise by offering to send him a gun from England; but to no effect, for he was quite wide-awake enough to know that if we fulfilled our part of the compact, it would never get beyond Cairo.

Finding then that he must draw in his horns, he changed his tactics, and gladly accepted a collapsing drinking-cup that looked very like silver, and a pocket-knife; and the discarded revolver, now eagerly coveted, was, as a punishment, only promised after our return here.

CHAPTER V.

Jan. 21.—A day simply dawdled away, for beyond paying the half-month's wages in advance there was nothing left to be arranged; but this was evidently no trifling matter, for the Sheik, after collecting a small crowd under an adjoining tree, devoted so many hours to the distribution of the dollars, that we began to think he had found our living so attractive that he would not let us be off at all to-day.

Gwayha is a most uninteresting-looking place, consisting of the usual straw-made huts crowded together, and though the men are if anything even a finer-looking race than the Hadendowa Arabs, with the same hair and costume, the women, judging from the few we saw, whatever their attractions may be have certainly not beauty as one of them; but a large ring in the nostril is probably considered to cover any little defect, and in this respect they must have at least the sympathy of Western nations, though these limit barbaric customs to wearing rings in the ears.

At 5 P.M. the departure from Gwayha was actually effected; but, much to our dismay, the Sheik decided upon accompanying us to a village, where he said we must halt for the night, as the Arabs will not travel at night from fear of wild beasts.

It was a great luxury to be mounted on our little horses; and lucky for us that we had bought an extra one, for, either by accident or design, one of them became dead lame very soon, and had to be sent back—with the understanding, however, that it should be replaced by another without extra charge. Our route to-day has been along the north bank of the Settite for about two miles and a half, and then turning to the left we passed through a small village, and shortly arrived at another, name Zahani, where we have encamped. As we quite expected, the Sheik has again been our guest at dinner. Afterwards he told us that he should very much like to come to England with us, and would not be put off by being told that the cold would kill him, for he said he had plenty of warm clothes, as well as kind friends there, and with great readiness mentioned the names of Baker, Arkwright, and Durant. It was very amusing to hear Albert giving him lessons in the pronunciation of our names, and he appeared most anxious to learn them also by heart. 'Lord Coke' and 'Mr. Myers' gave him no trouble to pronounce; 'Captain Vivian' was only accomplished after a hard struggle; but 'Sir William Gordon Cumming' was more than even his great mind could grasp, so he contented himself with a careful inspection of the individual with such an imposing name. He begged us to be very kind to his people whom he had given us, as they were his children; and never to use the koorbatch, or they would run away, and he would be unable to send us any more.

In the evening some hunters arrived who had been out elephant-shooting in the neighbourhood to-day. They had seen several and had killed one, and it was really almost annoying to find these Arabs so well armed. One man had a very heavy muzzle-loading four-bore rifle with the name of Williams and Co. upon it, which he said cost one hundred and thirty-five dollars, and almost always killed an elephant first shot at about twenty-five yards distance. The charge is ten drachms of their bad powder, and it is fired from a rest consisting of a forked stick. The other rifles they had were of very inferior quality, and were only used on an emergency to shoot at a wounded animal. It appears, however, that these firearms are almost the only ones in the possession of the Hamran Arabs, and are looked upon with much wonder; and one cannot help hoping they may remain so, for it would be a pity if the career of the renowned Hamran sword-hunter had to yield to the advance of civilisation in this respect. Sir Samuel Baker thus describes their exploits:[1] 'Provided with horses, the party should not exceed four. They start

---

[1] *Vide* 'Nile Tributaries of Abyssinia.'

before daybreak, and ride slowly throughout the country in search of elephants, generally keeping along the course of a river until they come upon the tracks where a herd or a single elephant may have drunk during the night. When once upon the tracks, they follow fast towards the retreating game. The elephants may be twenty miles distant;. but it matters little to the aggageers. At length they discover them, and the hunt begins. The first step is to single out the bull with the largest tusks; this is the commencement of the fight. After a short hunt, the elephant turns upon his pursuers, who scatter and fly from his headlong charge until he gives up the pursuit; he at length turns to bay when again pressed by the hunters. It is the duty of one man in particular to ride up close to the head of the elephant, and thus to absorb its attention upon himself. This ensures a desperate charge. The greatest coolness and dexterity are then required by the hunter, who, now *the hunted*, must so adapt the speed of his horse to the pace of the elephant that the enraged beast gains in the race until it almost reaches the tail of the horse. In this manner the race continues. In the meantime two hunters gallop up behind the elephant unseen by the animal, whose attention is completely directed to the horse almost within his grasp. With extreme agility, when close to the heels of the elephant, one of the hunters, while at full speed, springs to the ground with his drawn sword as his companion seizes the bridle, and with one dexterous two-handed blow he severs the back sinew. He immediately jumps out of the way and remounts his horse; but, if the blow is successful, the elephant becomes disabled by the first pressure of its foot upon the ground; the enormous weight of the animal dislocates the joint, and it is rendered helpless. The hunter who has hitherto led the elephant turns immediately, and, riding to within a few feet of the trunk, he induces the animal to attempt another charge. This, clumsily made, affords an easy opportunity for the aggageers behind to slash the sinew of the remaining leg, and the immense brute is reduced to a standstill, and it dies of loss of blood in a short time, *thus positively killed by one man with two strokes of the sword!* This extraordinary hunting is attended with superlative danger, and the hunters frequently fall victims to their intrepidity.'

The book from which this is quoted is invaluable to us as a general guide, although our route has not been quite the same; and so careful has the author been in all his minor details, that it is difficult to find much new material for insertion in this diary. The pictures are an endless source of amusement to all the natives, from the Sheik downwards, and it is quite absurd to watch the slow way in which they turn over leaf upon leaf, lest by any chance one should be missed.

Our four hunters are named Hassan, Essafi, Mohammed, and Ibrahim, and we have the satisfaction of knowing that they have some 'blue blood' in their veins. Hassan is the son of a notorious sword-hunter who was killed seven years ago by an elephant, and Essafi is the son of an old Sheik, and he is now the chief of a party of aggageers.

Jan. 22.—Another horse was brought this morning, but not without our knowing friend the Sheik succeeding in getting six more dollars out of us for the exchange. He came at breakfast-time, and was considerably sold about the parting meal, for, our tents being struck, he did not like to be seen by his people eating with us. At the last moment, however, he scored one against us by declaring that Hassan was on the point of having a fever, and must be replaced by another hunter he brought us, named Said, an extraordinary-looking woolly-haired negro, who, though strongly recommended, does not look much up to his work. Rumour says that Sheik Aghill has kept back Hassan as he wants him to do a little elephant-hunting on his account. Our progress has been very curtailed to-day, as we were obliged to encamp at midday on an open piece of ground named Gadamur, upon which once stood a village, as the country is so undulating and thickly wooded that there are only a few places available, and we have therefore to be entirely guided by our chief hunter, Essafi, he having been placed by the Sheik in authority over the others.

This is an important day in our calendar, for we have had the first ocular demonstration of the fact that we have actually arrived in the country of some of those animals against which we have come specially to wage war. After leaving the Settite, where we saw numerous crocodiles in the distance silently gliding into the water on our approach, we at once were pointed out innumerable tracks of elephants, besides other unmistakable evidences that they frequented the neighbourhood. Now, although we could not claim as the chief cause of our expedition to shoot elephants and lions the disinterested motives suggested facetiously before leaving England, that it was to protect the natives from their natural enemies, this was without doubt a most refreshing sight in a purely sportsman's point of view. Farther on we saw a large troop of dog-faced baboons keeping at some distance ahead of us, with thick dark manes, and much bigger than our Kassala friends. Our horses showed a most positive objection to approaching them, though our hunters told us they were as common as the pebbles. After luncheon we went to the river to look for a hippopotamus (an animal that for the future shall have the more convenient term of hippo applied to it). To get to their pool we had to wade across the river three times, and in one place the stream was so strong as well as deep, that it very nearly carried us off our legs, and reached up to or beyond our hips. Probably our protectors think it is safer to risk this than to walk into the jaws of a crocodile in still water. Our search was so far successful that we saw five hippos; but as they only put up their noses now and again for a moment to breathe, it was impossible to get a good shot at them. A crocodile was more accommodating, for, swimming along the surface of the water, he exposed himself sufficiently to allow a bullet to penetrate his thick hide, and then, after two violent convulsions, in which he threw himself half out of the water, he sank. The men say he must be dead, and that his carcass will float to-morrow. The programme for to-night is to wait 'at home' quietly, as our camp lies between two main elephant-paths to the river, and if they are heard trumpeting on either side of us, we are then to sally forth. Coke, however, prefers to take advantage of the full moon, and watch by the river.

Jan. 23.—Coke returned at midnight, having had no success beyond hearing an elephant, and seeing a hippo at the river-side that he thought was an elephant in the darkness until, after waiting in ambush for a few moments expecting it to approach him on its return, he saw it disappear into the river.

By drawing lots, our hunters have been disposed of thus: Said to Coke, Ibrahim to Cumming, Mohamed to Vivian, and Essafi to myself; and to-day, each of us having gone off at sunrise in a different direction with our respective protectors, returned about sunset, and over a capital dinner narrated our experiences. Coke, scorning a crocodile and finding no elephant, did not fire a shot. Cumming killed an ariel, and fired at a hippo and a crocodile, both of which he believes he wounded mortally, so the river will be searched to-morrow. Retracing my footsteps of yesterday, no dead crocodile could Essafi find, and the hippos being even less obliging than yesterday, I had to give vent to my feelings by a shot at a splendid grey crocodile that was basking in the sun on the opposite bank, at about one hundred and fifty yards distance. This only wounded him; but before he could struggle into the river, another bullet in the head turned him over on his back, and then, after two or three slow movements of the legs, he remained motionless. Owing to the depth of the river here we could not examine our prize at the time, and therefore turned our steps homewards for assistance. On our way, Essafi was so excited with the marvellous power of my rifle, that he wanted me to fire at every monkey that crossed our path; until at last, seeing a splendid old gentleman perched on a high bank about one hundred yards off calmly surveying us, he became so anxious for me to fire, that I thought it as well to so far please him, and, having taken a steady aim, I put an end to its existence. Unfortunately the bullet had completely smashed the skull, and therefore I had not even the poor satisfaction of keeping this in remembrance of, perhaps, what some people would call a cold-blooded murder. On our return to camp, Essafi's report of the death of an immense crocodile caused great excitement amongst the camel-men ; and as Essafi said it was far too big to be brought home whole, a party started off on camels to skin and cut it up. When they arrived at the place they found that the crocodile had turned over again, and as one man went close up to him, he slipped into the water and was lost. The experience therefore of yesterday and to-day is, that the express rifles with expanding bullets do not answer for crocodile-shooting.

On Vivian fell the honours of the day. Having decided upon a long day's elephant-hunt, he provided himself with a good supply of water ; and the horses being fed and watered, he and his hunter took a line of country directly away from the river in search of fresh tracks. The search was soon successful, and, after following them up for about an hour, Mohamed made signs that he could hear elephants ahead. The two horses were then tied to a tree, and stalking commenced as quietly as possible, though under considerable difficulties, owing to the overhanging branches of the mimosas with their hooked thorns, which, without 'elephants ahead' as a stimulus, have much too great a power of penetration to make walking amongst them an agreeable occupation.

Soon again the elephants were heard, and this time the body of one could be discerned in the close covert they had entered about forty yards off. At the same moment Vivian and his man were also seen, but a hardened ball from a No. 10 smooth-bore of Messrs Moore and Gray, hitting the only one of the herd visible in the right high, stopped him in his attempt to follow his friends, as, crashing through the trees, they made a general stampede. A second bullet in the shoulder made him turn round, when, seeing the enemy, he assumed the offensive and came on boldly with trunk high in air, until within fifteen yards of them. Now a third bullet, penetrating the front of his chest, made him come to a halt, and then, after swaying his huge frame to and fro for a few seconds, he fell heavily to the ground. Upon this they crept behind him, and, finding that he was still breathing, remained quiet until respiration ceased ; then creeping a little nearer, the eyelids could be seen to move occasionally ; but soon all was over, and Vivian had become the proud possessor of our first elephant. Great rejoicings in camp on hearing the good news, and it certainly was a singular piece of luck to shoot a full-grown tusker the first day, and promises well for the future.

Jan. 24.—Last night Essafi took me near to an elephant-path, hoping that some might pass on their way from the river ; but after waiting quietly for an hour or more, he shook his head, said ' mafeesh ' (nothing), and having examined the path, showed me that, as there were no fresh tracks, no elephants could have passed that way to drink earlier in the evening. Sitting quietly under the shadow of a tree whilst the moon is shining with intense brilliancy, and listening eagerly to every sound of crackling bushes in the hope each time that it may prove to be an elephant approaching in the distance, is in itself a source of no small excitement to an inexperienced hunter, though time after time it turns out to have been caused by an antelope, jackal, or other small animal that the surrounding trees had concealed from view. But the hunter's command must be for the present our law; so, on a sign from Essafi, I turned my steps homeward.

If this watching by moonlight is a very wakeful occupation, returning is just the reverse; and so in a dreamy way I followed Essafi until, emerging from a ravine, he suddenly stopped short, and, seizing me by the arm, whispered 'feel' in my ear. For a moment I could see nothing, but upon looking across the open ground in front of us, I caught sight of a huge mass coming out of the opposite ravine, about which there could be no mistake; and what was equally certain was the fact of its being in our path, and coming directly towards us. In a moment we were off the path, and crouching in some long grass under the shade of a tree to wait for its approach; whilst Essafi, trembling all over with excitement, would clutch at my arm and try to make me fire at it. Guided, however, by the experience of Baker and other African sportsmen, who have found that it is practically impossible to kill an African elephant by a forehead shot, I was determined not to lose such a chance in this way, as it was quite certain that, by remaining quiet, the elephant must pass within about five yards of us. Essafi's patience could not stand so severe a trial, and, becoming more excited as the elephant slowly but surely advanced, he made him observe us, and instantly turn round; but at the same time, having the full power of the moon upon him, he gave me a splendid broadside shot with my eight-bore. A crash, a cloud of dust, and, on this clearing away, a dark passage into the ravine, were for the moment the result; and one might have felt inclined to believe that it had been but a dream, save for the sound after a few minutes in the distance of a retreating elephant. Essafi then made signs to me that there were two, mine being left behind, and as it would have been clearly most dangerous to approach it in the dark ravine, I accepted his suggestion of 'bookra' (to-morrow), and continued our course homewards.

When the sun had risen we returned to the spot on foot, accompanied by Vivian; and though Essafi was positive he would be dead, no elephant, alas! could be found.

Following up his track, however, occasional pools of

blood proved that he had been severely wounded, and we became full of hope that in one of the ravines we should come suddenly upon him. Still on and on we went, Essafi now and again almost losing his track amongst the many others of earlier date, and then proving his correct eye by finding the gradually diminishing patches of blood, until these patches passed into drops, the faults became more frequent, and at last, stopping short, he shook his head, and with a woe-begone face had once again to say 'mafeesh'—the fatal word that told me the hunt was over, and that I had lost my first and possibly last chance of bagging an elephant, for the career of my eight-bore is now literally hanging on a thread. I omitted to mention that, when we were at Kassala, a Greek mechanic joined the broken ends of the stock so cleverly, that it was made as strong as, if not stronger, than it was originally; but a cloud still hung over it, for, a day or two after leaving Kassala, Cumming took it to try its killing-powers on guinea-fowl with a charge of shot, and his horse shying as he mounted, his foot slipped, and away went the gun. The fall cracked the stock right through the old place, but one of our soldiers managed to bind it together so firmly with twine, that it has been given another lease of life. Nothing has been seen of Cumming's hippo or crocodile, and no one has bagged any game to-day. Cold as we felt last night, we were greatly surprised to find the minimum thermometer registering only 33° Fah., and should have doubted its accuracy had it not been proved by the maximum at daybreak, when both stood at 34°. Comparing this with the maximum heat of to-day—viz., 81° in the shade, and 115° in the sun—the variation in the twenty-four hours is very great.

Three native hunters paid us a visit this evening, each mounted on a camel, and having an almost naked black boy perched up behind him carrying his rifle. They were on their way to Zahani in a very despondent state of mind, not having killed an elephant after three days' hunting. The chief told us that this was the best season for finding elephants in this neighbourhood, for a little later they migrate to Abyssinia, and that as we advance in our present direction we shall lose them, but in their stead find rhinoceros and lions; and if we go, as we purpose doing ultimately, to the Salaam river, we shall find lions as plentiful as sheep. Their rifles were very inferior to those we had seen. Ours were examined with great interest, and the breech-loading action quite astonished them.

Emanuel, with most of our available men and camels, left camp before sunrise for the place where the dead elephant lay, and spent the whole day there cutting it up and packing as much of it upon the camels as the time would allow. The Arabs left in camp have also been very busy making huge fires, as there is to be a grand feast to-night, for, much as they love raw gazelle, the flesh of the elephant reigns supreme to their dainty palates. The return to-night was hailed with great rejoicing, and now the camp is one scene of bustle and excitement, all sorts of preparations being made for the feast and for the future preservation of the precious food; and as we sit in our tent, groups of figures can be seen squatting round the fires that blaze on all sides of us.

Jan. 25.—No sport again to-day. Vivian and Cumming came unexpectedly upon a very fine lion, lying half asleep near a dead cow on open ground. He saw them, however, quite soon enough to let them only have a running shot as he bolted away, and thus managed to escape.

The 'game list' has had a small addition made to it by my shooting with a revolver a civet cat as it crouched in a hollow under the roots of a tree that had been torn up by an elephant. There are very extensive mimosa-woods near our camp, and many of the trees have lumps of gum exuding from them, generally of amber colour and semi-liquid inside. One species exudes a white gum, beautifully transparent where liquid, and having a much finer flavour than the other. Elephants evidently find it an amusing pastime twisting their trunks round these trees, and either uprooting them or breaking them down, for in every direction can be seen such innumerable evidences of their terrific strength. This part of the country is now so hunted by natives, that the elephants have been driven to coverts so far away from the river that our only chance of finding them by day would be to spend two days in tracking them. Coke, when bathing to-day, put his foot on a small crocodile, but failed to catch it; otherwise he might have been brought home and allowed to disport himself in the Serpentine, as a little pleasant excitement for morning bathers. Returning to camp this evening, all the cut brushwood that surrounds it as a protection from wild beasts seemed to have burst into leaf in our absence; but on closer inspection the leaves turned out to be long strips of elephant's flesh with which the Arabs had covered the branches, to dry them in the sun, and they were still busily at work hammering out the cut strips with a piece of wood, over the elephant's thigh-bones or on smooth stones. Mohamed the cook, and others of our more personal staff, have lost no time in taking advantage of the arrival of the civet cat, and have so smeared themselves over with the secretion from its musk-gland that they have given us good cause to groan over the introduction of so potent an animal into our otherwise contented family.

CHAPTER VI.

Jan. 26.—Again no sport; but we had the small satisfaction of finding a dead crocodile lying in shallow water, that had been shot two or three days ago. It measured ten feet, and was considered of only medium size. After hauling it on the bank, a piece of the skin was carefully cut out for a shield, and the rest left for those, whether man, bird, or beast, who like crocodile well kept.

Whilst we were hunting, our camp was transferred to new ground a few miles further along the Settite. It is an extremely pretty spot, named Imberaga, and we are established on a sand-bank in the bed of some dried-up tributary of the Settite, and about two hundred yards from it. On each side are low hills thickly wooded with mimosas and the 'nabbuk,' a tree equally thorny, that bears a fruit about the size of a cherry, with which it is now loaded. When ripe, as at present, it has a very pleasant slightly acid flavour, and is much liked by the Arabs and monkeys, who pick it up generally after it has fallen to the ground. Its colour is then light brown or yellow, with wrinkled surface and dry like a biscuit, with one large stone in it; and the only fault then to be found with it is, that there is too much stone and too little biscuit.

Vivian has made an important addition to our at present very meagre collection of the insect world, by finding a creature, in shape, colour, and almost in vitality, exactly like a piece of straw with giant legs, and having a body about four inches long. There is very little prospect of our making a good entomological collection, for after returning from shooting we are only too glad to rest quietly; and if there are any good specimens to be found, they certainly have an unhappy knack of keeping well out of sight, and would require much time to be specially devoted to them.

Jan. 27.—Again we have to thank Vivian for the excitement of the day, and for keeping our people in their present state of high spirits; for, besides shooting a 'ratel' that he made bolt from its hole by a lighted whisp of straw, and then knocked over with a ball from his big 'smooth-bore,' he has also killed the first buffalo.

His hunter Mohamed, after a quiet stalk, found him alone and asleep, and then, calling up Vivian, they managed to creep within sixty yards of him. At this moment he awoke from his morning nap and stood up, and, surprised to see visitors, steadfastly surveyed them. Again the ten-bore did its duty, and sending a bullet into his chest, he became powerless to move, though two more had to penetrate his thick hide before he was laid low. On Vivian's return to camp there were great rejoicings and shaking of hands, and one man with drawn sword rushed out, and with frantic gestures danced wildly before him. Everybody shakes hands in this country; if you meet a caravan, the whole party must go through this performance with you if you halt for a moment amongst them, otherwise ' Salaam aleikum ' is never omitted. The manner of the Arabs whom we have so far met in our rambles has been most friendly, and as if they considered us as their equals—no more, no less. Our little camp looks especially compact to-night. Near one end of the sand-bank are three large fires that light up the valley splendidly; round them men are lying asleep, so coiled up in their one sheet that they look like dirty sacks, whilst others are squatting about them eating elephant, an amusement that occupies most of their spare time; forming a crescent beyond them is an impassable barrier of camels packed closely together, with legs tucked under them and heads fixed as high in air as they can stretch their long necks, and all facing inwards. Beyond them our horses are tethered, and lastly come our two tents. These tents answer admirably for a dry climate; but, not having the support of ropes, an extra gust of wind gives us occasionally a little alarm for their safety, and one did collapse last night from this cause, much to the astonishment of those sleeping under it.

Jan. 28.—Moved our camp three hours' distance eastward along the Settite, to a high bank on the opposite (south) side, known by the name of 'El Effaara.' As usual, we went off in different directions, with the intention of returning by dinner-time, an hour fixed by the setting sun; but to-night there was a vacant place, for Vivian had not arrived. As time passed on, we began to fear that Mohamed had lost his way in the darkness, for it was said that he did not know just this part of the country well. Bonfires were therefore lit on the highest points of the hills near us, and guns discharged at intervals. At nine o'clock they were still absent, but a shot then echoing amongst the hills in the distance, followed later by others nearer, told us that Mohamed was persevering in the present almost total darkness to find his way, and that, guided by our beacons, they were gradually approaching us. At last a shout from a well-known voice from the opposite bank of 'Emanuel, make me some lemonade,' set our minds at rest, and immediately there was a rush to the river-side with torches, whilst some Arabs crossed over to light them better over the slippery way. Directly after leaving camp this morning, Essafi came upon a fresh buffalo track, and following it up for an hour, we arrived at a dense mimosa wood, where numerous similar tracks could be seen, perfectly fresh; and it was therefore evident we were close upon a herd. Shortly afterwards, Coke and Said arrived from an opposite point on the same hunt. It fell, however, to my lot to have the first shot, for Essafi pointed out a buffalo through an almost impenetrable bush, standing about forty yards from us. Hopeless as it was, I fired, for Essafi's excitement would not admit of any hope of creeping nearer, and the only result was that the ball probably glanced off a branch close to me, whilst I startled a large herd, which for a moment we caught sight of tearing across an open strip of land. We then started in pursuit; but, finding that the others were well ahead of us, we returned to the wood to get our horses, which we had tied up to some trees on the outskirts. On entering it we heard a shot ahead, and in a minute it was succeeded by a rapidly increasing noise in the brushwood. It then became evident that Coke had succeeded in turning the buffaloes, and that they were bearing down directly upon us. A few more moments and the noise became tremendous, though nothing could be seen until they were within twenty yards of us. As they crashed past us in their headlong career, and a very few yards off, they were treated to a right and left from my eight-bore, but, much to my disappointment, without apparently stopping any of them. Essafi, however, looked about him carefully, and soon found one standing about fifteen yards off. It had faced round, and was looking at us as if preparing for a charge, when another ball nipped these thoughts in the bud. Still, though bleeding profusely from the nose and mouth, it stood its ground, until, with another shot, it fell dead. More rejoicings on our return, and I had the honour of some wild dancing, sword exercise, and shaking of hands. All this at first is amusing enough, but if it is to be repeated whenever a big animal is shot, there seems to be every prospect of its soon becoming monotonous.

Jan. 29.—Cumming has added two new animals to our list of killed—one a fine specimen of antelope, named the têtel. It is larger than a red deer, and of a somewhat darker colour. Its special characteristic is a long ungainly-looking head, that looks far more suitable to a horse than an antelope, and not altogether unlike one. The horns are also ugly, short, and annulated, projecting at first outwards, and then curving upwards and inwards. Though not therefore altogether a handsome species of antelope, it has three good points—a skin valuable to the natives for carrying water, flesh excellent as food, and plenty of it. His other addition was a pig, but a poor lean specimen, with very small tusks. Judging from those we have yet seen here, it seems almost absurd to call them wild boar, for tamer creatures could scarcely be found. On first seeing us, their idea generally is to run up gently towards us to inspect the strange apparition in their wild haunts. Ibrahim's career has suddenly come to an end, Cumming having found out that he is totally ignorant of the country; and Emanuel has gone back to the Hamran village with him to-day, with orders to bring another hunter to replace him.

Another new arrival to-day in camp—viz., a very fine antelope that Vivian shot yesterday, but could not then bring home. Mohamed called it a maāriff, which, according to Baker, is the largest and most rare of all antelopes; but his description of it does not quite tally with the appearance of this one, so mine shall be deferred for the present.

Coke shot his first buffalo to-day near the camp, after an unsuccessful hunt along the Royan, a river that flows into the Settite a few hundred yards beyond our ground. This river, we are much disappointed to find, is now dry on the surface, excepting here and there some stagnant-looking pools; but there is water still flowing at a little depth below the surface-sand, so we have a slight chance of finding animals in its neighbourhood.

Elephant's foot for dinner has been a great success; it was boiled for twenty-four hours consecutively, and then very much resembled calf's foot, both in taste and appearance, excepting perhaps in size and shape, and it was appreciated accordingly. Our table is now very well supplied with dainties from the forest, and with the enormous quantity of meat at his disposal, our cook, Mohamed, produces soup of an excellence and strength,

so far as nourishment is concerned, that would put the most old-fashioned English cook to the blush.

Our men are having a grand entertainment to-night, and we for a short time joined the circle of spectators. It consisted chiefly in showing off their various modes of fighting with the sword, spear, and shield; whilst one man performed the most doleful music, consisting of a constant repetition of three notes on a stringed instrument named 'rababa,' and evidently belonging to the guitar tribe.

It was astonishing to see the great rapidity of movement and power of spring of these Arabs—one moment bounding forward at the imaginary enemy like an antelope, and the next crouching behind their shield so as to be completely concealed by it, whilst, by peering through a notch in the margin, they could follow the movements of the enemy. Each of our hunters was called out in turn, and they, in addition to what we had witnessed, went through the performance of protecting their respective masters. This was very amusing to look at whilst others were being protected, but when the sword was frantically waved over your own head in the torch-light, the pleasure was somewhat marred by the feeling that, with one little slip, it might be in a condition to be transferred to a plate. An apology was made by the chief of the camel-men for no more complete exhibition of these warlike exercises, and we were quite willing to accept his explanation that they were apt to get excited and fight in earnest, and that they would not like to do this in so dim a light.

Coke's buffalo fell an easy victim to his ten-bore smooth-bore, for he was able to stalk within seven yards of it whilst it was feeding in the high grass. Said is very different to the other hunters, and was originally brought as a slave from the Blue Nile. He is quite black, and, with his short woolly hair and nigger features, he is so like 'Uncle Sam,' that we have christened him accordingly. He has several little special ways of his own which afford his master considerable amusement in their daily wanderings together. To-day, Uncle Sam stopped at the tomb of a Sheik, prayed for some time, and having pulled out some hair from his horse's tail, put them on a stick over the tomb, and then continued the hunt. This performance, interpreted by Albert, was a special prayer and offering to this Sheik to give him good luck, as he had been several hours without showing his master any game; and as the buffalo was shot soon afterwards, Uncle Sam was no doubt quite satisfied with the efficacy of his prayers to the dead Sheik. Vivian tried his luck fishing this morning, and in a short time hooked five turtle; but, his tackle not being exactly fitted for this kind of sport, he lost four. The fifth was safely landed, however, and turned over on his back to wait for further orders; but in the meantime, whilst Mohamed was ruminating over a cup of coffee how best to cook him, he managed to right himself and to disappear into the river.

Jan. 30.—The prayer to the dead Sheik still holds good, for Coke and Uncle Sam succeeded in stalking close to some antelope, named goteer by our men, and succeeded in bagging two. One has such a magnificent pair of spiral horns, that it has made the rest of us feel very keen to get a similar specimen for our individual collections. The other was a doe, and without horns. This antelope is found in Southern Africa also, where it is named koodoo, and their horns are even finer than are found here. It is very handsome, standing about thirteen hands high, and has a mouse-grey coloured hide and three white stripes crossing the body vertically. According to Baker, it is also called the nellut. To-day a maāriff has been added to the game list by myself. The first shot with an express at about two hundred and fifty yards distance struck the shoulder, and he went off; but Essafi, seeing that he was lame, jumped on his horse and started off in mad pursuit, and ultimately succeeded in turning him, but in a direction far away from me. Essafi then returned for me, and very soon we were upon his track, with the satisfactory addition of occasional patches of blood. For more than an hour we followed him in this way over hill and dale, sometimes catching a glimpse of him disappearing over the crest of one hill as

UNIV. OF
CALIFORNIA

we arrived at the summit of another, when the distance would be diminished by a gallop, until, wearied out, we at last found the poor beast lying down in the bottom of a valley to rest, though not to escape from the keen eye of Essafi; and then, creeping within twenty yards of him, a ball from my eight-bore went right through his body, and so brought to a close this exciting hunt. When Vivian and myself compared notes about our respective maāriffs, we found a distinct difference in the slope of the horns, a difficulty which Mohamed (his hunter) tried to explain away by saying that maāriffs' horns sloped both ways. This, however, was not good enough for even our limited knowledge of the various species, so Essafi was consulted, and he at once said that Vivian's antelope was a méhédéhet; and upon a more careful examination of Baker's illustrations, it was very clear that such was the case. Both have annulated horns, but those of the méhédéhet curve outwards as well as backwards, and then forwards; and in this specimen are twenty-six inches long and seventeen and a half between the tips; whereas the horns of the maāriff curve gradually backwards, and with a very slight inclination outwards—so slight in this specimen, that though twenty-six and a half inches long, they are only eight inches apart at the tips, the widest point; then also, whilst in the one the concavity is forwards, in the other it faces backwards, and he markings in the two animals are quite distinct. The maāriff is the largest of all the antelopes of Central Africa, and having been apparently first observed by Baker, it has been classified by Herr von Henglin as the *Hippotragus Bakerii*. 'The colour is mouse-grey, with a black stripe across the shoulders, and black and white lines across the nose and cheeks. The height at the shoulders should exceed fourteen hands, and the neck is ornamented with a thick and stiff black mane. The shoulders are peculiarly massive, and are extremely high at the withers. Both the male and female are provided with horns; those of the former are exceedingly thick, and the points frequently extend so far as to reach the shoulders. It invariably inhabits open plains, upon which it can see an enemy at a great distance; thus it is the most difficult of all animals to stalk' (Baker). The méhédéhet is not so large nor nearly so powerful an animal as the last named. It is darker and has a more shaggy hide, and is free from such special markings about the head; and the female is without horns.

Emanuel returned this evening from the Hamran village with a new hunter for Cumming, named Hamet, and he has brought us the dread news that Sheik Aghill will pay us a visit to-morrow. At baggage-camel rate the journey lasted $9\frac{1}{2}$ hours, so we may calculate the distance at about 24 miles. Crossing the river on one occasion they found a dead hippo, the property of Coke or Cumming, but it had been dead too many days to be of any use even to an Arab.

Jan. 31.—Nothing special has occurred to-day. The Sheik has not arrived, but two even more unwelcome guests found their way into our tent.

These, however, were more easily disposed of, for one can kill a scorpion.

CHAPTER VII.

February 1.—We have changed our encampment to-day to a place named Emhaggar, on the south bank of the Settite, about twelve miles from El Effaara by camel-track. A prettier spot for a camp could not well be imagined, though the available space is perhaps too limited.

It is completely surrounded by trees with overhanging branches now in full leaf, and the river flows at our feet, though so quietly that it has more the appearance of a pool, in which on our arrival numerous hippos were seen to disport themselves. Thousands of small birds of very varied plumage are singing in the trees, and on the margin of the water are here and there to be found Egyptain geese and Marabou storks. The opposite bank presents one mass of green from the overhanging branches of some nabbuks in full leaf drooping to the water's edge. Our arrival, followed by a few unsuccessful shots at the hippos, made them very cautious about showing their noses above water; and as snap-shooting at them under these circumstances would rapidly reduce our ammunition, we have decided upon postponing for the present this sport, if such it can be called. Under a very wide spreading tree our staff have taken up their quarters, and a part of it is converted into a larder, and all seem highly pleased at having at last found such a shady retreat. The rule laid down by travellers never to pitch a tent or sleep under trees lest you may be attacked by animals at night, or have snakes drop upon you from the branches, is here utterly disregarded. As to snakes, we shall soon begin to think that Africa has taken a hint from Ireland, for not one have we seen or heard of excepting the demon of excited imaginations reported by Albert and Bob. Cumming bagged two buffaloes to-day, and one of them gave him great sport. The first shot having only broken a leg, he was able to bolt off across some open country for nearly half a mile, with Cumming after him on horseback; when the distance was reduced to twenty-five yards the buffalo pulled up and faced round, and for a moment stood his ground before charging. Instantly Cumming dismounted (the horse taking advantage of the opportunity to decamp), and when the buffalo was only ten yards from him a ball from his twelve-bore rifle brought him to the ground. Amongst several antelope killed by us to-day, I was fortunate in getting a méhédéhet with a superb head; but from henceforth the antelope will have a rest from our persecution, for of the common kinds we have all the specimens we require, and for the future shall only shoot them for food; and then, what is far more to the point, our thoughts have taken a higher flight by the sight of numerous tracks of rhinoceros, as well as by the report that we have arrived in the home also of the lion, giraffe, and ostrich.

We are becoming most learned in the study of tracks under the tuition of such masters of it as these Hamran Arabs, and hunting for the various animals in this way, even when attended with failure, is in itself a source of immense interest in the day's ride. There are no longer any fresh tracks of elephants, but on the high flat land away from the river, now so baked into a dry crust that it is split up by endless wide fissures, innumerable deep circular holes give evidence of how much it is frequented by them during or soon after the rainy reason, when the land is saturated with moisture.

Most of the tracks are very easily distinguished from one another, but those of the camel and giraffe are very similar. The soil is generally very favourable to tracking, consisting of a light sandy earth in which the impress of the hoof comes out very distinctly, but on the high dry ground no mark is left. The rhinoceros track will interest us most for the present, for though the track of the lion is by no means uncommon, we do not intend to pay the nominal monarch of the forest any attention until a new moon will give us a chance of watching for him in his nocturnal rambles.

Feb. 2.—A sudden outcry about midnight from those who slept under the big tree, and shouts from Emanuel of 'Sair! sair! bring gun, bring gun,' made us jump out of our beds, seize our weapons, and rush to the spot. Here all was darkness, for even the fires had been allowed to go out; but in the general confusion Emanuel could be heard declaring that a big animal had passed close to his head and was behind the tree, and begged of us to shoot it. The dying embers of the fires were soon blown into a flame, and then the big animal was looked for, but of course not found; and one began to believe that Emanuel had had a nightmare, until sundry haunches of 'venison' suspended from ropes in the 'larder' were seen to swing to and fro, and thus gave evidence of something having passed beneath them.

Looking at the assembled party, Bob was nowhere to be found, but when called for a faint voice from high up a tree answered, 'Yes, sir.' How he managed to climb to his perch in the dark he could not understand, but he gave the practical reason for doing so that he thought he could see Emanuel eaten by a lion safely from there. Albert's poor nerves were so shaken that the only relief he could find was by having two good fits of crying. No sleep after this event, for the whole camp became astir to make a big fire and laugh over the fright they had had, and for which there really was good cause; for when daylight appeared the tracks of a lion were seen about a foot from Emanuel's pillow. Hanging up a quantity of meat under a tree and sleeping with your head close to it, is about as simple a method of putting it into a self-made trap as could well be devised; and with his present experience it is not likely he will try the experiment again, though probably nothing of the kind would have happened had not our sleepy Arabs allowed the fires to burn out. But if we saw no real lion, we received a visit to-day from his representative amongst elephant-hunters; for, mounted on a most spirited little Arab, no less a personage than Jali arrived in camp. He is quite looked upon as the chief of the present race of Hamran sword-hunters, and his appearance quite justifies this, though living on elephant flesh has made him so fat and large round the waist that his agility must be slightly impaired. It did not seem so, however, as he sprang lightly from his horse, and in a most cordial way shook hands with us, quite as if we were old and long-parted friends.

He soon let us know who he was, and of his intimate acquaintance with Howagee Baker; and to prevent there being any doubt of his identity, showed us his left leg, which was shortened by fracture of the thigh-bone in an elephant hunt when in his service. He is a short but very powerfully-built man, with a fine-shaped head, now nearly bald, with good features and most jovial countenance, as if he had known but few of the cares of life in his wild exciting career, and he has a skin of a far lighter shade of brown than the usual colour of these Arabs.

He is on his way to Abyssinia, so he says, as chief of a party of hunters numbering twenty-six, all mounted on horses, to kill elephants and catch young ones for Sheik Aghill. In two days they will be in the Basé country, where they expect some fighting, and in seven days they will reach the present great home of the elephant. Baker gives a very spirited account of this man's skill as a hunter, and when he had to send him to his village in consequence of his misfortune, he considered that he had lost his best man. Jali speaks of his master also in the warmest terms, and has very far from forgotten the kindness he received from him after the accident occurred.

Vivian did a good stroke of business with him by an exchange of horses, adding ten dollars, his own having a very sore back. Jali had evidently not forgotten some of his English master's comforts, for he came quietly to me and whispered 'Cognac,' and then found in our whisky an excellent substitute. On his return he will try to seek us out again, for we shall not in all probability have moved far from our present ground.

Encamped close to us are some Arabs, who are chiefly ostrich-hunting. They have caught twelve, and one is a very fine black bird. Albert and Emanuel tried to purchase the feathers for twenty dollars, but thirty were demanded, an amount they could not raise, nor that we wished to give, not knowing at present whether our supply of dollars will more than meet our necessities. It was a pity we could not so far help them, for Albert declares the feathers would realise more than 100 dollars in Cairo. One of the Arabs' ostriches escaped yesterday, so they have begged us if we shoot one with a rope round his leg, to give it up to them. So far as our present experience goes, there is not much chance of our shooting one without a rope round the leg, for the only one yet seen was by Coke 400 yards off, and nearer it would not allow him to approach.

Creeping under a bank to-day for some distance, I managed to get a long shot at a hippo standing near the river's edge; but with no apparent result, for it succeeded in disappearing under water, and much to my annoyance the report caused about forty or fifty more, which must have been grazing quietly within a few hundred yards of me, to rush headlong over the shingle into the river.

Following them up I gave one a parting shot as he took his first breath, and certainly hit him in the head very severely; but after sundry tremendous splashings he disappeared, and time alone can prove whether he is killed. Vivian was on the track of a lion for several hours to-day, but never caught sight of him; and Coke had similar ill-luck with a rhinoceros. It is no easy matter to track quietly in these mimosa-woods, though there are many well-defined paths to the river made by animals, and generally adhered to by them; for the thorny branches that continuously block your way are now so dry that they break off with a snap on being moved; whilst the long grass, equally dry, requires most careful walking upon. But there are two ways of doing everything, and certainly watching a hunter wend his way noiselessly amongst them, and with his koorbatch gently push the overhanging branches on one side as if they were on hinges, soon makes one more expert at it; but there is a difficulty that even he cannot grapple with—viz., the guinea-fowl. On certain ground they literally abound in thousands, and there is then no escaping from them, for they run or fly at a respectful distance in front of you, making their hideous noise, and frightening away every animal in their neighbourhood.

Feb. 3.—Vivian brought home to-day the finest koodoo head of our collection. The horns measure $29\frac{1}{2}$ inches from base to tip, and 8 inches round the base. They have three spiral twists, and their tips are 41 inches apart. It was killed too far from the camp to be sent for to-day, so instead of covering it up with straw and sticks, as we usually treat our dead animals to keep off hungry birds or beasts, until the arrival of some of our Arabs with camels, his hunter skinned it and cut off the head. Before they had gone fifty yards from the remaining carcass it was so completely covered with huge vultures (more than a hundred), some of them standing on the backs of others, that it seemed as if it had been suddenly converted into a living mass.

Coke has had a shot at a rhinoceros with his ten-bore at twenty-five yards' distance, but it succeeded, though severely wounded, in making good its escape. Uncle Sam tracked it afterwards for more than a mile, and now and again they found small pools of blood where the animal had rested for a time; but they could not get within shot of it again, and finally gave up the hunt for the day, as Uncle Sam was very thirsty and wanted to return to the river for water. He is quite confident they will find it to-morrow, and probably dead. Upon myself fell the fortunes of the day, and singularly enough so; for when I told Essafi last evening that I should remain at home to-day, he begged me not to do so, as he was sure it would be his lucky day.

After a long ride to near the foot of one of the numerous low ranges of hills that almost surround us, we found the fresh tracks of rhinoceros, and upon arriving at a wood we dismounted, and, leading our horses, carefully followed them up for some distance, when Essafi pulled up, gave me his horse to hold, and went off by himself. Stealthily he crept along, stooping his head very low, so as to be able to get the best view under the low branches; and scarcely had he gone fifty yards, when he turned round and rejoined me, and then with an expression of intense excitement whispered in my ear the joyful word 'kharteet.' The next step was to tie up our horses, and then to follow his original path. Soon I could distinguish, lying under the trees about thirty yards from us, two mounds which, had it not been for Essafi, I should never have supposed were my long-sought friends. Essafi's breathing became here very hurried, and much too noisy to be agreeable, and at the same time he began making gestures for me to fire; but having lost an elephant, I was determined to profit by my experience, so crept on, Essafi remaining behind, until within fifteen or twenty yards of them, when I could just make out that one was lying with his legs towards me, and the direction in which his head would be. Whilst choosing the best spot to aim at something moved; it was only a little wag of the ear, but it announced that the sleeper had awoke, and instantly a ball from my eight-bore penetrated his thick hide under the right shoulder. The only effect for the moment was to make both animals spring to their feet and to start off, one to the right, the other to the left, in the direction they were lying. The wounded one, however, hardly went a yard before he faced round upon me, and with head high in air looked like meaning mischief; but another ball entering the front of his chest cut short his career, and he fell heavily to the ground uttering a faint cry, and was dead before Essafi reached him.

The eight-bore therefore, on this occasion, with a charge of seven drachms of powder, most certainly did its duty. The addition also of Messrs. Silver's vulcanite pad proved of decided value in diminishing the recoil, a point of no small importance when firing in a very cramped position, and when the second barrel has rapidly to follow. So far this pad has not been the least affected by the heat, as I was assured by the patentees, and their advice has been carefully attended to not to allow greasy things to touch it. Essafi's delight over the death of the rhinoceros was great, but so anxious was he to hurry me home that I had no time to examine my prize carefully or take his measurements. We galloped most of the way back so as to be in time for the camel-men to return there with Essafi to-day, but before doing this he could not resist applying for the stipulated backsheesh of two dollars. We have agreed to give the following rate of backsheesh to our hunters for the first we kill of certain animals—viz., elephant, two dollars; lion, two dollars; rhinoceros, two dollars; hippopotamus, one dollar; giraffe, one dollar; ostrich, one dollar. So this makes them very keen to show us new species, for, if they had their own choice, the hippos, rhinoceros, and buffaloes, where there are no elephants, would be most to their taste.

We had only just returned when Essafi ran up in great excitement, followed by all the camel-men, to tell me that my hippo of yesterday was dead. Albert then added that some Arabs from the next camp had seen one come out of the water as if to die, and as they knew that one of us had been shooting near there they came to report it, fearing to take possession of it. Two men were therefore sent off to search the place, and soon returned with the report that it was dead. The men now begged that a dragoman and a soldier should accompany them to the scene of future operations, to prevent there being a fight between the other Arabs and themselves over the flesh; and the request having been granted, Albert and our young soldier departed with them. We have been very fortunate in our two representatives of Egyptian authority. One is a very fine-looking young soldier, a negro, named Abdullah, of whom our Arab friends have a most wholesome dread. Munsinger Pasha let him have a picked dromedary, on which he careers over the country in grand style, looking uncommonly proud of himself and his fleet charger. He is dressed in a white uniform, which he keeps scrupulously clean, and wears a tarboosh. His rifle is always slung on the back of the camel-saddle when he is mounted, and round his waist he wears a belt having sundry articles fastened to it, besides a silver-mounted revolver and big knife. The other soldier is a veteran, who has long since seen his best days, named Hadji Basheer. He has brought his own donkey with him, or he would have been reduced to accept the position of being perched on top of one of our baggage-camels. In his way he is, however, very useful, for there are many little things in camp for which his talents can be turned to account, and the clever way in which he bound up my unfortunate smooth-bore proved that they were of no mean order. When the hippopotamus party arrived, they found a large assemblage of Arabs collected round the body, all anxious to get some of the dainty food, though afraid to commence operations without our sanction.

It was a very fine cow, and the ball had entered the head through the right eye. This ought to have been enough torture for the poor brute, but it was not allowed to die quietly, for it was driven out of its natural home by a crocodile that had already succeeded in gnawing off one foot. Joy reigned supreme amongst the outsiders on hearing that all should share equally with our own men, and they set to work in good earnest to assist in the flaying and cutting up. Albert stood by an observant watcher of the exciting scene, and, catching sight of a two-inch hippo, he laid claim to it, and afterwards brought it home in great triumph as an addition to our museum curiosities. It is now safely deposited in a bottle of spirits, one of a set we had fitted carefully into a box for such purpose before leaving England.

One would almost imagine that there was not another rhinoceros in the country, so great has been the row this evening in camp about the division of the hide—all wanting one of the eight pieces into which it had been divided for shields, the young soldier not being behindhand in putting in his claim—and it became necessary to administer a little law on this matter. We have settled that, after we have taken what we may require for specimens or for occasional presents to our own staff and to the two soldiers, each of our hunters will have in turn their choice of the remainder, according to which of us has killed the animal; and that our camel-men are to consider they have no claim whatever to the hides, for they have every reason to be well content with the enormous quantities of meat they are daily preserving for their families in the way already mentioned. Though we have ordered this drying process to be carried on well away from the camp, we have often much cause to object to it, for frequently a faint odour pervades the camp, especially the first part of the night, when the temperature is 80° or higher, and there is scarcely a breath of wind. The sun rapidly dries the long strips into chips, and when a large quantity of them is accumulated, they are packed in bundles and sent on camels to the villages; so, long after we have left the country, the natives will have good reason to remember us, if the rate of exportation continues as at present. There is no doubt it adds immensely to the pleasure of our sport to know that not a scrap of the animals we shoot is unnecessarily wasted, and indeed that all is turned to valuable account.

Judging by the minimum thermometer register, it might be supposed that our nights are very cool; but they are much the reverse until towards daybreak, when the temperature falls to the low point daily recorded, and it then remains pleasantly cool until the sun has well risen.

Eighty degrees Fahrenheit, rendered doubly oppressive by the perfect stillness of the air, on going to bed, and being disturbed in one's slumbers by a reduction of temperature to 50° Fahr., mean, in other words, lying down in a Turkish bath and waking up in an ice-house, and make it a point of no small difficulty how to calculate best for the night's repose. The recent nocturnal ramble of the lion has also complicated matters, for now such huge fires are blazing close to us that an ox might be roasted before them, and indeed our horses appear to stand some chance of being so. Cumming has unfortunately sprained his shoulder by the great recoil of his twelve-bore rifle, when firing a hardened ball, and it is so swollen that he will probably be crippled for some days.

Feb. 4.—This has been a very busy day for the Arabs, owing to the quantity of meat brought into the camp yesterday. A few have devoted their time to cutting up the hide of the hippo into long strips, to be ultimately converted into whips (koorbatches), whilst others have prepared the segments of the rhinoceros' hide previous to being sent to the village for conversion into the much coveted shields, or have cut up the remnant into sandals.

Excepting the pleasure of killing such big game, the Arabs have in fact all the advantage, for there is nothing of these animals worth bringing home as trophies beyond a specimen shield, the teeth of the hippo, and the horns of the rhinoceros. Ugly as these last-named are, there will be some satisfaction in keeping them, as they have at least an imaginary value in this country, and might consequently prove very useful in the future as presents. In Cairo they realise from six to ten pounds each, according to their size.

Their value is due to an Arab superstition of their complete power to nullify the injurious effects of any poison drunk out of them when converted into cups; so when an Arab is the fortunate possessor of one, he has no fear of drinking anything a stranger may give him.

Its supposed miraculous powers do not, however, end here, for if a man has been poisoned, a draught of water from one of these cups, with a little of the horn scraped into it, is considered almost equally efficacious. The rhinoceros of this part of Africa is a nearly black smooth-skinned animal, double horned, though bearing no comparison in this respect to one of its prototypes in Southern Africa; but, on the other hand, it is a much larger animal, and, according to report, infinitely more savage. Cumming and myself remained in camp, purporting to have a quiet day; but the Fates willed it otherwise, for whilst at our unusually late breakfast there was a sudden call to arms, every Arab rushing off frantically for his sword or spear, whilst Emanuel, Albert, and Bob shouted to us to bring our rifles. For a moment we thought that we were attacked by the Basé, but the cry from Albert of 'a lion! a lion!' as we ran up to the place where they were assembling settled that point. Here we found everyone laughing excepting one unfortunate Arab, who with far more expression of stolid indifference than of pain depicted in his face, held up to our view a horribly mangled hand; and then we were told that he thought he would like to see how our large spring trap worked, which we keep set at night, by touching it with a stick, and he certainly did have a practical lesson that he is not likely to forget soon. His yells were the cause of the sudden alarm amongst his friends, who thought he

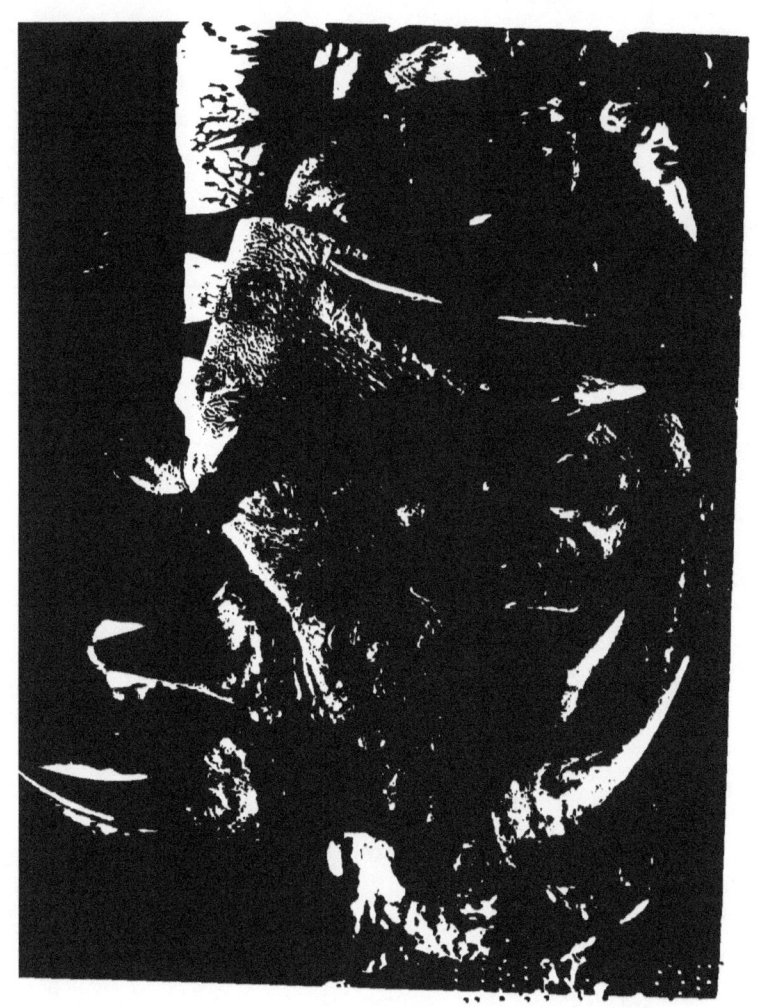

CALIFORNIA

had been seized by a lion; and though we should have considered the jaws of either highly objectionable, they seemed to think very little of the mechanical ones, and after witnessing the performance of plastering and bandaging, they quietly resumed their occupations. The trap caught his hand right across the centre, and though the flesh on both sides is much lacerated, there is no evidence of any bones being crushed, which is astonishing, for from the great strength of this trap, requiring two men to set it, one would have expected that the hand would have been completely severed by it.

Nothing important killed to-day. Coke tracked his wounded rhinoceros for several miles, and at last caught sight of him amongst some thick bushes. For a moment it turned as if to charge, but again went on its way unchecked by another ball from the ten-bore, which Coke does not think penetrated his thick hide. Vivian saw a lion, but could not get a shot at it.

Feb. 5.—An unlucky day for Vivian and Coke, for both were on separate rhinoceros tracks converging to the same wood, and, by singular ill-luck, as Coke had a close shot at his animal Vivian was drawing so near to his own that the report made it start off and only gave him a hurried shot, and neither were successful. Shooting in these closely-packed mimosa-woods, though the branches are dry and leafless, is very unsatisfactory, as the probabilities are great that a ball will be stopped or turned, however short the distance may be from an animal, and our chances of bagging these rhinoceros do not therefore seem great, unless we can catch them taking their morning nap. After a long morning's tracking, Essafi unexpectedly came upon some giraffes feeding about two hundred yards from us ; but the moment's delay in exchanging my smooth-bore for the express he carried was quite long enough to enable them to be out of sight and far away, and to leave me to make the best of the reflection that I had at last seen giraffes in their own home, minus the pleasure of leaving a card upon them. The Arab's mutilated hand is much swollen, and the poor fellow was in great suffering all night ; but I am glad to find that this is not due to any application of gunpowder to the wound, as I quite expected—another man having recently treated a wound of the leg in this fashion, and, it need scarcely be added, without materially aiding the healing process. The finest goteer head of our present collection was added by me this afternoon, measuring thirty-six and a half inches from base to tip of horn.

We are now in the full swing of experience of the industrious habits of the white ant, and a very disagreeable experience it is, for the earth is literally alive with them. Excepting metal, whatever rests on the ground for a few hours is certain to have an army of them doing their best to devour it, and they evidently hold to the opinion that there is nothing like leather. Fortunately most of our boxes are made of tin, and are therefore, so far as the ants are concerned, indestructible; but they have had a severe trial of strength in the frequent loading and unloading of the camels, and sundry bulgings and indentations tell their own tale of gradual destruction. We had very strong tin boxes made for us in England, nearly square in shape, with convex lids; but at Cairo we had others made—low, oblong, and with flat tops—by Russell's advice, as he thought ours would be very awkward loads for the camels.

Would that ants were our only plagues, for if they did eat up all our clothes we could go about as natives without much discomfort, and certainly with some advantage, so long as we remained in the country; but there is a far worse enemy in our present locality, a subtle one that strikes you in the dark, and, confident in his powers of baffling your efforts to arrest him, however strenuous they may be, adds insult to injury by trumpeting his approach. This monster of the night, after all, is only a mosquito; but he is a very fine species, and does his work so well that he must be felt to be fully appreciated. Fortunately his visits are limited to a portion only of the twenty-four hours, but the gap is not altogether badly filled up by one that should rather be termed an old friend than an enemy, so natural is it to see him. Go where one may, so long as the sun shines

—in the desert or out of the desert, in England or in Africa—he is the same in size and appearance and in his playful habit of annoyance, when, tired, one seeks some cool shade to be at peace for a little time, were it not for a fly.

CHAPTER VIII.

Feb. 6.—Having decided upon sending to Kassala tomorrow for any letters that may have arrived there, as well as for a few useful supplies, such as lemons, eggs, and honey, shooting has had to give place to correspondence, as it will probably be our last chance of communicating with friends at home, and proving to them how groundless so far have been the predictions poured into our ears before starting of the risk we were about to encounter to life or health through native tribes, animals, or disease. It is also a chance not to be lost to send back Mr. Cohen's faithful servant (slave?) to his master, for a more idle, useless being than he has proved could not be imagined, dividing his time solely between eating and sleeping. Mr. Pickwick's fat boy would have been a treasure compared with him, for between these two laborious exercises he was known occasionally to smile and to be a little 'wide awake,' whereas Abdullah always looks sulky when by chance he is awake. He proved himself, however, quite equal to looking after his own interest, when paid his month's wages of four dollars, by asking for baksheesh, but was instantly hustled off by Emanuel. He may think himself fortunate that his friends are not cannibals, for he is now in prime condition for killing. Emanuel thoroughly understands how to deal with our Arab party, and is just firm enough with them without using the koorbatch to make them really fear him and obey his orders, though they know they have in us a court of appeal. They muster strongly, for besides there being one man to each camel there are one or two volunteers, only too pleased to be allowed to join the circle and pick up what they can of the good things going.

I shot a very fine bull buffalo in the morning, after a most exciting chase on horseback. The first ball struck him in the shoulder and brought him to bay under a big mimosa, where he was finally despatched after a hard struggle for life. Though it was the finest head yet brought into camp, Vivian shot another in the afternoon which again surpassed it. They certainly are noble-looking animals with smooth black skins and well-developed hind-quarters, and the hide, especially about the neck, is of immense thickness. Their horns meet across the forehead, and are so wide at base that they almost entirely cover it; and then, after projecting directly outwards, rapidly diminish in size as they curve inwards again, and come to a point. *Filet de buffle* is one of our favourite dishes for dinner, but Mohamed turns him to account in many other excellent ways, the tongue being a special breakfast luxury; and even a marrow-bone is not forgotten. A chase after a buffalo bull-calf to-day afforded some of our men besides myself great sport, and he was ultimately caught and brought back after a fashion in triumph to camp, though not before he had had a little fun on his own account. After a rope had been fastened round his neck he positively refused to be led or pushed from behind, so the dragging process had to be adopted, and for a few moments successfully; but suddenly changing his tactics he made a charge, and, catching one of the Arabs exactly in the right place, sent him flying. This proceeding brought them to a mutual understanding; so as long as the rope remained taut the men pulled, but the instant it slackened they ran for their lives with the calf close on their heels; and so they progressed merrily on their way together until, the journey over, a frightful gash across the throat put an end at once to his part of the sport. We are now only waiting for the new moon to devote part of the night to watching for lions. That they abound here we have ample evidence, for not only can we hear them roaring at night round our camp, but we also see almost daily remnants of the large antelope and buffaloes which have been killed by them; and if any animals we shoot are so far from camp that they cannot be sent for the same day, there are always very distinct evidences on the following one of the visit of a lion in the interval. Last night we heard one roaming about close to the camp; and, as a pleasing variety in nocturnal visitors, we saw by the light of the fire a large snake glide under a bushy tree about two yards from one of our tents, and after putting his head out for a moment to have a good look at us, he retired for the night, and we left him in undisturbed possession of his establishment.

Feb. 7.—Hamet being laid up with a sore foot, I let Cumming try his luck with Essafi, and with a most satisfactory result, for through his guidance he had a shot at a rhinoceros, a buffalo, and a maāriff, and killed the two last named; and he also saw other species of antelope within shot, but was forbidden to take notice of them. Vivian, though not killing anything, very nearly succeeded in dislocating Mohamed's shoulder by hauling him violently up a bank. Probably he partly did so, for the arm became useless until a little additional hauling afterwards made something 'go in with a snap.' Coke finds tracking rhinoceros not very interesting, so for the present he intends confining his attention to the antelope, as he is anxious to get a good collection of their heads, and to-day he bagged some fine ariel.

The young soldier started for Kassala this morning, and calculates that he will be able to return here on the ninth day. It will be an important event for us, owing to the expected accumulation of the letters and newspapers of two mails.

Feb. 8.—Vivian has had quite an exciting day, for, starting out before sunrise in search of rhinoceros, he soon found the track of one, and almost immediately came within sight of him. He was then facing him, and not more than twenty-five yards off, and by holding up his head, and thus leaving his chest exposed, gave Vivian a good shot with his ten-bore. He then turned sharply round and went off at full speed, though severely wounded, for he was tracked partly by his blood for four or five hours, but he succeeded in escaping from his pursuers, much to their mutual disgust. However, fortune was to favour them, for returning home another fresh rhinoceros track was found, and soon afterwards, when still on horseback, they saw one feeding in open ground about thirty yards off. Vivian instantly dismounted, and, after approaching afew yards nearer, discharged the two barrels of his big gun at the right side. There was no running away this time, for after giving one loud whiff he charged straight down upon them. Fortunately a bushy tree was at hand, behind which Vivian sprang, and the rhinoceros passed on, but only to go about two hundred yards, for then, after faltering for a moment, he fell heavily to the ground and was dead before they reached him. He measured over six feet at the shoulder, and the first horn sixteen inches. The two bullets entered directly behind the right shoulder, and within four inches of one another. Vivian also saw two leopards, but could not get a shot at them.

Cumming has found unpleasant enemies in some bees that regularly set upon him and stung him about the eyes, but beyond temporary pain they have done no harm. He is very pleased with the proof he has had to-day of the killing powers of his twelve-bore rifle by Grant, charged with five drachms of powder and steel-tipped bullets; for of two buffaloes he killed one fell dead from a shot in the neck, and the other from two in the front of the chest. Hamet played him a practical joke by telling him that one was a rhinoceros, and he only found out the mistake after carefully stalking it for some time. Now that we have all shot buffaloes and know that they can always be found when wanted, they cease to give us any special interest, and we would rather avoid them in consequence of their interfering with other sport; but this cannot always be done, for our men will always try to show us some, as they set such a value on their flesh and hides.

Coke has also had a practical joke played upon him, but of a very different kind. Having apparently struck down dead with his express rifle a very fine têtel, he was so pleased with it that he stood over it for some minutes taking measurements and examining the wound, whilst Said was busily employed sharpening his knife on a stone previous to commencing his work of skinning, &c. The têtel, however, suddenly awaking to the fact of the unpleasant society he had fallen into, jumped up and went off on three legs at a highly creditable pace. Mounted on their horses, they soon came within sight of him again, and after a short chase he had to succumb to his fate.

Whether Said has an idea that chased têtel is like coursed hare is not known, or whether the run gave a special stimulus to his appetite, but at any rate he decided upon dining; so the skinning process having been completed, he opened the body and carefully removed the liver. This he cut up into small pieces, which looked so good that Coke almost felt inclined to taste it; but the dish was not yet prepared, for it was minus sauce, and on this point at least their tastes so decidedly differed that poor Said had to dine alone—a simple repast of pieces of raw liver with the gall squeezed over them, besides other additions which need not be mentioned. Our hunters afford us much amusement, and each has his own little peculiarities, but superstition reigns supreme with them all, excepting perhaps Essafi—unless he keeps them more to himself. The others have great faith as a source of luck in picking up a bit of the droppings of any animal they may be in search of, and after mixing it with an equal portion of tobacco and charcoal, they fold up the mass carefully in a corner of their garment, not, however, without first offering a little of it to their masters. Still, though our natural habits widely differ from those of our men, we are on excellent terms with them, especially at *our* luncheon. This also is a frugal repast, consisting of biscuits that we sometimes soften by soaking them in the river until they swell up to twice their normal size, a slice of Dutch cheese, and some figs and dates, and as an occasional treat a tin of preserved meat or a box of sardines; but, whatever it may be, master and man share alike whilst sitting under the shade of a tree or on the bank of the river. Filters are quite things of the past, for no water could look more pure and clear than the Settite in its present state where it flows over the shallows, and without doubt it is quite pure enough for all practical purposes, as it filters in its rapid course over the shingle. Our Arab neighbours sold us six fresh ostrich eggs yesterday at three piastres, or about sixpence each, their freshness having been first proved by knocking a hole into them and inspecting the contents. They have made a most pleasant variety to our daily fare, cooked in various ways. As an omelette they are excellent, but poached they can only be compared with plovers' eggs, with the great advantage of combining quantity with quality. These Arabs do not, as we supposed, confine themselves to ostrich-hunting, for they have caught a rhinoceros. The trap is a very simple arrangement, and is made thus: the trunk or branch of a tree measuring about six feet, and being about the thickness of a man's thigh, has a deep notch cut round it near one end, and a very stout rope made into a noose is fastened to this: the noose is fitted round a slight wooden hoop having thin wooden spikes passing from circumference to centre. The stump is then buried in the ground, and the hoop placed over a small hole dug in the line of some well-known track, and the surface is most carefully sprinkled over with earth. A rhinoceros or buffalo stepping into this hole is caught by the slip-knot, and if he is strong enough to drag out the stump it remains fixed to his leg, and he is thus easily tracked and ultimately killed with swords and spears, when worn out with his attempts to penetrate the woods with this obstacle to progression fastened to a leg, he is compelled to face his pursuers and suffer a slow and ignominious death.

Feb. 9.—Moved our camp two hundred yards further along the bank as a sanitary measure, for in consequence of the great amount of skin and meat drying our late ground has become a little odoriferous. The present encampment is a decided improvement in some respects, for it is divided into three parts well separated by trees. No. 1 is allotted to the Arabs and their camels, and it has been completely fenced in by cut brushwood, the gate consisting of a thick bush which is drawn on one side for entrance or exit. No. 2 has been given over to our immediate staff, and as it has a shady tree under which Mohamed can cook and drink coffee at his ease, he is perfectly happy. No. 3 has no special attraction for ourselves beyond the important fact that it is situated to the north of the others, for the wind generally blows, when there is any, from this quarter, and we thus escape from being made unpleasantly aware of the near society of our dark-skinned friends.

We cannot complain of not finding game, for Cumming saw three young lions to-day, and Coke a very fine old fellow; but as they could only get snap-shots from a distance, they were not successful in bagging one. I came suddenly upon a rhinoceros within five yards of me, but the bushes were so dense that I could not see the creature, and only knew it was there by its moving. For Essafi's special benefit, I let off the two barrels of my eight-bore, though it was practically impossible for any bullet to penetrate the thick mass of branches and then this creature's hide with any effect; and so, as I expected, it went off, giving three tremendous whiffs, and though we followed the track for two hours we could not find it again. 'Jali' paid us another visit to-day on his return from elephant-hunting, after a much shorter expedition than he had anticipated. He reports having killed six elephants, five by his own hand, and caught a young rhinoceros, which they are bringing back to the Hamran village, from whence probably it will soon depart upon its first and last visit to Europe.

Feb. 10.—The lions last night were specially entertaining, for three were heard roaring in different directions about the same time, and very near the camp. In the morning an Arab from the other camp came in great haste to tell us that he could hear a buffalo making a great noise as if caught by a lion, and that his people wanted us to help them to find it. Vivian being 'at home,' joined the party, and, advancing in line, they searched the country for some time, but found nothing. He, however, made them very happy by previously dropping a buffalo dead by a ball in the neck from his ten-bore. Coke has hit a hippo in the head, and believes that it is dead, but he could not remain long enough near the pool to see if it floated.

Myriads of small birds have passed eastwards over our camp both this morning and evening. Their flight is very rapid, and they are packed so closely that they appear like a cloud of dust, and in their swoops over the river they make a noise like a rushing wind. Hawks follow in their wake, and catch in the air or on the water any unfortunate stragglers. Every evening soon after sunset we have other winged visitors which fly at a tantalising height over the camp. In their flight and call they resemble geese, but the only specimen bagged by the occasional volley fired into them proved that they are more nearly allied to the heron. Certainly this is a marvellous country for birds, and in a measure gives a direct contradiction to the doctrine that numbers bring disease. Guinea-fowl are apparently in millions here, and in some places the ground is completely covered with them. The doves are only second to them in number, for they swarm by the river-side. The tamest birds are the Marabou storks, and there are generally about a dozen taking a walk leisurely up and down the river in front of us, waiting for anything that chance may bring them from our daily-replenished larder.

Feb. 11.—Coke's hippo has not floated, but there are great rejoicings in camp owing to the certainty that Cumming has killed one, if not two, to add to one I shot this morning, and which, to my surprise, floated in about an hour. An expanding bullet from my Rigby express entered the head two inches below the eye, and killed it almost instantaneously; for after a few seconds' tremendous splashing it turned over, and the legs appeared above the surface before it sank. Being close to camp, we were soon able to return to the place with all our Arab men besides our neighbours, who appear now to think they have some claim to a share of the spoils. The hippo was floating in the centre of a large pool, but no hesitation was shown to swim out to it, as with shouts and yells, and cries of 'timsah' (crocodile), they rushed wildly into the river. Having managed somehow to fasten a rope round a leg, the hippo was gradually hauled by the swimmers to shallow water, and then by sundry rolls they succeeded in getting it into two feet of water, when the cutting-up process was commenced in a thoroughly business-like way. An Arab, chosen by the assembly as being specially learned in the art, first marked out most carefully the various lines of incision by which the hide was to be divided into segments, whilst the others gave an extra edge to their curiously-shaped curved knives with the aid of a smooth pebble. With so many willing hands, the hide was very soon completely detached and placed in the shallow water to soak well. Then all the superficial layer of fat was most carefully removed and placed by itself. This was followed by an investigation of the interior, and after all the fat had been again carefully collected, every man appeared to think that he could act entirely upon his own account, and the cutting and slashing at the flesh became universal; and so complete was the operation that the storks, vultures, and other birds of prey which had collected in hundreds around us must have been grievously disappointed after our departure on finding how badly they were repaid by their patient waiting. It was during this performance that Essafi, whom we all looked upon as quite a superior being to the others, sank one degree in my estimation; for the man who day by day had sat by my side to share my luncheon and drink from the same water-bottle, I beheld for the first time feast with the rest upon the raw entrails, whilst with hands covered with blood he did his share of the work. Busy as he was I was not forgotten, for one man was told off to make a fire and cook slices of the liver and flesh, and when they were done Essafi brought them to me, and, squatting by my side, cut off small bits in turn for us both. How could one refuse so delicate an attention! The lion's share, however, fell to him, for I found that hippo-flesh 'toasted' before it had even cooled down after death was, though very excellent in flavour, a trifle too tough, and that a little went a long way, especially with the surroundings of which for some time I had been a spectator. Cooking *à l'Arabe* is a simple process. A fire is instantly made by breaking up a lump of dry elephant's manure always to be found, though sometimes reduced to a cinder by the sun, and after placing over it a few sticks, and on the top of these some big pebbles, it is set in a blaze when we are absent, by a spark from a flint on some tinder that one or other Arab is sure to have in his possession, but when present a request is always made for the burning-glass each of us carries, as its power of producing the needful spark is a constant source of astonishment and delight to them. When the stones are well heated, the strips of meat are laid upon them and rapidly cooked, and when antelope are thus treated the bones are 'devilled.'

Returning home I shot a crocodile, which only just succeeded in struggling into the water to die. Vivian has again seen a lion, but could not get a shot at it, as it almost instantaneously disappeared amongst the bushes. After dinner we were entertained by a large herd of buffaloes coming down the steep bank on the opposite side of the river to drink, and quite within shot had it not been too dark. Coke has been again unlucky in not stopping a rhinoceros. He succeeded in stalking within thirty yards of it as it faced him, and he therefore waited for a side shot expecting that it would approach him. This it did for five yards, but then being startled it turned round suddenly and only gave him a snap-shot at its side, and another as it galloped off at a part which nature has certainly done her best to render bullet-proof.

Feb. 12.—Coke is the hero of the moment, for not only has he killed the first lion, but he has also had quite an adventure; and as he has escaped unhurt, we are very much obliged to him for supplying us with some good material for our diaries.

Making an early start with the intention of shooting anything that 'Inshallah' might be sent to them, Uncle Sam in a short time pulled up suddenly, and pointed out a lion stealing away up a hill in front of them, and only twenty yards off. Coke fired, and though he could not see if he had hit him, he was led to think so by Uncle

Sam going lame and pointing to his thigh, and as the lion turned his course after the shot they ran forward to try to cut him off. This they effectually succeeded in doing, for the lion politely met their intentions half-way by facing round, and with one loud roar coming towards them at a trot. Coke then decided upon not firing again until it was close up to him, and knelt down for a steady shot, so on it came, and just as Coke pulled the trigger a tug from behind brought him nearly on his back, and of course sent the muzzle of his rifle in the air. There was nothing now left to be done but to run for his life, and off he went as fast as his legs could carry him, expecting every moment to feel a *gentle* pat on the back. Most fortunately there was a hill close in front of him, and having gained this he was safe, for his wounded enemy could no longer follow him; and whilst crouching in the grass at the bottom, and growling at his ill-luck, he received his death-blow. Uncle Sam in the meantime had bolted in an opposite direction, little realising that in trying to save his master from the jaws of the lion he very nearly succeeded in causing him to fall into them. When they arrived home he explained his conduct by saying that he thought his master's rifle must be unloaded, and as he was unarmed and could not protect him, he believed their only chance of escape was to run away.

We can now afford to laugh over his narrow escape,

but it will be as well for us all in future to have no repetition of such experience. One of the hippos shot by Cumming yesterday, and another by Vivian this morning, have floated and given the camp plenty of occupation. On our way home Vivian and myself met, and directly afterwards Essafi having found some ariel, we each shot one to please him. Our kindness was dearly rewarded, for some Arabs appearing on the scene a feast was decided upon, and yesterday's performance repeated, occasioning us considerable delay. Essafi again brought some toasted slices of liver, and this proved so agreeable to our palates that the culinary performance will probably be repeated next year in the Highlands.

Coke has had another escape from injury, though the enemy was easily captured, for after bathing in the river he found in the towel he was about to use a fine scorpion, which he carefully brought back and transferred to my 'cyanide' bottle. This bottle is always kept at hand in the tent, and any creeping thing introduced into it rapidly succumbs to its noxious fumes. There are a great number of scorpions here, but no one has as yet been stung, and they are rarely seen unless looked for. A sure find is under our boxes if they have not been moved for a few days.

CHAPTER IX.

Feb. 13.—Another stirring event for entry in the diaries, but with a less satisfactory termination than yesterday's, and Cumming is the victim. After spending some time in search of rhinoceros a fine maāriff crossed his path, and with two shots from his twelve-bore rifle he brought it to the ground. In the meantime his horse had started off and Hamet after it, and whilst alone, thinking that he might as well inspect the dying animal, he walked up to within three yards of it, when, finding that it appeared to have a good deal of life left in it, he turned round to get out of harm's way. Hardly had he done so when he heard a rush made behind him, and in an instant as he fired a chance shot over his shoulder he was sent flying in one direction and his rifle in another. Upon picking himself up he felt inclined to laugh at the occurrence, until on putting his hand on the outside of his thigh where he had been struck by one of the maāriff's horns, he found that it was covered with blood. It being now no laughing matter he went quietly to a tree close by, and having despatched the maāriff, which had such a strong objection to die that it required three more bullets in the head and neck, he laid down and waited for the return of Hamet. The leg had by this time become painful and stiff, but as they were two hours or more from home, there was nothing to be done but to ride home. Singularly enough, they had not gone fifty yards before they saw standing under a tree close to them the rhinoceros they had in vain sought for all the morning. All thought of the wounded leg in a moment vanished, and jumping off his horse Cumming fired one shot at the rhinoceros, and as it started off another at the hind-quarter without any apparent effect. They then started in pursuit, but very quickly pulled up on hearing a sudden crashing sound amongst the mimosas, and immediately they saw the rhinoceros with head down charging directly upon them, and only ten yards off. Another ball, this time in the head, turned it once again, and it was instantly lost amongst the thick trees. Tracking was renewed, though only for a few hundred yards, for now the wound in the leg began to tell, and Cumming was compelled to give up the hunt and come home as best he could, riding side-saddle. On his arrival in camp, there was found to be a large gaping wound in the outer and fleshy part of the right thigh of considerable depth, judging from the length of the external wound and the pointed nature of the maāriff's horn; and some of the lacerated muscle protruded through it. The skin on the inner side of the left thigh had been grazed also by the other horn, and he therefore must have had a most narrow escape from a fatal injury from one or other of them. He bore very patiently having the wound sewn up; and now, with the leg well supported with bandages and pillows, he is lying on an angarep quite at ease, though not best pleased at the unexpected interruption for a time to his amusements. Great interest is shown by all our followers in the wounded sportsman, and they were much disappointed to find that a deputation headed by Hamet was not allowed to give practical proof of the general sympathy by rubbing gunpowder into the wound.

In the evening they marched in a body, led by a musician playing the 'rababa,' in front of his tent to entertain him with some of their games. The ground, however, was too limited to allow them to perform much in his presence, so they were obliged to retire to a sand-bank, where a grand performance took place in his honour before the rest of the party. The moon was sufficiently powerful to allow them to go through their warlike exercises with great zest, and so excited did they become at times that it looked very much as if they were fighting in earnest; and considering that their swords are so sharp that they can shave with them, it was quite a relief when we saw their weapons of war laid down and another entertainment begun. This consisted of a species of wrestling. After sides had been chosen they stood opposite to one another at about ten yards' distance, and then each man holding up one leg behind him by grasping the foot with one hand (either the right foot with the left hand or *vice versâ*) charged the enemy immediately opposed to him, and tried to throw him over with the free hand, a proceeding that usually terminated by both rolling on the ground. Much to the amusement of all, Emanuel joined heartily with them in this game, and being a more strongly built and heavier man than many of the Arabs he was more than able to hold his own with them when he could catch them, but he was naturally beaten in rapidity of movement in this cramped position. Albert and Bob were too afraid of their rough ways to join in the game, the latter remarking, 'them not men, them monkeys.' To what hour they kept up the entertainment is not known, but long after we had left the scene and had 'turned in' for the night, it had been changed to a concert consisting of the most fearful screams and yells, with which the surrounding hills resounded. My crocodile floated to-day, and when it had been skinned and opened it was found to contain thirty-seven eggs with hard white shells, and about the size of a goose's egg. These were evidently looked upon as a great prize by Essafi and his friends, and as I laid claim to none in consequence of the length of time that had elapsed since I shot the crocodile, they were equally divided amongst them, excepting the odd one, which I broke out of curiosity.

We have recently found out another party of Hamran Arab hunters encamped near us, and we are on the most friendly terms with them, though, if the truth were known, we probably do them an infinity of harm by driving the big game away from their neighbourhood. These men devote themselves entirely to rhinoceros trapping, and to-day Essafi pointed me out four places where traps were set. Upon two of them he accidentally stepped, but so lightly that he only disturbed the surface earth, and this he carefully re-arranged with a stick, for the rhinoceros is supposed to be so wary that it will not tread upon ground over which it can sniff the passage of a human being. Cunning as the rhinoceros is in the opinion of these hunters, they consider the elephant far more so, and say that it will even turn back when on its way to drink sooner than continue in a path that has been even crossed the same day by a human being, and that it will never follow the same path twice in succession. It is therefore very difficult for the Arabs to know where best to dig pits for them to fall into. In cunning these animals must find some good competitors nevertheless in their hunters, and as an example of this I was much amused to see that an excellent imitation of a rhinoceros track had been made in the light earth over one of the traps as a special inducement for the animal to walk into it.

Feb. 14.—The news of the wounded sportsman rapidly spread to the other camps, and so much interest has been shown in him that numerous black visitors have called to inquire, and they have been given that most satisfactory of replies, 'that he was doing as well as could be expected.' It is no small satisfaction to him to know that his enemy has made a most important addition to his collection of antelope heads.

The sky to-day is quite obscured by light white clouds at a great height, which are quite a refreshing novelty, though we hope it is one that will not be repeated often, for the moon is now nearly right for night-shooting.

Feb. 15.—A more perfect morning than this has been could not be imagined, for the usual heat of the sun has been most agreeably diminished by the continued presence of light clouds, and at the same time a gentle breeze from the south-west has given a general freshness to the atmosphere. Birds with innumerable varieties of note, and some so small that a humming-bird might almost look majestic amongst them, are singing in every direction, trying not to be outdone by the everlasting cooing of the doves; whilst others, less harmonious, give us the benefit of a little screeching; but above, or rather distinct from them all, is the single deep and plaintive note of a bird that sounds as if this songster had all the cares of the others thrown upon its shoulders. What kind of bird this is we have not yet discovered, and, excepting for food, the feathered tribe are left undisturbed. I regret not having shot at four very fine birds I saw a few days ago in pairs on some high rocky ground, for I now find it was a rare species named the Aboo Goumba. This bird is fully described in Mansfield Parkyns's most interesting account of 'Life in Abyssinia,' and he gives an illustration of the male and the female. It is about the size of a very small turkey, and on the ground looks quite black, excepting a white spot on the margin of the wing, but when it flies it shows a very large amount of white in the wing. The beak is thick and long, and has a horny lump on top of it, and the male has in addition red-and-blue wattles. Tempting shots as they were to me, I would not change my cartridges, as I was at the time tracking a rhinoceros. The little birds that passed us the other day in such marvellous numbers remain in the neighbourhood, and with one shot this evening I killed thirty-five, and was almost surprised that more did not fall. This bird is much smaller than a sparrow, has a red beak, and feathers on the back like a lark, and is called by our Arabs 'Hadderdub.' Essafi says that they arrive here after the rains, and depart again before they set in. Vivian, when returning home to-day, killed seven guinea-fowl with a right-and-left.

Fortunately we are well supplied with books, so Cumming has some amusement whilst lying quietly on his bed under a tree. From his position he has a good view of the river, and part of to-day was spent watching the Arabs cut up the crocodile I shot on the 13th, which did not float till this morning; and afterwards seeing the gathering over the remnants of numerous Marabou storks, and, by their kind permission, of some small brown vultures. These storks have an absurd resemblance to thin old men in white waistcoats and evening dress-coats, with hands tucked under the coat-tails, and head thrown forwards as if weighed down by all the cares, imaginary or otherwise, of a long Parliamentary career. The Arabs killed a porcupine to-day with their spears, and with great parade it was brought to us as a present; but as all the best quills had 'dropped out,' we would not accept it.

Feb. 16.—A light mist almost throughout the day has been another atmospheric novelty, and by no means an agreeable one, for with a maximum temperature in the shade of 87° Fah. it has felt particularly oppressive.

It has been very oppressive also in another sense; for Albert is in disgrace. Some question arose between Essafi and himself this morning about a koorbatch which

Essafi had lent me the previous day, and could not be found, though this was by no means an uncommon occurrence; for when riding in the woods, the report of 'game-ahead' would make one dismount instantly, and the whip was somehow or other sure to disappear. A stimulus was given to the discussion by Essafi calling Albert a thief, and by Albert returning the compliment with interest, in declaring that all Essafi's people were thieves, from the Sheik downwards. Essafi now improved the situation by a similar reply, and at the same time cursed Albert's religion. This spirited conversation took place whilst Essafi, mounted, was waiting for me, and as I approached him I saw it come to a sudden termination by Albert with clenched fist striking him in the neck. With one bound Essafi was off his horse, and like a tiger would have sprung upon his foe had not Emanuel and Bob been on the spot, and held him back whilst I took Albert away. It was then useless to speak to Albert about his foolish conduct, for, white with rage, he would only exclaim, 'I am very fond of my religion, and I would kill any man who cursed it.' So in this happy frame of mind I left him under a tree to cool down, and rode off with his adversary. This was scarcely a nice commencement to a day's sport, and instead of the preliminary gallop and wild shout to Abd-el-Khadr, a patron saint, to bring him luck, with which our hunters always start off, Essafi now led the way silently and with head down, as if his mind were far from occupied with thoughts of how he could find *me* something to kill to-day. The neglected Abd-el-Khadr, however, was not forgetful of him, and though for some time Essafi listlessly followed a fresh rhinoceros track we soon came upon, a broken twig, so moist that it must have very recently been in the animal's jaws, was all that was required to make my impetuous hunter himself again, and thoughts of the past and future were at once merged in the present. The rhinoceros was very quickly found, but as he was facing us, and the trees were so dense that we could not stalk round him, he got away probably more frightened than hurt by the only shot I was able to fire at him. Later in the day we came unexpectedly on another to our right, not more than ten yards off, and seeing us first of all, he made us acquainted with his presence by charging straight at us. Fortunately the discharge of my smoothbore when he was unpleasantly close (for owing to the thickness of the covert I could not instantly get my gun to my shoulder) turned his course a little, and in a moment he was again lost to view.

On my return in the evening, Albert, having cooled down, received some wholesome advice about restraining his temper, and not striking the Arabs as he had done. He stoutly maintained that he could not consider himself wrong in striking Essafi under the circumstances, for the Greeks looked upon these people very differently to the English; but he was clearly made to understand that whilst he remains with us he is not to take the law into his own hands for any insult, imaginary or otherwise, that he may receive from these Arabs, but to report the circumstance to us, and if a good case is proved against any of them, we have a very simple and most practical punishment at hand in sending them back to their village, for with the inducements we can offer we have no difficulty in obtaining recruits or retaining their services. By his conduct on this occasion he has quite proved himself unfitted to hold a post of responsibility in this kind of rough life, having no command over his temper. Excepting, however, the few occasions mentioned, he has proved a most valuable servant to us, and in the ordinary routine work of a dragoman or courier one could not desire a better man. He is of superior birth to the ordinary dragoman, and though looked upon as a Greek, he is nothing of the kind, for his father was a Spaniard and his mother an Italian.

He spent several years of his early life in Gibraltar, and there acquired the English language, which he speaks perfectly, as well as Arabic, and in this respect is very superior to Emanuel, whose English is not altogether quite easy of comprehension, and we have every reason to have equal faith in his honesty. We may indeed congratulate ourselves on the whole of our staff. Mohamed the cook, from the hour he was engaged, has done his utmost to please us, and is always ready to turn his hand to any odd job out of his special calling, of which he is such a thorough master; and as he can even skin birds well, we hope later on to make him of use in this way.

Bob, Emanuel's right-hand man, and like himself a Maltese, appears never happy unless busily employed for one or other of us, and from morning to night is at work. He finds great scope for his intellect in mending our tattered garments for us until we cast them off, and then, by a special display of ingenuity in patchwork, he is able to transfer them to his own most limited wardrobe. A pair of trousers has quite an interesting career, for when Bob can no longer with anything like decency wear his master's present, he transfers the remains to Ibrahim, who, with his black skin, is not so particular about sundry holes; but a time comes when even he thinks he must discard them, and then the old soldier, with more mind than body, is sure to find some part of them useful to cover his lean shanks. Ibrahim has proved the greatest surprise, for he made a very bad start in consequence of Mr. Cohen having prejudiced us against him by giving him a very bad character after he heard we had engaged him, and so much so that we almost left him behind, until the happy thought occurred to us that perhaps Mr. Cohen's opinion was influenced by his desire that we should engage his bright specimen of a servant,

Abdullah. He is without doubt a most valuable addition to our party, as he always does the hard manual work; he takes care of the horses, helps to prepare the heads and skins, and seems able to turn his hand to anything; and, what is of no small importance to his usefulness, he requires no interpreter, having a very fair knowledge of French, which he learnt, as well as Spanish, during a period of four years he spent in Mexico as one of the Egyptian Contingent under Bazaine. The two soldiers also deserve a special word of praise. The old one, though weak, is very willing to do his best, and when not looking after his donkey—which he reared, and seems as fond of as if it were his own child—he is perfectly contented to sit all day on the bank fishing, but owing to the weakness of his tackle he seldom succeeds in landing anything. The young one has quite established his right to the position of one of our personal attendants, as he works like any of the others, and seems extremely pleased to be allowed to do so.

Cumming continues perfectly quiet on his bed, and the wound looks very well. The condition of the Arab's hand is also very satisfactory.

Feb. 17.—Uncle Sam seldom returns home from a hunt without having done something extraordinary and peculiar to himself, and the explanation after dinner is always looked forward to with much pleasure; but to-day he has outdone himself, and will probably soon be 'at home' again, or, more correctly, returned as a slave to his owner, who, according to Uncle Sam's account, is very cruel to him. After Coke and he had left a wood, they passed close by a very overhanging mimosa quite apart from any other trees, and under it they could just distinguish a lion lying asleep. Coke at once moved on a few yards to get a good shot as the lion came out; and when it did so Uncle Sam rushed in front of him, and absolutely gave chase to it. The lion merely went away at a trot, but so close was Uncle Sam behind it that Coke could not fire, and no amount of shouting would make him stop, until the lion, distancing him, gave Coke a long shot, which only had the effect of pulling Said up short on hearing the bullet whiz past his ear. It is difficult to imagine a more annoying occurrence, for it is very unlikely he will get such a chance again of bagging lion No. 2. Coke gave vent to his feelings by an outburst of very pure English, that Uncle Sam sufficiently understood to make him turn back and walk sulkily home, not taking the least notice of his master's movements. The explanation he gave for his conduct was more simple than satisfactory, and much the same as before—viz., that he thought his master's rifle was not loaded, and that he had better prove how courageous he was by driving the lion away. The after-dinner attendance of the four hunters is by no means an unimportant ending to the day's proceedings, and standing or squatting round us, with Albert to act as interpreter at their side, each reports in turn on the events of the day, and his intentions for the following one, so that they may avoid going over the same ground as much as possible. Their great desire is to show us the animals for which they have as yet received no 'backsheesh,' as they feel that these dollars are their own, whereas they do not know how much will ultimately fall to their lot of the hides, &c., after Sheik Aghill has set eyes upon them. Still it is very difficult to extract any really useful information regarding the prospect of finding different species of animals where they propose taking us, and questions of the kind only draw from them their one word, 'Inshallah' (please God); but they were kind enough to tell us that they prayed to God every evening to send them the animals they wanted for the 'backsheesh.'

Vivian thought he would try a little extra persuasion with his man Mohamed to-night, when the following conversation took place:—

Vivian.—Do you think you will find me a lion to-morrow?

Mohamed.—Inshallah.

Vivian.—Do you hope to find me a lion to-morrow?

Mohamed.—Inshallah.

This reply was perhaps more satisfactory than was

given to the guest of a Scotch laird by a deerstalker, when he made a somewhat similar inquiry :—

Guest.—Well, Mac, what do you say of the day—will it be fine or wet?

Mac.—Well, sir, I hope it will be a fine day.

Guest.—Oh, never mind what you hope : tell me what you think it will be.

Mac.—Ah! sir, that's another matter. I think it will be a very wet one.

It is becoming daily of more importance that we should know the kind of ground we are to be taken to, for our horses' backs are becoming sore, English saddles withal, and if we are not going to the woods frequented by rhinoceros, it is no use carrying our heavy smooth-bores; but we have been in this neighbourhood so long now, and have picked up so much Arabic, that instead of implicitly obeying the orders of our respective hunters we can afford to make them take a second place, and do a little hunting on our own account.

Feb. 18.—Abdullah has returned from Kassala, and after all our anxiety for the arrival of the mail it has been cruelly repaid, for instead of a pile of letters and newspapers, it only brings the 'Times' of January 1, one 'Punch,' and two letters, so when the others will reach their destination is a problem beyond calculation. The chances are in favour of their doing so on English soil towards the end of the year. Well, we have the immense satisfaction of knowing through said 'Times' that whilst we were experiencing the heat of an exaggerated English summer, our friends at home had a 'seasonable' Christmas, which, in other words, means one of thorough enjoyment and health to the young and vigorous, and of intense misery and death to the poor and infirm.

Munsinger Pasha has sent a few lines to let us know that there has been no alteration in the dates of departure of the Red Sea steamers. The time has now arrived for a great change to take place in our arrangements, one that has long been contemplated, and only delayed until the arrival of Abdullah. It is the division of our party into two, so that we may interfere less with one another's sport; and whilst Vivian and myself will remain in the neighbourhood of the Settite, Coke and Cumming have chosen to return to the Hamran village and make a fresh start to the Salaam, another tributary of the Nile to the south of the Settite. They could reach equally soon, if not sooner, by striking due south from here, but the camel-men declare that it would be a four days' journey without water, and they therefore refuse to undertake it. By mutual agreement Emanuel, Bob, and Abdullah go with them, whilst Albert, Mohamed, and Hadji Basheer with his donkey stay with us; and to make up for the deficiencies of the old soldier, we retain the valuable services of Ibrahim. The afternoon has been chiefly spent in dividing our stores and making ready for an early departure to-morrow morning in opposite directions. Cumming took a quiet ride to the hippo-pool to give our friends left in it a few parting salutes, and also to test the wounded leg; and, considering what a short time has elapsed since the injury occurred, it bore the ordeal remarkably well. He gave Hamet to-day a pair of drawers lined with red flannel, and Hamet is so proud of them that he has been strutting about ever since and has shown the red lining to everyone. It has proved an unfortunate present, for it has greatly excited the jealousy of the others, and they all want a similar pair, and are not disposed to be put off with the excuse that we do not all wear exactly similar garments. Our last evening together here has terminated most properly, with a lecture on the contents of a small medicine-chest fitted up by Messrs. Savory and Moore, together with a few general hints on medical matters, and with the understanding that in case of emergency Abdullah is to be sent post-haste to our camp.

CHAPTER X.

Feb. 19.—The last good-bye has been said; the ground upon which we have been encamped for three weeks is left to the vultures; our tent is pitched on a new site; and as Vivian and myself sit over our quiet dinner, we can fully realise what a great change has taken place in our existence. How long we shall be parted from the others depends entirely upon the sport we get in our respective localities, but we at least hope to meet at Kassala in April, and return to England together. A general feeling of sorrow pervaded all our staff on parting, and it was really pleasant to see Bob retire quietly to a tree to give vent to the tears he could no longer restrain. He had evidently taken a particular fancy to Vivian, and did not at all like being parted from him. His desire is ultimately to become a dragoman, and to all appearances he will be certain of success in such a career. Great excitement was evinced amongst our camelmen about their destination, as it was a serious matter; for those who return to the Hamran village now, will not be allowed by Sheik Aghill to go the Salaam. The consequence was that the ten best men were picked out to remain with us, and a nicer lot of fellows we could not desire.

Our present encampment is not more than a mile from the last, and higher up the river, which had to be forded twice to get to it. The place is named 'Henna,' and it is well known to Arab hunters as a camping ground.

Immediately beyond it to the east are the hills that mark the boundary of the hunting-grounds of Mek Nimmur, a native chieftain whom Baker described so fully when in this country. Essafi says that he was a source of great terror and anxiety to the Hamran Arabs, for, well armed and mounted, he went about their country with a party of his men, and coming upon them unexpectedly at night, would kill them and steal all their cattle. With his neighbours on the opposite side, the Abyssinians, he was on friendly terms, and they let one another alone until five years ago, when a report having spread that he had accumulated great wealth, they took a leaf out of his own book, and after killing him carried off all his possessions. The range of low mountains to the east marking the Abyssinian frontier can be very distinctly seen from the high table-land above our encampment; and nearer us on the north side is a low range of hills, beyond which extends the territory of the Basé. Essafi when he came for orders to-night gave us a long account of these people. He says they are the enemies of both Abyssinians and Hamrans, and that the Settite bounds their territory on one side. They have a Sheik, and live in houses made of straw when undisturbed ; but on the supposed approach of an enemy they burn these and retire into holes in the ground. They always keep a careful watch from their hills, fearing an attack from Abyssinians or Hamrans, to whom they are equally hostile, and all their stores of grain are kept far inland as a means of protection, whither their wives and children are sent as occasion may require. They have cattle, sheep, and goats, but no camels ; and almost their only trade is in seed and honey, which they send to a village situated on the outskirts of their territory, partly inhabited by their people and under the protection of Egypt. Their clothing consists of a skin round the waist, and their weapon of war is a spear. Their attacks are always made most stealthily and by night, and they will fight to the death.

From the way they retire into their underground homes, it is almost impossible to find them in their own country, so if the Hamrans want to fight them they wait for the month after the termination of the rains, when they come down to the river-side to feed their cattle. The Abyssinians seldom attack them, and when they do so it is only to obtain slaves from amongst their women and children. Essafi declares that the Hamrans would very much like to go in a large body under Sheik Aghill, and kill them and carry off all their cattle ; but they are afraid to do so, as Munsinger Pasha has ordered them to leave the Basé alone ; so the gradual advance of Egypt's power in this direction does appear to be bearing fruit, and now that a portion of the Basé country actually belongs to Egypt, and pays her taxes, it may not be very long before the whole of this wild race will seek her protection if she does not extend it unasked ; and when this is accomplished, Abyssinia, only lying beyond, will have reason to feel alarm for her safety in this direction from her great enemy. Excepting one or two, nothing would induce our men to go with us into the Basé country, and the very name of Basé seems to strike terror to their hearts ; and if the Basé are equally afraid of the Hamrans, there must be every chance of a mutual stampede on the sight of one another. Another of Essafi's statements is, that their cattle are so limited in number that they rarely kill any, and depend chiefly for meat on the assistance of lions and vultures ; for they watch the flight of the vultures, and are often guided by them to the body of a buffalo or antelope which has been killed by a lion, and they then bag all that their friends have not already demolished. Vivian has made a discovery, though not without some hesitation in the attempt, for having seen Mohamed frequently partake of raw liver, he has become so accustomed to it that he succeeded to-day in personally testing its merits, and he declares that it was excellent. Possibly, like many other 'good things,' a little was more than enough, for there is no evidence of his having done more than taste it. The country around us having been well hunted over, and therefore much disturbed, we have decided upon leaving it quiet for a time, and, by going southwards some few miles, to strike the Royan; for though it was dry near its junction with the Settite, Essafi declares that we shall find plenty of water where he intends to bring us.

Feb. 20.—After five hours' ride over a most monotonous and thinly-wooded high table-land, we arrived at a thick covert, and shortly descended a steep bank, when we halted in the dry bed of a river, apparently a mountain torrent; and as there were only two small pools left of such muddy water that the most old-fashioned pea-soup could hardly compare with it, we naturally supposed we had only stopped here for a temporary rest. Our astonishment was therefore great when, on the arrival of the baggage party, there was a general halt and unloading of camels, and the information was vouchsafed to us that it was our camping ground. Essafi was summoned, and on being asked what he meant by saying we should find plenty of water, naïvely replied that he meant plenty of water for animals to drink, and this we could not deny if they liked it nourishing. Our first idea was to return at once to the Settite; but upon finding that by digging holes into the sand a tolerably clear water welled up, we decided upon making the best of our position, and carrying out for a time Essafi's programme.

This is a well-known camping-ground amongst the hunters, and is named 'Birket Johda,' and it has an excellent landmark in a giant tree named Baobab or Dima (*Adansonia digitata*) which grows on one side of it. This tree we have occasionally seen in our walks, always solitary and scattered about at wide intervals—sometimes in the more fertile valleys, and at others on high ground amongst loose rocks—and in their leafless state looking like monster spectres that had abided from all time, and would last to eternity. On a closer inspection of them, however, whatever their age may be, their prospects of life are very poor, for their trunks are all completely hollowed out by decay, and have become the favourite home of the bees. So disproportionate are they in size to all other timber, that they look as if they belonged to a past era, and, so far as we have observed, there are no young ones to take their place. Though the trunk may measure from forty to fifty feet or more in circumference, the branches are few and very stunted. The bark is very like a cork-tree. Fortunately some of the fruit still remains, so we have had an opportunity of testing its merits, and we never pass a tree without knocking down a few pods with sticks or stones, as they hang suspended by a long stem from the branches. The fruit is a large green pod, about the size of a very small cocoa-nut, and when this has been broken open by a stone it is found to contain a number of irregularly-shaped seeds, enveloped in a thick yellowish-white powder, and held together by a fibrous network. This powder has a most refreshing taste, both sweet and acid, and tends greatly to quench thirst, and when mixed with water imparts a very pleasant flavour to it. Our present tree has numerous wooden pegs driven into it at short intervals, and is thus converted into a capital ladder for the Arabs to get at its precious stores of honey. Our men were not long in taking advantage of them to make an inspection of the hollow trunk, and much to their delight they found that the bees were still left in undisturbed possession of this year's store.

Whilst our people were trying to make the best of our present locality, we took a short stroll in the woods, but saw nothing to give us hope of any sport here beyond numerous tracks of giraffe and a few of rhinoceros. After dinner we were specially invited to witness the Arab method of taking honey. A fire was first lit close to a big opening at the bottom of the trunk, and made to give out large volumes of smoke that passed up it. Our oldest camel-man, an adept in the art, who declares that he has collected nearly two camel-loads of honey in one night, climbed up the tree, and with no other clothing upon him than a skin of leather round his waist entered a hole near the top where the bees were collected. Here he found so much honey that a second man was required to enter the tree at the bottom to hand it down. It now became evident that though one Arab's skin might be proof against stings, others were not so ; for the rest of the party kept well out of harm's-way, and showed a decided objection to offering any assistance until the ever-useful Ibrahim came as usual at the right moment to the front, and amidst general laughter performed this office. Here it was no laughing matter for him, for whilst holding up a lighted torch with one hand and a large pan in the other, the frightened and half-stupified bees fell in crowds upon him, and, though making their escape as fast as they could, many of them were not unmindful to let him pay the penalty of intrusion by a passing sting, that caused considerable contortions or splutterings, according to whether face or body was attacked. Still he did not flinch from his work until all the honey had been collected, and then the magic word 'backsheesh' made him at once forget his stings. As to the old man, he required no sympathy, for he is evidently one of the lucky people in the world whom bees won't sting ; and whilst everyone else was more or less attacked when examining the comb, still covered with bees, he stood quietly by without noticing the scores that crept over his legs and arms. Both honey and comb are in fine condition. A good deal of the latter is white, and though the honey is very thin—flowing more like water than ordinary honey—it is none the less sweet, and has a very delicate flavour, quite different to what we bought at Kassala.

Feb. 21.—Four of our men, with camels laden with our skins and heads, have started to-day for the Hamran village, where they will hand over our property to the care of Sheik Aghill, and, 'Inshallah,' they will be back again in four days with two new horses, a goat to supply us with milk, and dhurra for all our live stock. A horse, though not costing much, becomes in time an expensive commodity; for, whether with English or native saddles, their backs soon become sore, and they have then to be exchanged at great loss, or new ones bought. One of our original purchases stood the work well for some time; but lately, after a long day, it suddenly began persisting in turning to the left, and in a few days this tendency had so increased that it was useless, and had to be put on the sick-list. This horse gradually became so bad, that when standing he would almost fall over on the left side, and when trying to go by himself he only turned round in circles to the left. He was then sentenced to be shot so soon as a favourite haunt of a lion could be found, to which he might be led for execution. Somehow or other the shooting process has been put off from day to day, from our not liking to part with a tried friend, and he is still alive and with us; but how he managed to get here it is difficult to imagine. Now his career is likely to be brought suddenly to an end from an unexpected cause, Ibrahim wanting him to be shot, as he eats twice as much dhurra as the other horses, so the lions' prospects of having a turn at him are looking up again. Our two pools are full of small fish, and some of our men have amused themselves most of the day in catching them by the simple process of wading and feeling for them. No game seen to-day, excepting a leopard which sprang across Vivian's path, and was instantly lost in the long grass. Now that the old soldier has lost his chief amusement of fishing, all his thoughts are turned to his donkey, that he calls 'Jarrone,' and often he can be heard holding long conversations with him as he grazes quietly along the bank, and 'Jarrone gives practical proof of understanding his master, for he will always come to him when called, walking or trotting, according to order; and if eating and sleeping are *the* ways, in a donkey's opinion, to enjoy life, then Jarrone must indeed be happy.

Feb. 22.—Vivian and Mohamed have ridden over a great extent of country skirting the Abyssinian hills, without seeing any game, and for several hours Essafi and myself did the same; but as we were returning home and riding along the bed of the Royan, Essafi, on turning a corner, pulled up short, and whispered 'dāābee.' Dismounting quietly, I was most fortunate in being able to have a steady side-shot at a lioness from eighty to a hundred yards off, as she halted when crossing the river's bed in front of us, and merely turned her head in our direction to look at the intruders on her solitude. The express was equal to the occasion, and she fell dead on the spot where she stood from a bullet that entered the chest behind the right shoulder, and passed straight through it. At the same moment a lion sprang out from behind some long grass near her, and instantly disappeared again. It is curious to see how much these Arabs dread the lions, for they show no fear of the other animals; and on this occasion, though Essafi saw me standing over the dead body, he crept up to it stealthily, and hamstrung it with his sword as it lay stretched out at full length. Pleasant as it was to stand over the body of one's first lion, or rather lioness, it was almost disappointing that it had been such a very tame performance, hardly furnishing even any material for the diaries, and it is about time that there should be a startling novelty for insertion.

During the process of skinning, in which I joined, odoriferous as was the performance, two shots were heard close to us in the direction of the Abyssinian hills, and I thought they were fired by Vivian; but on saying so to Essafi he shook his head, and began talking in a very excited manner, frequently pointing to my rifle. Not a word could I understand, and therefore could not solve the mystery; but I observed that during the skinning performance he frequently got up, walked away a few paces, and looked anxiously around him, and when it was finished he hurriedly mounted and took me away from the place without ever hinting at 'backsheesh,' so much was his great mind occupied with other matters. On our return to camp, Essafi asked Albert to find out if I had understood what he said to me, and then gave the following explanation.

The shots were fired by Abyssinians, and, as he was afraid they would attack us, he wanted to tell me that if he saw them approach, and I heard him call out 'haräam,' I was to fire at them, as they would be robbers, and would kill us; but if either side called out 'amäan,' I was to understand that they were friends. Under these circumstances, it was fortunate that the extent of my knowledge of Arabic was not put to the test.

In our necessarily silent rides or walks there is not much opportunity given us to pick up the language of our hunters; but having learnt the names they give to the various animals, and having established a fine code of signals, we manage very well to make them understand us.

Emanuel and Albert both said that they found it at first difficult to understand their Arabic, as it was very different from what they had been accustomed to, and we certainly find the 'Egyptian Travelling Interpreter,' by Gabriel Sacroug, Cairo, is only of slight assistance to us here, excellent as it is in giving a general knowledge of the more common Arabic words and phrases.

Of the various species of antelope in this country we have so far killed ten. The têtel are, as a rule, by far the most tame, and they will sometimes stand at not more than fifty yards' distance, and look at us as we pass them, or canter off quietly in their own peculiar way, as if their hind-legs were too long, or their horse-like heads were too heavy for them. Next in tameness come the hind koodoos, and they appear to be as thoroughly aware that their hornless heads offer us no attraction as that their duty in life is to keep their lords and masters, with their magnificent heads, well out of harm's-way. All the other antelope, great and small, have a very good idea of what distance constitutes safety from the rifle, and require careful stalking. I should except one which, though occasionally shot, has not as yet been mentioned, as we find it about the Royan less wild than usual. It is the Dorcas gazelle, and besides being a little larger than the common gazelle, it has as a distinctive mark a horizontal black line on each side.

One gazelle to-day was particularly friendly, and after allowing me to pass within twenty yards of it, to my surprise it trotted up close to me, and then followed me for some distance. Fortunately the larder was well stocked, or its confidence would have been poorly repaid. Essafi's report of having heard the Abyssinians firing has so frightened our camel-men that they refuse to accompany us higher up the Royan than our present encampment, declaring by way of excuse that they have strict orders from Sheik Aghill not to do so; but as Essafi and Mohamed are willing to come with us, we have decided upon making a two days' excursion without the camel-men. Albert says they would not be afraid if they were always with us; but when we are out all day, they will be left in camp without anyone with fire-arms to protect them, whilst too few in number to protect one another; and in this line of argument there is some reason. They have escaped from the neighbourhood of one terrible enemy, the Basé (or Barea), to fall, they would have us believe, into the hands of our present neighbours, the Abyssinians, whom they call El Makada, and dread even more than the Basé. Probably a good deal of all this is assumed, so that they may not be far removed from their villages; but there must be some truth in it, for late to-night Albert called us out to look at them, and we found them all crouching behind a sand-bank watching for El Makada robbers, whose approach they suspected by a sudden fright amongst the horses.

Feb. 23.—The great march has been effected, and,

wonderful to relate, three camel-men were bold enough to accompany us, and we are now encamped on some rising ground above the Royan, named Immam, southeast of Birket Johda, and perhaps eight miles farther up the river, and within the boundary line of the Abyssinian frontier. Albert and Ibrahim have come with us, whilst the cook Mohamed and Hadji Basheer are left behind in charge of our stores, and by special request they have been given a loaded gun to frighten away any trespassers. When more than half way we crossed the Royan, where there are well-known pools of good water, and sundry evidences of its being a favourite camping-ground of Abyssinians or Hamrans. It has a name, which Wad-el-Hallan will about represent. *En route* Vivian had a shot at a maāriff as he drank at a pool, and though hit in the shoulder he was able to go off with only a limp, and be lost in the woods. Essafi and Mohamed were at once on the track, and after many faults succeeded in following it up until they cleared the wood and came upon a flat piece of open ground, with here and there a solitary tall mimosa. We had not advanced far over it when Essafi pointed out the maāriff standing still a long way off. Away we galloped after him, but were soon distanced by Essafi on his perfect little grey horse, and on approaching the animal, which stood its ground boldly, he leapt off, and with drawn sword went quietly towards it. We soon arrived at the same place, and then were witnesses of an uncommonly pretty spectacle, that we preferred to see played out rather than cut short by the rifle. The maāriff allowed Essafi to come quite close to it, and then charged him with great ferocity, making Essafi turn on his heel and run for his life for a few moments, until it was too exhausted to follow him. In vain did Essafi try to get round it to hamstring it; the maāriff, with its unpleasantly pointed horns, was master of the situation, until Essafi by degrees enticed it to follow him to a tree, when, standing close behind the trunk, he allowed the maāriff to charge him again, and as it did so he dodged round the tree, and with one spring his sword had severed the tendon, and his enemy was vanquished; and then with one thrust he sent his favourite weapon far into the chest. On our witnessing the terrific force with which the maāriff threw back its head when it thought Essafi was within reach of its horns, we could not help thinking what an escape Cumming had from more serious injury from this species of antelope.

Vivian, wishing to preserve the skin of the neck with the head of his first specimen of this rare antelope, gave an order that the throat was not to be cut across as usual by his hunter, and the result is the Arabs will not eat the animal. Now that they are well supplied with meat, dried or otherwise, their religious scruples are cropping up again, but they never stand in their way when a hippo is found floating. It is said that when the maāriff was first found by Baker, he asked an Arab what he called it, and the man replied something to that effect, and it was named by Baker accordingly; but as the Arabic for 'I don't know' is 'ana maarafshi,'[1] it has been suggested that, however good the name, the Arab's answer had this meaning. Whoever gave it this name, however, it is certain that Essafi was quite familiar with it. Just before dinner our hunters petitioned us to shoot some guinea-fowl for their supper, as of late years, they said, they had given up their custom of not eating them; so Vivian, taking his ten-bore loaded with shot cartridges, very quickly complied with their request, and those which survived sufficiently long to have their throats cut were soon feathered with the assistance of hot water, cut up, and put into a pot to stew with elephant's fat, and of all the varieties of fat the Arabs carefully collect that of the elephant is by far the most prized.

Feb. 24.—Since our departure from the Settite we had lost the music of the night, so pleasant to the hunter's ear—the lion's roar—until last night, when at an early hour it was heard close to our encampment. Essafi and Mohamed came to us at once, and off we started in pursuit, the rising moon giving enough light to guide us on our way to a pool, towards which the lion was

[1] Gabriel Sacroug.

apparently directing his steps. To reach it we were obliged to wade through some shallow water, and directly afterwards had to crouch in a part of the damp river-bed which was sheltered from the moon, upon hearing that the lion was approaching us. After the fatigue of a long day under a scorching sun, this under ordinary circumstances would have been rather a severe trial for the health; but momentarily expecting the appearance on the scene of a lion, which is only concealed by a thick bush within ten yards of you, just makes all the difference, and so it was with us. Concealed under this bush he remained, though kindly informing us of his presence every few minutes by a very fine roar, that resounded amongst the low hills, and was almost too close to be pleasant. On each side of the bush there was a path down the bank, and as we felt sure he would come to the pool by one or other, we each guarded one, whilst remaining so quiet, with our men close behind us, that we hardly dared to breathe for fear of disturbing his plans. Stir, however, he would not from his snug retreat until at last—when, from our remaining so long in our cramped position, he might have had an easy victory—the moon brought the *séance* to a close, by rising over our heads and bringing us fully into view, and immediately afterwards the roar of a retreating lion told us that we also might return home. Retracing our steps, we were quite of opinion that there were more pleasant occupations than even watching for lions by moonlight, and though we have long waited her coming we are not now likely to take much further advantage of her presence with us.

The Arabs frequently get small wounds, which they always come in a party to have dressed, and in Vivian and Albert I have two most willing assistants. Albert is quite an authority on the eye, for he spent one winter in Egypt with an Italian oculist, and at the expiration of their travels together received from him a very flattering testimonial as to his knowledge of the external diseases of the eye, and also a complete case of eye instruments. This oculist, Albert says, having made himself very notorious in Cairo by some successful operations there, determined upon taking advantage of his rapidly spreading fame in the country, and started up the Nile with Albert in a 'dahabeeah,' laden with small bottles, and having a good supply of sulphate of zinc. Thus fitted out, he drove such a thriving trade in that most invaluable of eye lotions to Egyptians, whilst making a short stay at all the towns bordering the Nile, that the stock of zinc became exhausted, and then the curative powers of bottled *eau de Nil* were allowed full play, and with the same satisfactory results in a pecuniary sense, according to his assistant's account. The charge for each consultation was a dollar, and as the patient had to present this amount before one was granted him, there was no chance of an accumulation of bad debts. Albert is evidently much impressed with his late master's powers, and says that besides the above-mentioned drug he used many other local applications, and with such wonderfully good results that the natives flocked to him, and never grumbled at the silver key that opened his door to them.

One of our Arabs to-day very nearly succeeded in cutting off a thumb whilst we were in camp, and he was brought up in triumph by his friends to have the wound dressed. Sewing it up caused them immense astonishment, as they had never seen such a performance; and the victim, far too much interested to mind the pain it caused, disdained having his arm held steady by Vivian.

We have ridden to-day separately over a great extent of country, in the low ground amongst the Abyssinian hills, without seeing any kind of game beyond antelope. Our men say this is due to the Abyssinian hunters having driven it away, and Essafi certainly did point out to me marks of numerous recent encampments, and stumps of trees that had been cut down for rhinoceros trap blocks. Taking honey was the entertainment of this evening, to which we were specially invited, as it was to be done somewhat differently to the last time.

On this occasion the tree was a small one (not a baobab), and though hollow had only one hole near the bottom for the entrance of bees. This hole having been closely plugged with a skin, the men set to work in turn to make another about four feet higher up; and very hard work it was, for they had only brought with them a little native hatchet, and the moon not as yet having risen, with only the light of a small fire to guide them. When this feat was accomplished, the lower hole was opened and some burning wood pushed into it, and immediately the bees came pouring out of the upper one. After allowing them a little time to disperse, an Arab thrust his hand into the newly-made hole, which was situated directly above the hive, and brought out piece after piece of well-filled comb in excellent condition, until no more could be reached, and then we returned home with the spoil.

CHAPTER XI.

Feb. 25.—We have returned to Berket Johda and to our two mud-pools, but merely to pass the night, for to-morrow we intend moving farther down the Royan to try our luck there. Mohamed, the cook, made a great display of delight at our safe return, though his fears were evidently more nearly associated with want of confidence in the combined cooking powers of Albert and Ibrahim than with thoughts of Abyssinians. A rhinoceros took a mean advantage of our absence by paying a visit at night to our pools, and was not easily driven away by the guardians of our property.

This has been a very unlucky day for most of us. Thanks to Essafi, I lost the only good chance I shall probably have of shooting an ostrich, for, coming round a sharp bend of the river, I saw from behind a tree a têtel and a black ostrich close to one another, and not more than eighty yards off. Just as I was going to fire at the ostrich, Essafi pulled me and said 'la' (no), believing that I had only seen the têtel and was aiming at it. At the same moment the ostrich perceived us, and was off like the wind, running as only an ostrich can run, and escaped unhurt. Returning here, I placed my eight-bore under the special charge of Ibrahim, as I knew I should not want it for rhinoceros, and on my arrival I learnt to my dismay that the stock and barrel had parted company, through the carelessness of an Arab to whom Ibrahim had given it to carry for a short time. The only explanation I could get from this individual was that God must have broken it. Still it is of little importance how or by whom it was broken, for now some of the steel is smashed, and its chequered career is definitely brought to a close, so far as this country is concerned, and with it my prospect of killing any more big game. But there has been a loss far more grievous to the individual concerned than mine, for the old soldier has lost his donkey, Jarrone having decamped with the sick horse during the afternoon unobserved by anyone, and is now nowhere to be found. Hadji Basheer has spent the entire evening by himself, crying piteously; but he has been somewhat comforted by the promise of two horses to-morrow, that with an Arab he may follow their tracks, and it is generally believed that if they do not meet any lions or hyænas by the way (N.B. hyænas are reported to be particularly partial to donkeys), they will be found at our last encampment on the Settite; and if they have gone there from sheer disgust at the water they have had to drink here, they ought not to be blamed for showing such good taste. The loss of the sick horse is of no importance, beyond the fact that we might have saved our old friend a painful death ; and that if the lions do eat him, it is a pity that we shall not have a chance of hastening their digestion. The worst news of the day, however, has been brought from the Hamran village by the men we sent there on the 21st, and it has thrown a great gloom over the camp. No laughter or singing can be heard to-night around the camp-fire, not even the dulcet sounds of the everlasting 'rababa,' but the men are seen to be talking together in a low tone, well out of hearing of the old soldier, whom they look upon as their common enemy. This is an unnecessary precaution for them to take to-night, whilst plotting and planning for the future, as Hadji'Basheer, poor old fellow, if he has not cried himself to sleep, is far too much absorbed with thoughts of his lost Jarrone to pay attention to what they may be saying against the Turks, as they call the people of whom he is the official representative with us. The report which has burst like a shell upon our men is that Wadd ab Sin, the Sheik of Khartoum, through whom the Hamrans pay taxes to the Khedive (or Sultan, as they call him), has just sent some soldiers to Sheik Aghill to tell him that from henceforth their taxation will be doubled. This announcement, communicated by Aghill to the various villages under Egypt's rule through their respective Sheiks, has caused utter consternation and dismay amongst them, ending in some instances in flight, and complete dispersion of whole villages. Sheik Achmet, who received Emanuel and his party on our first arrival in the country, at once decamped with all his goods eastward to a territory near the river Gash, but beyond the present boundary of Egyptian rule, and the people under him have fled in different directions. Several families have already disappeared from Sheik Aghill's chief village, Gwayha, and he says that he will pack up his traps and be off if this new order should remain in force. The Sheik of Zahani has moved his quarters near to Kassala, so that he may be directly under Munsinger Pasha. It has interested us much to hear in what high esteem Munsinger is held by these Arabs. They look upon him as a very just man, and the wish is universal that they might have him placed in direct authority over them, instead of his representative at Khartoum. Of Wadd ab Sin they speak in very different terms, believing that half the taxes they pay remain in the hands of himself and his emissaries. To add force to their opinion of Munsinger, they say that their camels, if they could speak, would ask for him. The present Sheik of Khartoum is one of twenty-four sons of the great Aboo Sin, who at one time governed a large portion of Upper Egypt; and all his sons have been made Sheiks. The new taxation will amount, our men say, to twenty-four dollars per head, excepting for the very poor; and the general feeling amongst them is that, as this cannot be paid, their homes must be broken up and their families scattered. No wonder, then, that sorrow reigns supreme here now. Sheik Aghill has sent us the two horses we required, and we have reduced his price from thirty to twenty-five dollars apiece. Another valuable addition to our live stock is the goat, for which we have paid two dollars and a half. Having brought amongst our stores a large stock of Anglo-Swiss condensed milk, this has answered all our purposes very well, and it has only recently occurred to us that the presence of a goat would add to our personal comforts. Now, however, the time has arrived when our stores are beginning to show a serious diminution in some of their pleasant rather than necessary items. One especially, from its extreme popularity both amongst our attendants and ourselves, is all but consumed; and, considering that it has been by special request the invariable daily wind-up to our dinners, it is almost surprising it has lasted so long. I refer to some dried apricots, which, when stewed ('mishmish') and served with rice, have found such great favour with us.

Both here and at our last camp we have seen numbers of fireflies, and when it is dark, during the early part of the night, before the moon has risen, it is pleasant to follow them with the eye by the light they evolve as they fly amongst the bushes. One tree to-night was so covered with them that it looked as if innumerable fairy lanterns were suspended from it. The light from this fly appears to be more brilliant, though smaller, than that of the glowworm.

Feb. 26.—Unlucky Friday! Hadji Basheer started off soon after sunrise with an Arab, in search of Jarrone—both being mounted on horses, according to promise—and at once came upon the track of his pet and of the sick horse together. For two hours they followed them in the direction of Emhaggar, then came a fault, and though their tracks were found again, it was soon followed by another, and so on until the declining sun warned them that the search must be given up, and that they must turn their horses' heads homewards. Now all hope of finding Jarrone is practically at an end, and it is really most painful to witness the old man's grief as he mourns over his great loss. He has spent the whole evening under a tree, telling the Arabs, as he calls them one by one to him, the oft-repeated tale of how he had reared Jarrone from his birth, and loved him more than his own children, for Jarrone, he said, he had always with him; and then, after declaring he was sure that if God had wanted to perform a miracle He would have chosen to make Jarrone speak, came the grand climax of a flood of tears. We have tried to induce him to feel some hope yet, by offering a handsome reward to the

Arabs if they bring him back, but without producing much effect upon him. Just now he said to Albert, 'The gentlemen will want me to go to Kassala soon for them; but how can I return to my home without my Jarrone?' Excepting ourselves, there is probably not much sympathy thrown away upon him, for Albert does nothing but laugh when narrating his griefs, and the Arabs would be equally pleased if he and his donkey had disappeared together. After taking a direction south-west from Birket Johda for about four hours, we have now pitched our camp on a bank, near two small pools in the bed of a river named El-la-Mab. No reference is made by Baker to this river, though it forms a very important tributary to the Royan, which it joins a little beyond and to the north-west of our camp. At their junction in the form of a V it is quite as wide as the Royan; but its banks are by comparison low, and it is equally dry.

By a stupid misunderstanding between Essafi and Mohamed, the latter took Vivian to the wrong place, and it was late in the evening before they found us out, and not before they had caused us some anxiety as to their prospects for the night. Whilst waiting for our arrival, they were soon more fully than pleasantly occupied; for, having seated themselves unconsciously between two swarms of bees—one in a tree and another in the cleft of a rock—they completely fell into the enemies' hands, and were punished accordingly; and after making good their escape they were able at their leisure to pick out one another's stings. Fortunately these bees do not cause much more than momentary pain; but whether this is due to a weakness in their own powers, or to the process of tanning that our skins have undergone, is a problem much too scientific for us to solve, though hardly a day passes without our experiencing a practical proof of the fact.

In the afternoon Essafi took me on foot to a wood near here, and, after wandering about in it for some time, we came unexpectedly upon a buffalo lying down about thirty yards off, and facing us. I had with me Vivian's single Henry ·577-bore, loaded with hardened ball, and as the buffalo looked up before rising I shot him in the front of the neck, and death was so instantaneous that, beyond falling over on one side, he never moved again. It is the finest head I have yet obtained; but what is of most importance is the fact that this fatal shot has given me such confidence in the killing powers of the rifle that I shall try it upon the next rhinoceros I find. Vivian would lend me his ten-bore alternate days, but after the ill-luck of my big gun I fear to use it, and prefer taking my chance with the Henry, though it is but a single one. We have also in reserve a twelve-bore rifle, but we fear it carries too small a charge of powder to be of any use.

On our return for camels to bring the buffalo home,

we were told that two of the horses, Essafi's being one, disappeared directly after our arrival here, and could not be found, though four Arabs had been in search of them. It was now Essafi's turn to look grave; but not being one to brood inactively over his sorrows, he instantly picked out two or three special friends, and went off in pursuit. Those told off to seek the dead buffalo begged me to accompany them, and were highly pleased at my mounting one of their camels with only a native saddle on it. After dismounting on our arrival at the wood, it only required a few minutes' search to tell me that I could give them no assistance in finding the buffalo; and our tracks having frequently recrossed one another, the men gave up the search very soon and returned home. Essafi and his friends were equally unsuccessful; but no one seems to doubt that the horses will be found to-morrow, when there will be more time to follow their tracks, either at our last camp or somewhere on the Settite.

Feb. 27.—A party of Hamran elephant-hunters paid us a visit to-day, headed by the great hunter Roder Sheriff—now quite an old though hale-looking man. So he is not dead after all, as originally stated. They are on their way to Abyssinia, being sent by Sheik Aghill at the special request of an Abyssinian Sheik, who requires their assistance in consequence of the presence of great numbers of elephants in his part of the country. These

Sheiks enter occasionally into regular contracts, of which the Hamran Sheik has no cause to complain, for whilst his men are hunting in Abyssinia both they and their horses have to be fed by their host, and fresh horses found by him if theirs fall sick, and an equal division is made of all tusks and hides. We can answer for it that they will have one horse unfit for work, for Roder Sheriff managed to do a stroke of business with us by an exchange of one plus eight dollars, and now we have four really sound horses for personal use. With all our care, it is most difficult to keep their backs sound; but we find the native saddles the least injurious, and as in purchasing a horse saddle and bridle are always included, we have no lack of them.

Essafi and Mohamed went off at a very early hour in search of the strayed horses, so Vivian and myself did a little hunting on our own account, in opposite directions, though not straying very far from home, for even with the assistance of a compass in times of doubt it is a most difficult country to find one's way about in, owing to the high table-land, the large woods, and the absence of any specially defined hills. Beyond antelope we neither of us found any game, but it has proved a day in my calendar not likely to be soon forgotten. Keeping my eyes fixed on the ground close in front of me, I was deeply engrossed in my occupation of following up the fresh track of a buffalo, in a path through the wood I was in yesterday, when I was suddenly startled by a rustle in the grass, and looking up I saw reared up before me, and not more than a yard off, a cobra. It was directly facing me, and, with outstretched hood, must have been on the point of striking. In an instant my rifle was discharged, more to frighten it from its intentions than for any other reason; but, to my astonishment, its head was laid low, and beyond a considerable writhing of the body it could not move from its place. When it was clearly dead I examined the wound, and it is a most singular fact that, though the bullet was a twelve-bore spherical one (I had taken out this rifle hoping to test its powers on a buffalo), and therefore of good size, it had passed through the neck so exactly in the median line that it left a thin piece of skin intact on each side—attributable no doubt to the hood being outstretched. My recollection of the boy at Cairo with his performing cobras made me at once recognise my fallen enemy; and, thankful for the narrow escape I believed I had had, I brought it home in triumph. It measures five feet four inches, and will come in most opportunely, as I promised a friend in London to present him with a snake for a new museum he is forming.

Our hunters found the horses at Emhaggar, and on their way home they disturbed three lions feeding on the carcass of a buffalo. No time was therefore lost in returning with us to the spot, but so far as seeing any lions was concerned we might just as well have stayed at home, for they had dragged the remains into a thick jungle far above our heads, and in its dry state it gave them timely notice of our approach. Guided by the vultures, who were eagerly watching the feast from the surrounding trees, we entered the jungle from different points, and happening to catch a glimpse of the back of a lion as he sprang through the grass close in front of me I gave him a salute, to which he replied with a roar as he continued his course onwards. Vivian heard another go away in his direction. We then remained in ambush near the buffalo, keeping a very sharp lookout in all directions for any movement in the jungle until after sunset, but we neither saw them nor heard them again, and then in the rapidly supervening darkness we had to follow our men home as best we could. They did not at all realise the fact that our eyes have not the cat-like powers of their own, and we consequently had some narrow escapes from breaking our noses over roots or fallen branches. Mohamed on one occasion, in letting go a small mimosa branch which he had carefully avoided, very nearly succeeded in doing serious injury to Vivian, as in swinging back it gave him a very sharp blow across the right eyelid. Had it struck the eye his chances of sport would have been brought to a summary conclusion.

The wounded hand has already quite healed, and the

Arabs are amazed with the success of the sewing-up treatment, saying that according to their method the whole arm would have become swollen, and the man would have been crippled for a month or more. Backsheesh was of course asked for the return of the horses, and given; but the special petition of Essafi's father (who is on a visit to us) for some because he prayed for their safe return, was a little too good to be encouraged, though he claims to belong to the priesthood. Essafi senior is a fine-looking old man, who at one time held a very influential position as a Sheik and an owner of several camels and cattle; but troubles falling heavily upon him, he lost his position and his property, and is now dependent to a great extent upon his son. He came to us originally bringing grain for his son's horse, and he is perhaps not the only instance on record of a man who, finding his quarters as a guest very comfortable and being in nobody's way, is loth to depart from them until he receives more than a hint that his room would be preferred to his company.

Feb. 28.—Vivian has had an exciting day's sport, and is therefore to be congratulated, as it has been rather slack of late. Hoping to see our friends of yesterday again, he left camp very early with Mohamed, and upon arriving near the jungle was pleased to see the ever-watchful vultures patiently waiting their time, and therefore showing that the feast was still attended by other guests. Owing to the extreme dryness of the long grass, it was impossible to prevent their approach being heard, and away went a lion without giving the chance of a shot. They then made a short cut to the bank of the river-bed, hoping thus to head him; but he had the start, and on their arriving there they found he had crossed it, and could see him some way off trotting along quite leisurely. A shot was then fired with the hope of making him stop; but he declined, and crossing another bend of the dry bed of the Royan was for a moment lost to view. Following in his course, and mounting the bank beyond which he was last seen, he again came into view; and now another shot had the desired effect of bringing him to a standstill. Vivian then crept towards him under cover of one of the large anthills, and from this point he could just see the head as, crouching in the grass, the lion faced him. This time Vivian hit him, and quite altered his tactics, for with one fore-leg crippled he sprang forward, and at the same moment Vivian fired again but without effect. Vivian's only chance now was his second rifle, but on turning round to take it from Mohamed he found to his disgust that hunter and rifle were rapidly disappearing. By this time the lion was within ten yards of him and still advancing, so with an unloaded rifle there was nothing left for him to do but to follow Mohamed as fast as his legs would carry him, hoping that he could outrun his crippled adversary, and upon gaining the opposite bank he was glad to find that the hunter was no longer the hunted. After administering a severe lecture to Mohamed they retraced their footsteps, but the lion was nowhere to be found. On Mohamed's return he reported having seen pools of blood in the direction taken by the lion I fired at yesterday, and as Essafi believed that both Vivian's and mine might be found dead in the jungle we decided upon returning there and setting it on fire.

Thanks to a light breeze, the flames spread with marvellous rapidity, and a magnificent spectacle was the result. Dense volumes of smoke, due to the less combustible nature of the green trees, made a splendid background, and against this stood out grandly the brilliant plumage of the birds as they flew backwards and forwards in front of the advancing flames, and apparently in dangerous proximity with them. No roast lion could, however, be found, and when we left the scene of devastation the flames were still travelling onward, though not in one unbroken line; and it was curious to observe how here and there over the charred ground small patches of jungle were left untouched which a spark would have ignited. I omitted to mention that Albert very nearly succeeded in consigning all our property to the flames last evening. We had told him to light a bonfire near the camp to guide us on our return in the dark, and so successfully did he carry out our orders that he also accidentally set the short grass on our ground alight, and it was only with great difficulty that we prevented the flames creeping onwards and surrounding us.

March 1.—Beyond shooting antelope for the special benefit of lions, we have had no sport to-day. I proved the killing powers of the Rigby express by dropping two fine têtel out of a herd with a right-and-left, and, reloading rapidly, bagging a third before they had time to get out of shot. Having obtained such a good supply of tempting food for our friends the lions, we decided upon lying in ambush and watching the result. This proved highly uninteresting, for the vultures soon surrounded the more distant têtel, whilst others covered the trees near us to wait patiently for our departure from what was far from being a hiding-place so far as they were concerned, and no lion appeared on the scene.

Albert entertained us to-night with a fuller account of his career as an oculist's assistant, and there can be no doubt that he gained a great amount of useful information, and indeed practical knowledge, from his master. Feeling confident in his powers as an oculist, and thinking he might turn them to good account, he decided upon making an experimental trip up the Nile the following winter; and having hired a dahabeeah and supplied it with an ample store of bottles and sulphate of zinc, he induced a friend to accompany him as dragoman; and that his costume should be in keeping with the character he was about to assume, he particularly informed us that he purchased a black frock-coat and a high hat. It was an easy matter to get the report spread that again an oculist was about to ascend the Nile, and on his arriving at the various villages and towns on its borders an anxious crowd of sufferers was waiting to consult him. The silver-key system was again put in force, but, with a modesty worthy of Albert, he only demanded a half-dollar fee; and to prevent any unpleasant accident arising, he wisely limited his treatment to the external diseases of the eye, and thus ran no risk of destroying sight. His success was far greater than he had calculated upon, and in some towns he found work for several days; and after this fashion he gradually ascended the Nile until he reached Assouan, near the first Cataract, when considering his professional career was at an end, he went out for a quiet stroll to think over his successful venture. During this time an old woman of the village called to have a bad eye attended to, and the dragoman, thinking that he ought not to lose so golden an opportunity of bagging a patient, placed her in the professor's chair, and whilst holding her head well back dropped into the affected eye what he supposed was a solution of sulphate of zinc. The effect was wonderful, but not quite what he anticipated, for the eye seemed at once to smoke up and collapse, and to his utter horror the old woman with a yell of pain rushed frantically away to her village. Albert soon returned, and had no difficulty in solving the mystery, for he found that his friend had poured strong sulphuric acid (oil of vitriol) into the old woman's eye. The question as to what ought to be done under the circumstances was quickly settled by the arrival of the Sheik of Assouan, who carried them off and made them prisoners, to await orders from Cairo. In the meantime they were sent to Thebes, and from here they managed to escape in a native boat to Alexandria, though at the cost of losing all they possessed on the dahabeeah, and so by one unfortunate slip their labour was for nought.

Many people might say that Albert was justly punished for starting upon such an expedition; but it should be remembered that he knows Egypt well, and with this knowledge holds the belief that though the Government doctors are all men of good repute, there are others to be found who would not quite care to follow their profession were they much under the eye of the law; and Albert had at least good reason to be confident in his powers to do real service to the natives in the limited extent to which he purposed to confine himself.

March 2.—Again a blank day. I had a very long shot at a giraffe with the Henry rifle, and wounded it so severely that it could only hobble away. Unfortunately we were on foot, and as the heat was very great, and about midday, it was a hard matter giving it chase. Still we did so over an immense plain, taking an occasional random shot at it, for more than a mile, when I was obliged to cry 'enough,' and, quite exhausted, to lie down. Essafi, nothing daunted, after seeing me comfortably settled under the shade of a small tree, went off home to get our horses to continue the hunt. He left me alone so long that I became almost impatient for his return, but the delay was explained on my seeing him approach with a party of Arabs on camels. We then renewed the hunt by following the tracks for two or three miles, when we came to a thick wood in which they soon were lost, and there we were obliged to give it up as hopeless.

CHAPTER XII.

March 3.—The presence of numbers of the common varieties of antelope, and the occasional roar of a lion at night, have not been sufficiently attractive to keep us longer in the neighbourhood of the Royan, and this evening finds us once again on the banks of the Settite, about two miles above Emhaggar, where we were so long encamped.

Though our visit to the Royan has done little to swell our game-list, we are very glad to have been there, for besides its having all the appearance of a splendid resort for big game, we have gained so much more knowledge of this portion of the Soudan. Returning to the clear water of the ever-flowing Settite is indeed a luxury after the Royan pools; and now our camp is pitched on a sloping grass bank almost level with the river, looking beautifully fresh and green, whilst the soil is dry enough for all practical purposes, and here we shall probably remain for some time. The spot is called 'Eddebabeha,' meaning, we are told, a slaughter-house. There is an island close by to which this name more especially applies, for it is known to be a favourite haunt of buffaloes, and when found there by the Arab hunters they are driven round and round by dogs until tired out, when they fall easy victims to their swords and spears. The dogs we have so far seen are miserable-looking creatures. They are a species of lurcher, very small and almost reduced to skeletons. When approaching the river, Vivian and Mohamed disturbed two lions in a wood feasting on a koodoo, and, as Essafi and myself were close at hand, they beckoned to us to join in the hunt. The trees were here so overspreading and close together that the pathways were nearly dark, and it was almost impossible to walk along them; and as I entered the wood I did not see I was walking directly up to a lion until I was close to him and caught sight of his glistening eye as he sprang on one side. I fired a chance shot into the brushwood, to which he responded with a growl, and then escaped, probably untouched, as Vivian caught sight of him going away at a good pace. So far our experience in lion-shooting does not tend to make us look upon the lord of the forest as a dangerous animal to encounter, for, hunting on foot as we do alone, we should have but a poor chance of escape if he chose to assume the offensive before being wounded; and it is more than probable that many have sneaked away on our approach, according to their natural tendency, without our having seen them at all. I have been told by

Indian sportsmen that the tiger also will always retreat before man if not driven to desperation, and that the man-eater is not a tiger in its normal state, but one that has by some unlucky accident tasted human blood, or that has through age become unable to obtain its natural food by killing wild animals, and therefore has been driven to attack human beings.

Whilst waiting for dinner, an Arab rushed to our tent in great excitement, crying out 'feel! feel!' (elephant), and, seizing our rifles, we followed him through some very close covert behind our camp, with the rest of our party in rear making such a row that the prospect of a shot would have been hopeless. The supposed elephant proved to be only one of a herd of buffaloes, and they of course took advantage of our noisy approach to make good their escape. Hardly had we settled down to dinner, when the roar of a lion close to us caused another call to arms, and again, much to our annoyance, everyone turned out. After getting our evening clothes, not *quite 'de rigueur,'* half torn off our backs by the everlasting thorns, as we struggled through the narrow paths between the bushes, we were kindly informed by another roar that our friend was only separated from us by one or two bushes at most. Halting here for a time to watch the spot from whence the sound came was without result, for he managed to escape, and well he might in the darkness, without being seen.

Nature has done her best to make this a perfect hiding-place for lions, for the mimosas and nabbuks—larger here than we have usually found them—have their widely-spread branches bending to the ground, and the interstices are so completely filled up from below with the long dry grass and above with a creeping cactus, that each tree is converted into a perfect den, quite dark, and only having one or two holes in its wall for the exit and entrance of animals. As a rule, each tree is just sufficiently apart from its neighbours to allow animals to pass between them, and there are innumerable beaten tracks winding amongst them leading to the river. Our prospects of finding, or rather seeing, lions 'at home' are therefore not great, and we must rather hope to meet them accidentally in our mutual morning rambles near the river.

March 4.—The excitable Essafi is rather in disgrace to-day. After following some fresh tracks for several hours, he pointed me out a rhinoceros moving quietly amongst the trees about forty yards off, and quite unaware of our presence. Creeping a few yards nearer, I saw a second one lying down, and whilst trying to get close to it Essafi said 'adroop' (fire), and softly as he did so it was quite loud enough to startle this rhinoceros, and in an instant he was on his legs and off, though not without being made aware of the powers of a Henry rifle to penetrate his thick hide. We found blood in his track for more than a mile afterwards, but we were then obliged to give up the hunt owing to our great distance from home.

Our present pretty encampment has its drawbacks, which we found to our cost last night, for whilst the white ants were doing their utmost to devour our goods, including the tent-pole, the mosquitoes swarmed about us like bees—intent on doing their best to devour us if we had obliged them by falling asleep. Careful as our friends were to warn us of the risks to life from wild beasts, natives, or disease, they omitted to mention the slow devouring process of the insect world; and though of varieties there seems to be a legion, we find there is one property common to them all, that of wishing to taste the blood of an Englishman—and of this our bodies now from head to foot tell their sad tale.

Mosquito-curtains, cleverly adapted by Albert to our beds, will defeat one great enemy here, and our old system of raising everything off the ground another—the white ant. The red ants are almost equally numerous, and though far behind their sickly-looking relations in their powers of annoyance, they manage to make themselves highly objectionable in their more general voyages of discovery, and often have to pay in self-destruction the penalty of inquisitiveness. Even if a can of water is left uncovered for a few moments, they are sure to have tumbled into it in scores. Thanks to them, it is very difficult to preserve any butterflies or moths, for if allowed the slightest chance they soon devour their bodies. There are numerous varieties of ants, both in colour and size. The black are by far the biggest, and their chief occupation in life appears to be, though a hopeless one, to keep down the surplus population of their white relations, and they make war upon them accordingly. There are some beautiful butterflies, though few in number, especially a very large one with speckled body and variegated brown wings, and another of a very brilliant yellow colour. The most common is a small white butterfly with a red tip to the wing. To catch them, of whatever kind they may be, requires the practised skill of an entomologist, and even he would require the patience of Job, for they have an aggravating habit of flying close to you amongst the mimosas, where, if you are foolish enough to try to catch one with a net, you not only meet with signal failure, but also have your net caught by a thousand thorns; and whilst you are pleasantly engaged releasing one portion of it, another probably gets more entangled. Still, like the animals and birds, they have their time for visiting the river to drink, and about noon they may generally be seen going through this performance. Now is the time for the skilled man of the net to catch his game in its hurried flight to and from the river; but he indeed must be an enthusiast who will wait under a scorching sun for the visit of a butterfly, and, besides, he has then to catch it. In one of my feeble attempts at this, I have been told, exciting sport, I caused considerable astonishment to the natives, as they watched me rushing about with my outstretched net after a butterfly that had a strong objection to visiting its interior, and I soon came to the conclusion that it was cruel work destroying the lives of such innocent and beautiful creatures.

March 5.—Vivian has been very fortunate in finding a rhinoceros standing under a big mimosa in otherwise open ground, and so well concealed was he that both Mohamed and himself walked almost up to the tree before observing him. Seeing probably that there was no chance of escaping quietly from his hiding-place, he allowed Vivian to walk round him for a side-shot, and this, though well-directed, produced no apparent effect beyond making him give a loud whiff. A second shot from the ten-bore with six drachms of powder was more than even a rhinoceros could bear quietly, and out he came at Vivian, but with a very feeble attempt to show fight, and then a third bullet dropped him dead. Vivian has a very good gun-bucket, made of leather, which is suspended by two straps from the saddle on the off side, in such a direction that when the stock of a gun rests in it the muzzle points upwards behind the right arm, and after a little practice the gun comes to hand most readily. This pattern bucket is specially described by

Messrs. Lord and Baines in their valuable book entitled 'Shifts and Expedients of Camp-life,' and it is used, according to them, by the Hottentots.

This book, though rather bulky for a traveller with light baggage, is so full of practical hints that it well repays a careful study; whilst Galton's 'Art of Travel' is more valuable as a pocket companion, in containing much useful information in a condensed form. A petition from the Arabs for a hippo, as they are in want of fat, induced me to pay a visit to a pool, where, at the expense of two cartridges from the express, I was able to carry out their wishes.

The worst of killing a hippo is that the day is over so far as having your hunter is concerned, for he at once returns to the camp to announce the joyful news and bring the men back to the pool, where, by the time they arrive, the body is found floating, and then he must preside over the cutting-up performance. On this occasion I remained at the pool to note the time of floating, and it occurred in just under an hour and a half. To my surprise, the Arabs hesitated to swim out to the hippo as it floated in the middle of the big pool, from fear of crocodiles; but after a great deal of shouting and splashing with stones four of the boldest entered the river, whilst the others kept up the shouting and stone-throwing, and having fastened one end of a rope round a leg, they returned safely to shore with the other, and then all joined heartily in hauling the monster to the bank. Having already made a careful study of the after-proceedings on such occasions, I preferred leaving my friends to their own strange devices, and, after finding a good place of concealment under some overhanging nabbuks along the bank, awaiting the arrival of any antelope. I very speedily came to the conclusion that there were many less pleasant ways of spending the hottest part of the day than this, although amongst the numerous visitors on each side of me, as well as on the opposite bank, not one arrived of sufficient importance to tempt me to disturb the peaceful gatherings. It was a pretty sight to watch the gazelle or ariel coming to drink. At first one or two timidly descend the covered way, and after listening attentively and looking well around them to be sure that the coast is clear, they make a short step forward over the dry bed, and then, with increased confidence, scamper down to the water's edge. This becomes the signal for the others, and down they come in rapid succession until almost within reach of the desired goal, where they may moisten their parched tongues, when the displacement of an extra loose pebble causes a panic and the rapid disappearance of the whole herd. It is only, however, to lie in ambush close by for a few minutes, until it is discovered that it was a false alarm, and then gaining wisdom by their mistake, they advance more boldly to the river. Here they linger but for a few moments to have their fill, and then lose no time in returning again to obscurity. The gazelle are frequently seen by the river-side, and probably drink two or three times a day; but the large antelope, such as the méhédéhet, têtel, and koodoos, so far as we have observed, invariably come to the river in the afternoon, and the têtel are frequently found there with the ariel. Maāriffs are so rarely seen that it is difficult to say when they leave their distant haunts in the high ground, but Vivian's was found soon after midday drinking, and mine was also near water at the same time. We often hear the buffaloes come down the bank two or three hours after sunset, and this is supposed to be about the time that all large animals visit the river, the rhinoceros being the latest arrival.

However wrong their religion may be, it cannot be said of our people that they neglect their prayers, for, not only at sunrise and sunset, but five times a day do they pray, this being the othodox number, and when 'at home' it is probably within the mark, so frequently are they seen at their devotions, standing like statues, with faces turned to the East, whilst muttering some passages of the Koran, or kneeling down and burying their foreheads in the dust. Mohamed's and Essafi's religious performances are sometimes a little inconvenient, for if we have taken the trouble to rise specially early to be off before sunrise, it is not pleasant to have to halt near the river at sunrise and wait whilst they wash feet and hands, and then devote several minutes to Mahomet.

Mohamed the cook, though a Nubian, is equally regular in his devotions, but at the same time he evidently has an eye to business. In the midst of them this afternoon he called out to Vivian, 'Governor, two goose!' and then, without cutting them short, watched Vivian fire a right-and-left with effect, and joined heartily in the laughter caused by Ibrahim in his unsuccessful efforts to catch a wounded bird which had fallen into a shallow offshoot of the river, and there exhibited its diving powers with great effect. In this offshoot we have discovered a delightful bathing-place, where we need feel no fear of the presence of a crocodile. Over one part the stream flows rapidly and is pleasantly cold for the morning bath, and in another there is a small though deep sandy pool, which almost answers all the purposes of a warm bath, if, after a long day's ride, we return home wearied and feel disposed to have one.

Passing this afternoon near a new encampment of Aráb hunters, we saw under a tree in the distance a donkey very like Jarrone, and on telling this piece of news to Hadji Basheer he begged us to keep it a great secret until to-morrow morning, so that he may go to their camp before any of our men can communicate with them. He believes that if the Arabs have found Jarrone, they would not give it up to him unless compelled to do so. Essafi and the hippo party have not returned yet (9 P.M.), and Essafi senior is in a great state of anxiety about his son's safety, fearing he may have fallen into the hands of the Basé. It is far more probable that, having gorged themselves with hippo, raw and cooked, they have found sleeping on the spot more conducive to their personal comfort.

March 6.—The hippo party returned home safely last night at a very late hour with three camels well laden with the precious food. We have now laid claim to an equal share of the fat, for after it has been melted down as a means of preservation it makes excellent dripping, and all our things are cooked with it. At first Mohamed objected to use it, preferring to send occasionally to the Hamran village for some horrible-looking mixture of fat, milk, &c., which he honoured with the name of butter. Since, however, we have found the hippo-fat so excellent, we have positively refused to buy him any more of his pet compound, and now we have at least the satisfaction of knowing what our butter is made of. Would that we could always do so in future !

Vivian has had a long stalk after a herd of maāriffs, and ultimately succeeded in killing a fine doe with a splendid pair of horns. They are much thinner and more regularly annulated than the buck's. I spent the day hunting in vain for rhinoceros. Returning home, Essafi suddenly dashed off at his horse's best speed in the direction of some vultures swooping about so far off that I could barely see them. Upon arriving at the place round which they were rapidly collecting we found a dead rhinoceros, and recognised it as the one I wounded the day before yesterday and tracked to within a few hundred yards of where it was lying. Essafi says that, directly he saw the vultures, he was sure he would find it there. Some camel-men belonging to another hunting expedition, under Jali, have paid us a visit on their way home, and report having been attacked by the Basé, who rushed down upon them from their hills as they passed along the valley of the river near here, and demanded half the produce of their spoil, consisting of the hides and tusks of three elephants; but they were ultimately content with the present of a third portion. This modesty scarcely agrees with the general character given of our black-skinned neighbours. We hear that they are a much darker race than the Hamrans, and have quite different features. Hadji Basheer, dressed in his best attire—slightly the worse for wear, though very picturesque in its patchiness—and mounted on one of our chargers, paid the Arab camp a very early visit, full of determination to impress upon the hunters the power he wielded, and to claim his own, his long-lost child ; but his energies were wasted, for the donkey was not Jarrone, and he had to return discomfited. He has been much more resigned of late to his loss, and is gradually transferring his affections to the goat; and a charming goat she is, for already she is on the most friendly terms with everyone, and finds in our biscuits a special inducement to pay us a visit regularly at breakfast and dinner. Besides supplying us with four cups of milk every morning, she never fails during the day to have a smaller quantity in store when called upon, and comes up to Albert to be milked with great willingness. She is left quite loose at night, and has a remarkably good idea of what constitutes safety, by sleeping amongst the camels, where she finds protection from her special night enemies, the hyænas. Nothing will induce her to go to the river to drink, although we are within a few yards of a very shallow place, so great is her fear of crocodiles; and when thirsty, she will not allow Albert any rest until he gives her some water in a basin. The Arabs never allow their goats to drink at the river, owing to the crocodiles, but make small pools for them near its margin, which they fence round with a low mud wall. The baboons have a thorough appreciation of the cunning of their natural enemies the crocodiles, and before coming down to drink make a very careful survey of the river from a high bank or from the overhanging branches of the trees, and always prefer dipping their noses into a little hollow made by the hoof of a rhinoceros or hippo.

P

They often can be seen by day moving in troops along the banks, a few fine old gentlemen with long manes marching one behind the other majestically in front, whilst the rest follow in general disorder—mothers carrying their little ones on their backs; and from the amount of screaming and screeching we sometimes hear amongst the general community, it is evident that rows are not uncommon in the family circle of our Darwinian brethren. They pay us the great compliment of taking a lively interest in our proceedings when they pass near our camp, provided that they are separated from it by the river.

There is at the present moment (6 P.M.) a tremendous storm over the Abyssinian hills, and we are having the benefit of the thunder and lightning, the latter being very vivid. Some very ominous-looking clouds are creeping onwards towards us, but the Arabs say that there is no chance of the storm reaching us so early in the year.

No reference has been made to the pearly whiteness of our Arabs' teeth, and it deserves a passing notice, universal as it is amongst Eastern races, for the Hamrans have their own way, at least so they think, of producing this satisfactory condition. It is simple enough, as it merely consists of rubbing the teeth when chance offers with the smoothly-cut end of a twig of some small tree now in the green state, the fibres of which gradually get separated in the rubbing process, and converted into a brush. If Essafi passes such a tree in the day's hunt, he always cuts two tooth-brushes, one for me; and the rest of the time he seems never to tire of the cleaning process. It has a pleasant taste, but from want of faith in the result I soon give up the performance.

What a valuable tree this would be to cultivate in England, if the native toothbrush were only required to give us the native teeth! Mohamed occupies his time more with the useful than the ornamental, and starts off in the morning with a strip of hippo-hide for conversion into a small koorbatch. This, though white and stiff at first, becomes after the labour of hours, or rather days, extremely flexible and quite black, by the simple process of being pulled through the closed hand; and whether he is riding, or walking, or sitting over the fire at night, like an old knitting woman he has always his work in hand.

March 7.—Our mosquito-curtains have answered so well that we are now perfectly content with our encampment on the green sward; but our people have raised such an objection to it, on the plea of the absence of shade from the great midday heat, that we have yielded the point, and have agreed to move a few hundred yards, to encamp on the island called Eddebabeha. If the truth were known, it is probable that they object far more to the proximity of the nightly roar of the lion than to the absence of shade. The island is a very favourite camping-ground, as it is quite free from lions, and there certainly are some good trees for shade. Sometimes it is no easy matter to find a place under the trees so completely shut off from the sun as to allow me to obtain the correct temperature in the shade, and a hollow in an old trunk is prized accordingly. A party of Hamran Arab hunters passed onwards to-day from the Royan. They declared they had caught nothing, and had had no meat for fifteen days, and attributed their want of success to our having driven all game from the country by our guns. We sent them on their way rejoicing, by giving them a freshly-killed ariel; but whether their statement was true or not our men don't care, for besides feasting daily on fresh meat, they are accumulating an immense store of it in the dried state in their villages. One Arab said the other day that he had not eaten so much meat in thirty years as he has done since he came to us; but as the Arabs who stay at home only eat meat when their cattle die from disease or old age, it is not surprising that the total consumption during this long period should have been so limited.

March 8.—We have been giraffe-hunters to-day, but beyond seeing our game three times half a mile off it has been a very blank day. The tiresome part of giraffe-hunting is that it is a long day's ride to get to their woods, and the trees are sufficiently scattered for them to see our approach from a great distance, and with their big eyes and long necks there is little chance of getting the best of them in a stalk, however much a favourable wind may curtail the powers of one special sense. The rhinoceros woods are a little nearer the river, say from three to four miles, and here also are the buffaloes frequently found, though they are not so particular about making long journeys from the river before settling themselves down in the shade for their daily nap during the great heat. Rhinoceros have a curious habit of depositing their manure in the same place, and consequently, in some much frequented woods, large mounds of it are found along their chief thoroughfares.

March 9.—Lions were especially entertaining last night, so at an early hour this morning we went in different directions in search of their tracks, and after a time a distant roar, heard by both parties, drew us towards the same point. Essafi very soon found a fresh track there, and followed it with his usual energy, and he certainly never seems so happy as when on a good track. One moment he turned round to specially point it out, exclaiming 'kebeer,' meaning a big lion; farther on, to keep up my interest in the performance, he showed me a place where the lion had scratched up the ground, saying 'gheean' (hungry), and so we progressed until our path joining another, he pulled up, and with a most disappointed expression of face pointed out the fresh and well-known track of the Vivian boot. It was quite evident, in fact, that Mohamed and Vivian were ahead of us, tracking a lion in the path ours joined. Still Essafi persisted in going forward, pointing out that there were the fresh tracks of two lions, and after some time had elapsed we heard a double report, and immediately afterwards caught up with our friends, whom we found resting under a tree, whilst a dying lion lay stretched out under another about twenty yards off, where Vivian found him asleep; and though he never rose after the first shot, Vivian gave him a second as a precautionary measure. This has been by far the most satisfactory hunt for a lion we have had, for tracking them as a rule is quite a hopeless proceeding. If this was the one we were originally tracking, Essafi's opinion that he was hungry was well supported by the fact of his having recently fed on a porcupine, from want probably of something better, and for this he paid the penalty of getting one quill stuck in his neck, and numerous small pieces in his front paws. It is a very fine lion, though rather deficient in mane. Continuing in the track of the second lion was soon put an end to by the arrival of Jali and his horsemen on their way home. He looked fatter and more hearty than ever, and reported their only having killed three elephants, as his advanced party had done, and we allowed him to remain in ignorance of the recent pressing claims of the Basé upon them. The new moon was seen to-night for the first time, and our men have been praying to her most industriously, not omitting to ask her to bring us good luck, and now (11 P.M.) there is a fresh breeze, almost amounting to a gale, from the north-west.

March 10.—Vivian has had a good proof of the difficulty of killing a buffalo, for a fine old solitary bull would not succumb until he had received a fourth bullet from the ten-bore, though all were close shots, and penetrated the chest. But the antelope also show great powers of vitality. The other day, with an expanding bullet from the express, I made such a hole in a koodoo's side that the lung protruded as it breathed, and I stood close by for some minutes expecting it momentarily to fall, when to my surprise it took a new lease of life and suddenly disappeared, and gave me some little trouble to find it again. On another occasion a gazelle managed to gallop off more than one hundred yards, after most of its interior had been knocked out by a low shot with a similar bullet. I wounded a very large hyæna to-day, but it managed to escape by swimming across a deep pool without being even caught by a crocodile, and then managed to secrete itself amongst the roots of some trees under a steep and wooded bank. After wading across the river in a shallow part, we were a long time in finding out its place of concealment, and then by climbing along some branches I was able to shoot it between the shoulders as it lay beneath me.

We then waited quietly for all evidence of breathing to cease, and after sundry prods at it with a stick without its showing any signs of life, we were on the point of descending from our perch, when a convulsive spasm turned the body over to the edge of the pool, and in an instant it disappeared into the jaws of a crocodile, which without doubt had for some time taken a very considerable interest in our proceedings. I regret losing it as a specimen, for it was far larger than I had imagined the hyæna was ever found, and even than Essafi had previously seen. Possibly it saved one of us having a more intimate acquaintance with the watchful crocodile. Arabs will never stand near the edge of a pool, from fear of being switched in by the tail of a crocodile, and wonderful stories they tell of how women and children fall victims in this way to its cunning. The mail for Kassala left to-day; in other words, Hadji Basheer started on horseback for the great capital with our letters, and if in two days' stay there he will find sufficient time to recite his grief to his friends on the loss of Jarrone, we calculate upon his return in ten with our long expected budget of letters and newspapers. Hadji is a title he has obtained by a visit to Mecca.

March 11.—Vivian has severely wounded a rhinoceros, but without any practical result; returning home he had a long stalk after a herd of buffaloes, and succeeded in killing a fine bull. Essafi and myself went to an island below Emhagga, specially to search for lions, as it had not been recently visited; and directly after our arrival there, when walking in a path through some high grass, Essafi suddenly pulled up and whispered 'daābee;' for a few seconds I could see nothing, until my eyes rested upon the face of a lion flat on the ground confronting us in our path and exactly the colour of the grass, whilst no other portion of him was visible. The distance between us being only from ten to fifteen yards, I fired, and then beyond a portion of the face becoming hidden by the grass no movement occurred, so I knew he must be dead; but Essafi thought otherwise, and to please him I fired again at the only part visible, the nose. As I did so, another lion stepped over the dead body and disappeared, to my great annoyance, for I had foolishly omitted to reload before firing the second shot, and consequently lost the chance of bagging a brace. The first bullet (express) struck the forehead and smashed the skull, and the second entering below the eye passed out under the chin. It proved to be a splendid male, as to size, though not grand-looking from being almost entirely devoid of mane, as lions frequently are in this country. From nose to tip of tail it measured nearly ten feet (115 inches), and from shoulder to extreme point of paw, forty-five inches. When opened it was found to be as fat as a prize ox, and every atom of this valuable commodity was carefully collected and brought home with the skin and head by Ibrahim and the Arab, who were sent out on camels for this purpose. Though the Arabs do not eat the fat, they find it very useful in many other ways.

March 12.—A hyæna paid our tent a visit in the night, and stayed for a few moments at the foot of Vivian's bed, but retired very quickly on his stretching out an arm for his revolver. After shooting two ariel for the larder, and whilst waiting for my luncheon on the liver, &c., of one *à l'Arabe*, I amused myself with the small kites. These, with the black and white crows, are always the first birds to be seen at such an entertainment, and the former are so courageous that they will even brush past us with their wings to pick up a piece of meat. My chief occupation was throwing bits into the air, which the kites seldom failed to catch in a claw before reaching the ground, so accurate were they in their swoops. The next to arrive are the vultures, soon to be followed by the Marabou storks, which from a region far beyond the reach of human vision keep constant watch over the movements of their friends beneath them. Twelve Arabs, headed by an old man named Ali, have arrived here from Gwayha, hunting as for a wild animal a young female slave who has recently escaped from Ali. They have tracked her from their village to this point step by step, where she stopped to drink, and beyond this they are afraid to go, fearing that they may fall into the hands of the Basé, her people, with whom she is now probably safe. They wanted us to assist them to continue the hunt into the Basé country, and were very much astonished to hear, on the contrary, that we were very glad she had escaped from their clutches, and that had it been in our power we would have given her every assistance to do so. Albert says they have a suspicion she is now in concealment with us, and it is a little curious that they should have tracked her here and no farther. She is supposed to have lived during her hurried flight upon the nabbuk-berries she could pick up by the way. Ali looks very miserable about his loss, and it is a great one to him, as he paid an Abyssinian sixty dollars for her only two years ago when with others she fell into the hands of those people in a frontier fight with the Basé. From the information we can gather from the Hamrans there must still be considerable trade in slaves in these parts. Essafi's father has frequently volunteered to procure for us a little boy and girl to take back to England, for the very modest sum of twenty dollars apiece, and cannot understand why we should refuse so good an offer, as he thinks they would be so useful to us. According to him there are plenty of slaves always for sale at 'El Kadarif,' a trading town one day's journey from 'Gwayha,' where they are brought by the Abyssinians after a successful raid upon their neighbours. There is another place much nearer home, named Tentah, a station between Cairo and Alexandria, where the slave trade goes on quietly. A great fair is held there annually about August, lasting thirty days, and during this time fifty or sixty slaves may be waiting for sale in a single house; at least, so our informant says, but with what truth there is much reason for doubt.

CHAPTER XIII.

March 13.—Vivian has been on the track of a lion all the morning, and had the small satisfaction of only seeing him sneaking away in the distance. Essafi took me quite a new beat into the Basé country, though not looking very happy about it, and especially when he pulled up once to show me some tracks of naked feet and gravely said, 'Basé.' Still on we went, and coming upon a fresh rhinoceros track all thought of the enemy vanished. Very soon he stops short and points upward, but there was nothing that I could see excepting a very small bird with a peculiar chirping note flitting about in front of us. No time then for an explanation, for we dismounted immediately, and having fastened our horses to the nearest tree, began creeping stealthily through some long grass for a few yards, when Essafi pointed out a rhinoceros lying asleep close to us, and almost completely hidden in the grass. Now was the time to test the twelve-bore rifle with its hardened spherical bullet and small charge of two-and-a-half drachms of powder, so as he sprang on his legs he received a right-and-left directly behind the right shoulder. To my surprise these shots produced no effect beyond making him bolt off with his companion, till then quite hidden, and at an equally good pace. The country being thinly wooded we ran after them, and as they fortunately turned round a hill we were able to make a short cut, and so gain upon them, until giving me a broadside at over one hundred yards I took a chance shot at the wounded one with the 'Henry,' and to my delight he stopped short, and after swaying to and fro he fell to the ground. The last shot struck the head below the eye, and seemingly low to have produced so fatal an effect. The other wounds I could not examine, as he fell on his right side. We always give special instructions to the Arabs sent to our dead game to bring back any bullets found in the body, and to observe their position; but they are generally so taken up with their own interests that ours stand a poor chance of being remembered.

Essafi explained in the evening that the small bird we saw and heard indicated distinctly to him that we were close to rhinoceros, for it is their frequent companion, and by its note gives them warning of approaching danger. In this respect it had to-day the misfortune which occasionally falls to the lot of other good-natured individuals, who, in trying to do a kindness for their friends, prove in the end their greatest enemies.

Some men we sent to the Hamran village the other day have returned with dhurra for our horses, and another goat to supply our increased demand for milk. They say that the people are still leaving the villages, expecting 'the Turks' to arrive daily, but that Sheik Aghill remains at his post. There is a strong feeling amongst them just now to migrate to Abyssinia, as they would only have to pay one dollar tax annually to the chief of the tribe they should join. The vultures have again done us a good turn by directing Mohamed to the body of the rhinoceros which Vivian severely wounded the day before yesterday. The sport for the week ending to-day, Saturday, has been therefore exceptionally good, and comprises two lions, two rhinoceros, three buffaloes, one wart-hog, two hyænas, nine antelope of various kinds, and numerous guinea-fowl.

March 15.—A blank day, excepting that I wounded a rhinoceros with the single 'Henry,' and lost him from not having a second charge to give him in time.

March 16.—An Arab from an unknown camp of hunters called this evening to ask the 'Hakim' to visit a sick man, who was so very ill that his friends could not bring him here.

Vivian, Albert, and myself, with some guides, at once started off on this mission of mercy, and from the report given of the case there was reason to hope for great results. Much to our annoyance, instead of their camp being near us, as the messenger stated, we were dragged through endless thorny paths, with only one lantern to give us light, and with clothes on by no means intended for this kind of night amusement, until we were just going to turn back in despair, when the barking of dogs announced the near approach to our destination. It was a very snug retreat, well away from the river, completely hemmed in by thick bushes, and specially adapted for protection from any night attack by the Basé. On our arrival, we saw the sick man separated from his comrades, and, whilst squatting on a mat, evidently writhing with pain.

Standing by his side, we were soon surrounded by the rest of the camp, numbering twenty, and a very picturesque group we formed, as the solitary lantern partially lit up this cavernous-looking place, and just enabled us to distinguish its individual members. Albert of course did the part of interpreter, and great interest was shown in the conversation between the sick man and himself. It happened to be a case in which an operation would give immediate relief to suffering, whilst the omission could only result in a gradual increase of it, until in all probability death brought it to an end. With these facts told him plainly and repeatedly, and every persuasion used to obtain his consent, not only through Albert, but also by his own people, only one answer could be obtained from him—viz., that it was by God's will he suffered, and that he would therefore accept his fate, whatever it might be. In fact, we had stumbled upon a ' Peculiar ' Arab. Albert of his own accord then said, 'Well, you must tell the "Hakim" you are quite well, if you want him to leave you ;' and with an expression of face which but too surely belied his tongue he thus addressed me and thereby consigned himself to a fate from which, in his blindness, he could not see he had been unexpectedly sent the means of relief. It was a hard matter to leave him thus, and one felt at first inclined to compel him by force to yield his wishes to ours, but it was decided otherwise ; and Albert's argument, that if anything were done and the man died, the Arabs would declare we had killed him, guided us greatly in the decision.

Our visit to the camp was not altogether unsuccessful, for we heard that they had found a grey horse, and upon our examining it there could be no mistake about its being our sick friend, slightly improved in his walking powers, though still showing great weakness of left side. They gave him up to us without any demur, and we led him home in triumph, and now the long-intended fate we had in store for him, and which by his wanderings he for a time escaped, will probably soon befall him. We could not hear any news of the donkey, but the old soldier has a hope that by a visit to-morrow he may extract something from them as to his fate. These Arabs have come to our neighbourhood in consequence of their belief that the reports of our rifles have driven the Basé into the interior of their own country, and we hear other parties are coming here from the villages to hunt under our protection in this neutral territory.

March 18.—An an early hour one of our old friends, the ostrich hunters, came to tell us that he knew where there was an ostrich-nest, and that if we would give him good backsheesh he would take us to it. After a certain amount of squabbling we came to reasonable terms, dependent on success or otherwise, and started off without delay on this novel expedition; and owing to the distance, and the consequent possibility of our being away all night, we provided ourselves with a limited supply of food and water, and with the friend of our dinner-table —the little whisky-barrel. A long ride over the high table-land in the direction of the Royan brought us evidently near our destination; but here arose a difficulty, for owing to the similarity of the ground, consisting of thinly-scattered mimosas and high grass, with here and there small spaces where it had been burnt up, our guide wandered about for a long time before he could find the trees that were his landmark. When he succeeded in doing so we tied up our horses, and tried to creep quietly along in line, but with the crackling of the grass at each step this was impossible, and we had the disappointment of seeing a black ostrich rise from the nest and instantly disappear, when we were a long way from it. We then went up to the nest, and found that it contained sixteen eggs, the proper complement being twenty-five, according to the Arab. The nest, if such it could be called, consisted merely of a very shallow depression in the hard-baked soil in the centre of a small burnt-up patch of ground, surrounded by high grass, and though the eggs were closely packed together they covered a considerable space. Vivian and myself were then carefully concealed in the grass on opposite sides of the nest to watch, and I was so thatched over that I literally could see nothing but the nest. After an hour of this very monotonous amusement, two visitors in the form of vultures pounced down upon the nest, and, apparently quite satisfied with the certainty of a quiet feast, commenced operations by a personal hunt amongst their own feathers, then a general survey was made of the white objects before them; and, finally, having retired for a moment, each returned with a stone in its beak, and set to work to hammer a hole through the shell of an egg. But the talents of these experienced old thieves were not allowed to obtain their just reward on this occasion, for whilst thus occupied an ostrich was seen by Vivian approaching the nest, and he fired at it, but, wounded or otherwise, it made good its escape without being even seen by me, and the vultures also of course disappeared at the same moment. It was a pity that the arrival of the ostrich should have so abruptly terminated this interesting *séance*. It was then useless watching any longer, and after our men's arrival and the robbery of two eggs, we retired to a little distance to enjoy a frugal repast of baked ostrich-egg, biscuits, and sardines, and afterwards go to bed, or rather roll ourselves up in our blankets and lie down on the ground. Here we felt quite sure that our sleep would be undisturbed by visitors, being far from the haunts of animals, excepting the harmless giraffe, and so, without taking any special precautions for safety, our hunters and ourselves soon dropped off one by one into the soundest of sleeps. The horses fortunately were of a different opinion, and a sudden chorus of snorts in the middle of the night made us spring to our feet, and then find that, thanks to them, two rhinoceros, instead of walking over us, had turned their course a little, and were rapidly vanishing into space. At daybreak we paid the nest a final visit, but no ostrich was to be found there; and as the eggs were quite cold, and probably deserted for good, our party divided the spoil, and we turned our steps homewards, both being of one accord, that ostrich-shooting after this fashion was not amusing. The excursion has taught us one good lesson—viz., before leaving camp always to examine the water-skins, for our men had brought a new one, which they no doubt thought was in perfect order, but owing to the materials with which it had been tanned and otherwise prepared, it imparted such a very unpleasant odour and taste to the water, that even when almost parched with thirst it was with great difficulty we could gulp it down. Most of us suffered more or less from thirst for a time after our arrival in this country, and found the water-bottle slung over our shoulders an indispensable companion. This has long since ceased to be the case, and we are able to abstain from drinking anything till luncheon-time with perfect comfort. Once, however, tea, or more especially water, has touched our lips, then for the rest of the day the water-bottle has to be in frequent requisition, if only to moisten the throat and tongue. During our absence, according to order, though with the most determined opposition on the part of the camel-men, our camp has been moved two miles farther up the Settite, to a bank a little raised above the river, named Hel-Egheeme. Essafi, senior, has been in a wild state of excitement since his arrival here, brought on by thoughts of his proximity to the Basé, who killed one of his sons, and, dancing about last evening whilst waving a sword over his head, he was heard shouting for them to come on that he might kill them; and in fact he worked himself into such a state of frenzy that Albert began to fear, for want of a Basé, he would fall foul of a friend. Returning very tired after our long ride and scarcity of provisions, it was most annoying to be told that Sheik Aghill had arrived yesterday, with two uncles, also Sheiks, and that he intended remaining until to-morrow; so the long-dreaded visit has at last come to pass, and he has of course chosen the present time to make sure of getting his dollars, as it is the termination of the camel-men's month.

Before making him receiver-general, as he asked to be, we sent for the chief of our party to know if this would meet with general approval. Essafi distinctly objected to receiving his wages through the Sheik, as he was sure the Sheik would try to borrow what he did not claim, and therefore paid him four dollars out of his savings at once, to be quit of him and his extortions. Nothing satisfies this voracious ogre, and he tried his utmost to extract some extra dollars from us on the most trifling pleas, even begging for one because we sent a man to Kassala; but we know our friend too well now to be humbugged by his energetically kissing our hands in turn, or by any other dodges to induce us to open the dollar-bag again.

During the process of pleading it was very amusing to see him trying to get round Albert by soft words and winking after his own fashion by completely closing one eye; and when he found this plan unsuccessful he became very angry with Albert for not taking his part, and, having pushed him aside, appealed again directly to us.

Determined as we were not to recognise his false claims we tried to entertain him, his uncles and followers, and in this respect our success was undoubted. The pictures in our books, and especially in the frequently examined 'Baker,' attracted as much interest as ever. In this book, each man represented has been given a name to add to the interest, and there is of course no difficulty in pointing out 'Howagee' Baker in each group; but amongst the numerous half-naked Arabs it is not easy to remember on each occasion to whom we have given the name of Aboo Doo, Taher Sheriff, Roder Sheriff, or other celebrities, yet a change of name is quickly detected by them. The pictures in other books do not attract half the interest of these, and even the great Sheik is quite as contented to look at any others upside down as the right way, and possibly more so, for he is most frequently found studying them in this position. One and all have quite made up their minds that we shall write a book on our return to England, and give illustrations of their exploits also. There is one picture which far surpasses in interest even the invaluable 'Baker,' and when once seen the study of it never appears to weary them, although, after all, it is only the reflection of their own faces in some little looking-glasses we brought out as presents for them. The air of perfect satisfaction with which the Sheik inspects himself in one whilst stroking his small beard, or exposing to view his really beautiful teeth, is delightful. One of his men had never seen his own face before, and after a very long study of it he was not apparently over and above pleased, remarking that he had seen a great many other faces like it. The next entertainment on the programme was one new alike to all, and we therefore held a levée of the whole camp, and having placed them in a circle no less a marvel was produced than a galvanic battery. From the Sheik downwards each in his turn had an opportunity of testing its astonishing powers so long as they had any inclination to do so; and the very varied effects and the extreme contortions of their faces were a source of endless amusement and produced shouts of laughter amongst the spectators. All tried their best to endure the torture, believing that it would give them new life, and the violent contractions of their muscles before they cried 'enough' proved there was no lack of pluck in their constitutions. One old Sheik declared that if we took this wonder of wonders to the Abyssinians they would say we were magicians. Interesting, however, as it may be to amuse in this simple way a party of Hamran Arabs, it would require a very strong constitution to continue the performance for a long time whilst the thermometer stands at about 100° Fah.

in the shade, and 145° Fah. in the sun, with a perfectly still atmosphere, and when owing to the closely packed crowd one seems to inhale nothing but oil of a most unsavoury kind. We therefore sent them all off very quickly when all had had a trial, though they would gladly have stayed for another round, excepting our old friend Aghill, and there was no chance of shaking him off till after dinner. As we sat down to this repast he took a last look at himself in Vivian's looking-glass, and asked for it to be given him, and on Vivian refusing to do so he pushed his plate away and said he would eat nothing. To set his mind at rest a half-promise was made that it might ultimately be given him, and he at once hid it in the numerous folds of his robe. After dinner Vivian, referring to the glass, asked Aghill what he would do if it were taken away from him, and his reply, needing no interpretation by Albert, was as prompt as it was suggestive, for he instantly put his finger down his throat, and the glass without a moment's loss of time became his own. For a wonder he then had a liberal fit, and offered to give us two wives each if we would remain in his country; and it is almost a pity that we have not accepted the present, for it will probably be the only one, as he thinks his only duty in life is to receive, that nothing is too good for him, and that he ought to be given everything he asks for. A very convenient doctrine! He is very anxious to go with us to Cairo to seek a personal interview with the Khedive about present Hamran troubles, and to petition him to place all the people of this country, who are as yet under Egyptian rule, directly under the government of Munsinger Pasha. He has begged us to assist him in this laudable project; but not to commit ourselves to a mistake, we have only promised to refer the matter to Munsinger, and if he approves the Sheik will be allowed to travel with us to Cairo.

March 19.—After breakfast, as a parting gift, we gave some of our store of presents to our guest and his uncles, consisting of handsome Venetian beads, Cairo beads, looking-glasses, ribbons, and scissors, and pertaining more therefore to the lady department, but equally acceptable; and as there seemed no prospect of our visitors being the first to move we took the initiative, and left them under Albert's watchful eye to check the rather restive tendency of their hands. Aghill has succeeded in wringing from the Arab who showed us the ostrich-nest the three dollars we gave him, and two or three from another who sold Albert a rhinoceros horn; but Essafi with all his cunning has been the great sufferer, for the Sheik has succeeded in borrowing from him his month's wages of twenty dollars, and the general opinion is that he will never see a penny of them again. Soon after Vivian's departure he found a young lioness under a tree, and not being able to see any other members of the family he relieved the country from one encumbrance in the future. Later in the day the sharp eye of Mohamed discovered a lioness lying under a mimosa which they were passing, but her retreat was so dark that for some time Vivian could not see her. Upon doing so he fired without being able to aim very clearly at any part, and with only the result of making her spring out of her ambush in an opposite direction to where they were standing and disappear. Immediately afterwards, Essafi and myself on our way home appeared on the scene, and as it was very evident from the blood in her track that she was wounded, we agreed to join in following it up.

For a long time the two hunters were mutually keen, but Essafi was the first to despair of success, as he had not the stimulus of its being his master's lion. Mohamed at last was on the point of giving up the hunt, when as we walked along the dry bed of a mountain torrent we saw the lioness crouching on the bank under a large 'baobab' about thirty yards off. Vivian then took a steady shot at her and literally rolled her over, and she finally landed in front of us in the bed of the stream, and though not dead she appeared quite done for. We fortunately were very cautious about approaching her, and did so very slowly, whilst throwing a few stones until within fifteen yards of her, when with a low growl she sprang up and came straight at us upon three legs, though at a pace by no means alarming; and then a bullet in the front of the shoulder from my express dropped her dead. In the meantime our hunters had taken their usual precaution of retiring rapidly to a distance. Whilst they were busily employed afterwards concealing the lioness with dry grass and wood from the watchful eyes of the vultures, we took advantage of the opportunity to measure the baobab, as it was about the finest we had seen, and we found its circumference to be over sixty-five feet near the base. Those who question whether it is by sight or scent that the vultures and Marabou storks find out their food, could not remain very long in doubt, one would think, in this country, for if our Arabs can manage to cover over our game quite loosely with some branches and grass before it has been observed by the feathered tribe, it will remain perfectly safe from them; but in addition the Arabs are always most particular to specially conceal any marks of blood on the body or in the neighbouring track. If, however, we can see at the time any vultures soaring about high above us, the Arabs know that their labour will be in vain. These remarks do not apply to the black-and-white crow, for this bird has a wonderful knack of being in at or soon after the death, independent of sight apparently; and, with a generosity worthy of example, vociferously 'caws' all its immediate relations in the neighbourhood to the feast, from the top of the highest tree it can find.

At last the sentence of death by shooting has been carried out upon the sick horse in a favourite haunt of lions, where it was led by Essafi after sunset, but the result was most disappointing; for, after the execution, Vivian and myself remained in ambush near it far into the night without receiving a visitor of any kind. Another great proof that vultures, &c., are guided by sight, not scent, is that they only soar about during the day, and if towards sunset we kill an animal there is no need to cover it over, for it then becomes an unnecessary precaution against their greedy proclivities, and quite useless to save it from being scented out by its enemies of the night, the lion and hyæna. Our Arab neighbours caught a giraffe yesterday, and made us a present of some of the flesh, and as Albert caught a fine fish, a 'baggar' (Baker), our dinner to-day has been more varied than usual, consisting of giraffe soup (which by Mohamed's careful cooking was, like his usual soups, reduced almost to an essence, and had consequently a rather too strong flavour of the menagerie for the palates of such connoisseurs as we have become in the delicacies of the forest), boiled 'baggar,' a very fine fish and the best of the inhabitants of the Settite, a buffalo mince, a giraffe steak, ariel cutlets cooked in hippo-fat, and a sweet omelette made with an ostrich-egg and apricot jam; and, to have everything in keeping, our lantern is supplied with the prepared fat of the lion. The Arabs declare that they know many of the lions by sight which frequent the Settite, from seeing them often follow their cattle when they bring them up the valley after the rains, and say that my fat one was a very old offender, having robbed them of many a cow, and that the news of his death had spread through all the villages.

March 20.—Vivian has shot a maāriff with a most curious pair of horns, and we are at a loss to know whether their condition is the result of a well-fought battle or of abnormal development. One horn is only represented by a short stump, as if it had been broken off, whilst the other is so completely twisted out of its natural position that instead of curving backwards it turns directly outwards, and is otherwise misshapen. It will form a valuable addition to his collection of heads. On our return home in the afternoon we heard, much to our astonishment, that Cumming had been to the camp to see how we were getting on, and then returned to the Royan, where his party had just arrived from the Salaam. All quite well, but they have shot nothing of importance beyond a giraffe, owing to the almost total absence of game there, excepting têtel and méhédéhet. They intend, therefore, to return to the Settite in a few days, and we shall then be able to hear more of their doings since the great separation. I have continued to keep a daily record,[1] when practicable, of the maximum temperature

[1] *Vide* 'Chart.'

in sun and in shade by day, and the minimum by night, and all gradually tend upwards with occasional variations; and now that the lowest temperature at night is only 65° we find it more refreshing to have our beds outside the tent, and thus get the full benefit of any movement of air during the early part of the night, when the heat is rather oppressive. The maximum in sun and shade to-day has been respectively 145° and 100° Fah. During the past week we have seen frequent thunderstorms over Abyssinia, and this afternoon very dark, ominous-looking clouds have hung directly over our heads, whilst we have had thunder and lightning in the distance on all sides of us. At one time it appeared scarcely possible we could escape a good drenching, but not a drop of rain fell over the camp, and the sky has now returned to its usual cloudless condition. We already feel the effects of the storms in Abyssinia, by a very decided rise in the river; and if this continues to increase, our fords will soon become impassable on foot. There are few things to mar the pleasure of life on the banks of the Settite, and the threatening approach of the rains tells us but too truly that we must make the most of the time still left us for a safe sojourn here; but there is one performance, sometimes repeated three or four times a day, which is far from agreeable, and the shorter the individual the more he has cause to object to it. I refer to wading across the river at varying depths, from above the knee to an occasional plunge to the waist or higher. When feeling fresh in the morning there is no cause to find fault with the performance, for it is then rather pleasant than otherwise, and the sun very soon dries the wet clothes; but in returning home after a long day on foot in the scorching sun, when we are more or less fatigued, the water strikes very cold, especially if it reaches the waist, and it requires a brisk walk to restore the circulation properly. Sometimes I have been almost surprised at no ill effect being produced by it, but nothing seems able to disturb our rest or our digestion.

March 21.—Last night, just before we were going to bed, an Arab told us that a herd of buffaloes were drinking a short distance above our camp, and dressed as we were we started off after them; Vivian in shirt-sleeves, pajamas and slippers, and myself in a thin dressing suit. The moon, partially obscured by clouds, only gave us sufficient light to allow us to distinguish an immense black mass, until we crept up to within perhaps thirty or forty yards of them, when we could make out a general outline of the nearest, and into these we fired our four barrels. Never could buffaloes have been more startled from their peaceful occupations than were these, on seeing such volumes of fire suddenly bursting upon them; and, leaving two wounded companions behind, they tore along the bank in headlong

UNIV. OF
CALIFORNIA

flight, raising such a cloud of dust that they were instantly lost to sight. To please our men, all of whom had turned out, we went on, and when the buffaloes left the bank and entered the woods we soon gained upon them, for owing to their great number, exceeding certainly one hundred, the trees checked their advance greatly, until another volley made them rush up a hill with a noise almost like thunder, as the branches were smashed in their mad career. We still followed them, and on reaching the crest of the hill found them again within sight, and, the moon at the moment aiding us, we were each able to pick out a fine bull and drop him. We had now used all the ammunition we had snatched up before starting, and were resting quietly before returning home, when we noticed that the herd had also halted, and like a regiment was drawn up in line on the high table-land beyond us. In another moment a wild cry from the Arabs that the buffaloes were coming proved only too true, and so rapidly that it became a case of *sauve qui peut*, and down the hill we tore and some way beyond it before we felt quite sure of having distanced the enemy. With faces, hands, and clothes, such as they were, telling their own story of the rapidity of our flight amongst mimosa thorns, we now returned home to get a further supply of ammunition, to assist our men in terminating the sufferings of the wounded; and in the subsequent proceedings how we all escaped without being shot, or otherwise injured, is somewhat surprising. The Arabs were wild with delight at the buffalo slaughter, and from the numbers reported to be wounded we ought to have hit about two per shot. A grand search was made for these under the low trees, and everyone was very bold at first, even Albert; but directly a buffalo was found and it was heard to move, a general scamper occurred right across our guns, leaving us in a much more uncomfortable position than themselves had one charged. Essafi very cleverly drew one out from under some trees by dancing about before it, and making thrusts at it with his sword, whilst we stood in a good position for a shot, and as it charged at Essafi he kept clear of our guns, and it was at once rolled over, most probably by Vivian's ten-bore. In another instance we had an opportunity of seeing with what great accuracy and force these Arabs can throw their spears, for having found a wounded buffalo in open ground, a deaf and dumb Arab belonging to another camp begged to be allowed to finish it off in his own way, for our special edification. Having been granted this privilege, he crept up stealthily, and at five yards distance away flew his spear, and striking the buffalo behind the shoulder it penetrated the chest to a depth of several inches. It did not finally succumb to its persecutor until by sundry cuts with a sword, lent by Essafi, across the back of the neck, he severed the spine there. Though it was far from any pleasure to us to aid in such a night slaughter of buffaloes, it was one not likely often to have its equal, for in nine shots we brought down five, and we have no cause to regret it, for our people will take care that not a scrap is wasted. It has proved a fine opportunity to fulfil a promise to our hard-working Ibrahim, to give him an animal all to himself, for one of the buffaloes was found quite dead, and the Arabs therefore did not grumble at his having the whole of it for his friends at Kassala. The deaf and dumb man is a splendidly-made fellow, and is quite the 'Ibrahim' of his own camp, as he does most of the hard work, and he is considered their boldest hunter. By various signs his friends understand him perfectly, and, much to his delight, he finds in Albert a new friend with whom he can hold a long conversation with even greater ease. The fact of Albert being able to talk to him with facility astonished us greatly at first, and it proved, if proof were wanting, that when language is of no avail the minds of human beings, of whatever race they may be, naturally turn to a very similar method of giving expression to the thoughts; and it has also brought to light another of Albert's numerous talents. At Shepherd's Hotel, Albert was one day told that a Russian gentleman wished to see him in his room, so he went up stairs and knocked at the door, and receiving no reply came down again, believing that no one was at home. The landlord told him to go up again, and open the door and walk in, and having obeyed these instructions he found himself in the presence of the Russian. Apologising for thus intruding, he felt annoyed at receiving no response, and was about to retire when, by signs made to him to sit down, he perceived that the Russian was deaf and dumb. The result of the interview, sustained by writing in French, was that Albert agreed to travel with him for six months, a portion of the time to be spent in Cairo, and the remainder in Italy. Albert describes this engagement as the most trying of any he has accepted in his career of dragoman or courier, and especially during the first month, for he never was away from his master's side, and began almost to fear that he also would lose the power of speech. As time went on, writing gradually gave place to signs, and so completely towards the end of the engagement, that they could hold long conversations with great ease in the latter way, and when they parted Albert considered himself quite a proficient in the language of signs. He now finds a fine opportunity to renew his experience, and to show off another talent to us. The deaf and dumb Arab lives more in our camp than in his own, and is always delighted if allowed to assist Ibrahim in cleaning and preparing heads and skins, and returns home quite happy if given an odd remnant of hide to make a pair of sandals. It is painful to watch him holding a conversation with Albert, for he makes during the whole time a peculiar whining noise, and sometimes gets so excited that he looks far more like a raving lunatic than a sane man. Albert runs him very close in this respect, by the distortion of his features, and by the wild and rapid movements of his arms. It is quite evident that they must understand one another perfectly, or they would not be so frequently seen going through their gymnastic performances. The Arab unfortunately thinks that because Albert understands him we ought to be able to do so, and is rather fond of a chat with us on our return home; and as we have paid him the compliment of learning his signs to represent the different animals we shoot, and whether they are male or female, we are able to tell him some news, and a few mutual nods and grins help out the conversation wonderfully.

Albert, wise in his generation, takes advantage of having been born in Gibraltar, and registers himself every year at the Consulate, Cairo, as an English subject. For this he pays 5*s.*, and by so doing escapes other taxes. In his speech he might be mistaken for an Englishman, excepting for an occasional mistake, such as one last night, when he called a bee a honey-fly. He says he can speak seven languages, and most of them fluently.

March 22.—Surprised as we were the other day to

hear of the visit of Cumming, this news was as nothing to the announcement of to-day that Ranfurly and Arkwright had arrived at Emhagga, our old camping-ground down the river, so in a few days we shall be quite a large party here.

CHAPTER XIV.

March 23.—I went out early with Essafi, and came unexpectedly upon a rhinoceros in some jungle, and as he looked at me with his head up I fired at the front of his chest with the 'Henry,' but without producing any apparent effect. We then tracked him for some distance by observing the freshly-trodden grass, and walked up to within five yards of him before he was seen. He was again facing us with head up, and I fired as before, and to my unpleasant surprise the cartridge missed fire. Keeping my eye upon him I reloaded, and in a most liberal manner he allowed me to take another shot at him without moving, and this time with an immediately fatal result. The bullets had entered the chest side by side, the last being a little to the left and probably striking the heart. In the afternoon there was a great gathering in our camp, for Coke and Cumming arrived from the Royan, being already disgusted with it, and Ranfurly and Arkwright paid a 'morning call.' It was very amusing to compare our respective experiences, and Vivian and myself have no cause to find fault with the way Fate has treated us.

The Massowah party give a very unfavourable report of their sport in the Bogos country, having found no elephants, as they had fully expected, nor scarcely any other game, excepting buffaloes and gazelle. They therefore returned to Massowah, and having heard from the Governor, Arekel Bey (the nephew of Nubar Pasha), to whom they had received letters of introduction, that Munsinger Pasha had telegraphed to him very favourable accounts of our doings, they decided upon coming into our country, and engaged fresh camels for the desert journey to Kassala. This extended over two months, in consequence of their making excursions into the Basé country; and owing to the almost complete absence of antelope, they ran very short of their meat supplies. Ranfurly shot a fine lion *en route*, and between them they killed a boa-constrictor measuring fifteen feet, which they found coiled up in a bush and believed to be temporarily blind, as it had just shed its skin and the eyes were still covered with a portion of it. At Kassala they accepted a guard of six soldiers, and after arriving at the Hamran village, and being fleeced by Sheik Aghill, they departed for the Salaam river, Arkwright preferring to visit a new district than to return to his haunts of the previous winter on the Settite. Having decided to strike the Salaam at a point well within the Abyssinian frontier, they took a line of country between the Settite and this river, until, arriving at a favourite camping-ground upon its bank, they pitched their tent there for a time, and then gradually descending the river they came to the camp of Coke and Cumming, where they spent a week before proceeding here. Their sport was no better than their neighbours', but in one respect they nearly succeeded in having a very different experience.

Arkwright is very partial to fishing, and one day he started off with his rod, rifle, and Tokroori attendant (a Mahometan negro tribe belonging to Darfur), to a pool about a mile above their first camp in Abyssinian territory, and set to work to see what it contained. In a short time his man suddenly sprang up, and in a wild state of excitement cried out the 'Hhábeshi' (Abyssinian) robbers are coming. It was then too late for escape, so seizing his rifle he quietly allowed the enemy to approach him. He counted thirty-six men mounted, all armed with spear and shield, and he was in a moment surrounded by them; and as he looked up and saw all their spears pointed at him he felt his position to be extremely critical, and especially as at the same moment one of the party seized hold of his rifle and tried to wrench it from him. In this emergency he found in the Tokroori a faithful friend, for the man stepped forward, and speaking in their own language told them that they dared not touch his master, for beyond a tree which they could see was their camp with a party of Egyptian soldiers; and if they attempted to do any violence to him they would all certainly be killed.

The effect was magical upon them, for they at once dropped their threatening attitude, and declared that they meant no harm, and were merely hunting for buffaloes, and they rapidly decamped upon being pointed out by the Tokroori the direction in which he said he had seen some fresh tracks. That night the soldiers kept up a careful watch, fearing a surprise, but without cause, for nothing more was heard of them.

Whilst Arkwright and Ranfurly have decided upon remaining in their present camp below us, Coke and Cumming have chosen some ground about a mile above us, for we have decided that it would be better for us not to rejoin, as Vivian and myself wish to turn our steps homewards before they do. They give a most favourable report of Emanuel, Bob, and the young soldier Abdullah; but their Arabs have given them much trouble, and Emanuel has been occasionally obliged to resort to the native method of enforcing obedience—the koorbatch. The general meeting was most cordial, and Emanuel and Bob were specially demonstrative in their delight at finding us safe and well. Cumming has been attacked with dysentery, but it only lasted a few days, thanks to the careful management of Emanuel, who, after administering a good dose, kept him very quiet, and fed him chiefly on rice-water and arrowroot. He is now perfectly well, and though the edge of the wound in the leg has not quite healed, it has caused him no inconvenience.

March 24.—Our deaf and dumb friend came early this morning to ask us to assist his people to kill a rhinoceros which had been caught in one of their traps, and had travelled a long distance into the Basé country with the block of wood attached to a leg. Vivian being in camp went off with them, and when once on the track it was very easy work following it up, owing to the trailing mark made by the wood. When first they came within sight of him he was eighty yards off, in open ground, and much to Vivian's surprise he galloped off without appearing to be the least impeded by the huge addition to one hind-leg. After another hour's tracking, Vivian was able to creep close to him, whilst the Arabs took good care to keep at a respectful distance; and though the first shot did not prevent his going off, a second one settled his fate. The Kassala post arrived this evening, and again no letters from England, nor even papers on this occasion, excepting some copies of the 'Mail,' which Munsinger Pasha has most kindly let us have.

The mistake about the letters is very annoying, as

we took every pains at Cairo, where it probably occurs, to arrange for their transmission to Souakim by the Egyptian steamers, and a friend promised to keep an eye to our interests there. At Souakim we left a money deposit with the Egyptian postal agent, to ensure their transfer across the desert, so we do not expect the delay arises there, and now there is little hope of getting home news until our return to Cairo.

Hadji Basheer does not bring good news from Kassala, for small-pox has broken out there, and is so rapidly spreading that the inhabitants are leaving the town as fast as they can. He had consequently great difficulty, and in some instances failed, in fulfilling our small commissions. The camel he took with him has not returned quite unladen, however, as he managed to buy about two hundred small hens' eggs—distinctly of the 'cooking' variety, and therefore requiring considerable care in their selection—lemons, onions, coffee, and sugar in loaf. Emanuel was very proud to be able to lend us from his stores some of the last two items, to show how careful he had been with his half of our original division, notwithstanding the extra drain upon them by the visitors from Massowah. But he has not had a black cook with him like Mohamed, who from morning to night is drinking coffee as strong as it can be made, and as sweet as syrup. The lemons are very small and have little juice, but they impart some flavour to the water, and when to this is added a little honey, a refreshing drink is readily made for our daily return from hunting. Honey has also quite taken the place of stewed apricots as an addition to rice, which is in great demand both at dinner and breakfast, now that the supply of our best biscuits (Lehman's) is consumed, and we are tired of the commoner kind, 'hard-bake.' Rice has also a great advantage over biscuits, in combining better with the large amount of milk our two goats kindly supply us. There has been one thunderstorm at Kassala. Another piece of news brought by the old soldier is that the Shukoriah Arabs, who are under the Sheik of Khartoum, have recently attacked their neighbours, the Hadendowa Arabs, and after killing six of them they carried off ten herds of cattle.

The Hadendowas are consequently in a very excited state, and have sent a deputation to Munsinger Pasha, by whom they are immediately governed, to beg him to leave them to settle the matter without his interference, for they wish to kill their enemies, or die in the attempt. In consequence of this disturbance, Munsinger has had to return to Kassala from a tour of inspection that he was making in the country under his rule. A report has spread amongst the Hamrans that the late King Theodore's son has been brought back to Abyssinia.

March 25.—We have had on the whole good cause to be satisfied with the amicable relations existing between the members of our establishment (even Albert and Essafi soon forgot their bloodthirsty intentions towards one another), though we could have wished that Albert had more power in checking Mohamed's extravagance in the consumption of our stores; but lately we have seen that Mohamed was becoming daily more jealous of the notice we took of Ibrahim, and to-day it culminated in a row, which would have had a very serious termination had not Vivian returned home at the right moment. It began by Mohamed claiming a large skinning-knife from Ibrahim, which undoubtedly belonged to Ibrahim, as he proved by a private mark, and a struggle ensued of a desperate kind, though Ibrahim was by far the stronger of the two. Vivian brought it to an abrupt conclusion by appearing on the scene, though a moment too late, for the plucky old soldier in trying to separate the black combatants paid the usual penalty of getting the most injured; for Mohamed in drawing the knife away made a frightful gash across his hand between the first finger and thumb, from which blood spurted in torrents. They then wisely set to work to bind the thumb to the finger as tightly as possible, and thus partially check the bleeding, and messengers were sent off in search of me. I was fortunately returning home, and aided by my assistants the arteries were tied and all bleeding arrested; and then, faint from loss of blood, the old soldier was laid quietly down in the best shade to be found. The business terminated with a severe lecture to the combatants, and a warning that if there was any more fighting between them the one most clearly in the wrong should be at once sent back to Kassala. Afterwards we heard from Albert that Mohamed had received a present from Kassala of some 'booza' (a kind of native beer made from dhurra), and that he had been decidedly 'boosy' the whole day. Last night we dined with Coke and Cumming, and this evening we returned the compliment, and Coke entertained us with an account of a most spirited adventure he had just had with a rhinoceros. When some distance from home he suddenly came upon three in some low grass, and was able to creep within a few yards of them without being seen; and conceiving the bold design of trying to bag them all he gave two a right-and-left, and reloading rapidly before they had discovered their enemy took a shot at the third. The first two decamped, but this one, whilst more boldly looking about him, received another ball from the ten-bore in the side, and then catching sight of Coke charged straight at him. Coke, guided by the current belief that a rhinoceros never turns when he has once made off, stepped a little on one side to give him plenty of room to pass on; but instead of doing so he changed his course accordingly, and there was nothing left for Coke to do but to run for his life to the nearest mimosa-tree, at the same time dodging about from side to side to elude his persecutor. This was without effect, though the rhinoceros once lost ground by a tumble; so upon reaching a small mimosa-bush he made a wide circle round it. Still the rhinoceros followed, and round and round the tree he chased Coke, the circles becoming gradually smaller, until the latter, finding that the distance between them was also diminishing, whilst he was rapidly becoming exhausted, made up his mind that his only hope of escape was to get to a neighbouring wood, and he therefore made a push for it. The rhinoceros now cut off a corner by trampling down the mimosa in continuing the chase, but Coke reached the wood first of all, and falling down amongst the bushes quite exhausted he managed to elude the eye of his would-be enemy as it passed on. After a short rest to recover his breath, and when rejoined by his hunter, he followed up the track, and very soon found the rhinoceros lying under a tree, and then with one shot put an end to its dangerous propensity. This account makes us look upon rhinoceros-shooting in a rather different light, for though often warned of the danger of shooting them, our experience had led us to believe that it was more imaginary than real, from their invariably turning on receiving a charge in the face, though their first intention might be to assume the offensive. It is necessary to see a rhinoceros in its native home to realise the rapidity with which such an unwieldy-looking creature can spring to its feet, the pace it can go, and the very quick way it can turn, beating some say in this respect a horse.

On seeing the malformed maāriff's head in Vivian's collection, Coke at once recognised it as one of an old friend he had unsuccessfully stalked five miles beyond the Salaam, as lately as March 15, so it must have crossed the river and travelled over forty miles during the short time that elapsed before it was shot.

March 27.—A hippo which was killed last evening by Vivian was found at sunrise, and very soon afterwards it was surrounded by more than sixty Arab hunters, so greatly have they multiplied of late; and owing to the large amount of meat we have in camp, our men let the visitors have all of it excepting the hide and fat.

This is the third hippo we have killed this week for the Arabs' benefit; and with our experience we seldom require to expend upon each more than one expanding bullet, small as it is, from our express rifles, for if it strikes a hippo in the eye or within two or three inches below it death is sure to follow. The programme is to sit near the edge of a pool, allowing a little intervening space if the bank is a low one, to check the too eager advance of a crocodile, and to wait patiently for the momentary appearance of a hippo's nose and eye, for more is rarely seen. With luck the first hippo may be accommodating and remain up long enough for a steady shot, but after the first they become very wary, and our plan then is, after seeing the spot where one has risen to breathe, to keep the rifle directed to it; and when the hippo rises again, as he frequently does in the same place after two or three minutes, or more if the pool has been disturbed, to take a snap-shot at him, and if he is hit his desperate struggles under water generally set the whole pool in commotion; but sometimes death is so instantaneous, judging by the quickness with which they float, that there is no immediate evidence of their being mortally wounded.

Curiously enough, after a long morning's tracking, and at last, guided by the little bird already referred to, Essafi and myself for the first time found three rhinos together. Two were asleep close to us, and another was feeding at a little distance off. I again tried the effect of a double discharge from the twelve-bore rifle behind the left shoulder of one, but without any effect; and as it bolted with its companion it was so hidden that I could not give it a 'Henry' bullet. No. 3 stood quietly looking at me, so I fired at it with this rifle, and instantly on it came towards me.

Coke's experience of yesterday was much too recent for me not to be affected by it, and I found myself rapidly following on the heels of Essafi, until, on looking round, I saw to my relief that the rhino had not changed his course. Reloading quickly, I gave him a parting shot, and afterwards followed him for a time; but as it was getting late, we had ultimately to leave him in peace. Arkwright sent us a very large 'baggar,' weighing about twenty pounds, this evening. He is the only one who cares for fishing. We have not found it very interesting, for if we fish with a rod and line a turtle is just as likely to take the bait as a fish, with a result not very satisfactory to the fisherman when his supply of tackle is limited, for something has to yield, and the probability is that it is not the turtle. The other expedient is to use a hand-line of considerable thickness, having a monster hook on it baited with half a pound of meat or more, according to fancy, and by sundry whirls over the head to throw it a long distance into the river, and wait the result. As a precautionary measure, after allowing for plenty of slack line, it is advisable to fasten the frame on which the line is wound to something immovable. A few gentle nibbles, then a jerk, and probably a turtle is again hooked, and it is merely a question of hauling to bring it to the bank, when it has a playful way very frequently of making good its escape. Possibly a turtle is not in the neighbourhood of the bait, then woe be it if, when holding the line in your hand, your thoughts stray, for before you have time to let the line go a monstrous fish may have darted off with the bait, and dragged the line at such a rate through your fingers that it must be felt to be fully appreciated. On one occasion I had a nasty cut in this way. After one run, if there is one, it would be just as amusing to pull a dead weight out of the water as to catch the enormous fish that inhabit the Settite. The most common one caught by our fishermen, Albert and Hadji Basheer, is a hideous creature with an almost black skin, called by the Arabs 'bayard.' The head is very large compared with the body, and it has four long feelers in the upper jaw and two in the lower. Though ugly it is very good to eat, and we generally have it sliced and fried. The finest yet caught probably did not weigh more than twenty-five pounds, but Baker mentions having frequently seen them from sixty to seventy pounds' weight.

CHAPTER XV.

March 28.—We have to-day turned our steps homewards, leaving the special home of the rhinoceros and lion to the new arrivals, and have encamped upon our old ground, named El Effaara. Approaching it, we saw immense herds of cattle being driven into the country from the villages to feed on the dry grass, and our hunters at once galloped off to the drivers to get some milk. This entailed our following them for some distance, until the halting-ground across the river was reached. The cattle, parched with thirst, on approaching the river rushed headlong down the steep bank to drink, and afterwards so enjoyed fording the river that they took their time about it, wandering up and down in mid-stream until driven out; whilst the calves, of which there were a goodly number, finding it necessary to swim, lost no time in reaching the opposite bank. These cattle are very varied in colour and shape, and are as a rule about the size of an Alderney. They have the one general characteristic of marvellous leanness, and as regards their milking powers, one good English cow would be a match for twenty of them as to quantity, and as to cream the whole herd perhaps would not produce so much. Still, a good draught of milk from the united efforts of sundry Soudan cows is not to be despised after a long ride under a tropical sun. We thoroughly enjoyed it, though not able to repeat the performance so often as our men expected, for bowl after bowl was brought us, until we were obliged to point to our throats to prove to them that our capacity to swallow milk had a limit. We soon arrived at our old camp, and then took a stroll to find something for the larder, and bagged two Dorcas gazelles.

Vivian's hunter Mohamed, surnamed, we find, Fagerole, has obtained three days' leave to go to his village to pray for his father, of whose death he heard to-day from the cattle-drovers. The news has not apparently distressed him, nor was he anxious to go if Vivian wished to keep him.

March 30.—Our second visit to El Effaara has quite settled the important fact in our minds, that there is no game to be obtained here excepting by very long journeys from the river, and then only antelope, and these keep in such open country that no amount of stalking is of avail in its present burnt-up state. Even our very domestic friends, the têtel and hind koodoos, keep well out of shot, and indeed, were it not for guinea-fowl, we should soon find ourselves on the short commons of rice, milk, and honey for dinner. I took out to-day as guide and gun-bearer, in the temporary absence of Essafi, a camel-man, and very proud he was to be so raised in the social scale above his fellows, though a man more unsuited to this work could not be imagined. He is our finest specimen of the Hamran Arab, standing about six feet three inches, and splendidly made in proportion down to the knees, but in calf and form of leg below knee he shows the usual defect of his people. Notwithstanding this, his carriage is very perfect, and his head is protected with as fine a crop of hair as the most fastidious Hamran could desire. Walking as erect as a statue in front of me, his idea seemed to be that the faster he got over the ground the more game he could show me, but he signally failed to see anything, and three times I had to pull him up, though too late, to let me get a standing shot. At last I had a distant shot at a méhédéhet and wounded it, and away went my giant guide, 'El Minna,' after it as fast as he could run, and he so successfully drove it far out of sight that it was quite hopeless for me to follow one or other, and I therefore returned home. Albert says 'El Minna' is very proud of his performance as a hunter to-day, and is anxious for a re-engagement. One day Albert told him that if he would go to London with us, and exhibit himself in his war costume, with the addition of a few ostrich feathers in his hair, that he would make an immense fortune, as everyone would pay a dollar to see him. At first he liked the idea very much of earning dollars so easily, but when he heard that the climate might kill him, he came to the conclusion that it would be better to live on dhurra in his native home than run the risk of inflicting so great a loss on Hamran society.

Ibrahim had also a great treat to-day in being allowed to take a gun to shoot some guinea-fowl. After a long round in the woods and a rather large expenditure of ammunition he brought home two, and was greatly pleased with his success. Hadji Basheer, however, threw cold water on his great achievement by declaring his conviction that he must have found one guinea-fowl dead and the other stone-blind. Joy reigns supreme in the camp, for no less important news was brought this evening than the dethronement of Sheik Aghill by the Khartoum authorities, and the appointment of an uncle, at present Sheik of a small village, in his place. The report goes on to say that the new Sheik has already been to Khartoum to be adorned with a special robe, tarboosh, and turban, and is now on his way to Gwayha to turn Aghill not only out of office, but also out of his home. Aghill, on the other hand, is reported to have sent a deputation to Khartoum to ask if they intend to deprive him of his money and possessions, for if so he will at once go to Abyssinia; but if left alone he will remain quietly in his own village. Aghill has the credit of being a very rich man, for, besides having saved money, his father left him a large sum. There can be no doubt of the pleasure this news has given to our people, who hate as much as they fear Aghill, and his power of extorting money from them was well exemplified when he took away all the dollars we gave the ostrich man because he had kept our present a secret from him. They speak very well of his successor. Essafi, senior, is especially happy, as he now sees a prospect of his son getting back the twenty dollars he lent Aghill, and he intends to stay with us till next pay-day and take Mohamed Fagerole's month's wages instead of allowing him to transfer them to Sheik Aghill in repayment of a debt of his own.

Hadji Basheer's hand is already nearly well, and never has a wounded extremity been kept more quiet or given a better chance of healing, for whilst tenderly nursing it in the other hand he has spent nearly all his time lying down in a semi-somnolent state, or perhaps grieving over his practical lesson on interfering in other people's quarrels.

March 31.—Another move in a homeward direction, and our tent is now pitched close to our old ground at Emberaga, but beyond hanging up our rifles, &c., in it the tent is no longer of any use to us.

The not unusual report soon after arrival at a place

of 'horses strayed' has again been announced, and this time all six have walked off, but their tracks have been found in the direction of El Effaara, and early to-morrow a party of Arabs will be sent after them. We have come here with no small expectation of finding elephants, as large herds are reported to be in the woods. Unfortunately, the moon is in the wrong quarter for night-shooting.

April 1.—The horses being absent, Vivian paid the first visit to the supposed elephant-haunts on a camel, accompanied by an Arab similarly mounted, with the intention of tying up the camels upon arriving there and walking through the woods. If the camel had been told that it was the first of April he could not have better succeeded in adapting himself to English customs, for directly he was required to lie down he made such a tremendous row that no elephant would have remained within miles of him, and he also succeeded in driving away two black ostriches at which Vivian thinks he might otherwise have had a shot. We have not often seen ostriches in our rambles, and then only on the high table-land at half a mile distance from us.

April 2.—At Essafi's special request, I stayed out all night near the river to watch for the arrival of elephants at a favourite drinking-place, but none came, and we had only the questionable satisfaction of finding this morning by some fresh tracks that elephants had drank about a mile below our station. Later in the day we heard that one had been caught in an Arab pit, and this so frightened the others that they crossed the river. I have no reason to grumble at my night's lodging, however, for Essafi made me a very comfortable bed by clearing away the loose stones in a dry part of the river directly under the bank, and covering it with a thick layer of partially dry reeds. My ever-useful water-bottle became my pillow, and thanks to this glorious climate the sky was the only coverlet I required. Essafi then performed the same office for himself, making his pillow of a bent branch, and soon fell into the soundest of sleeps whilst I took the first period for watching. Essafi has his own particular pillow in camp, which consists of a concave piece of wood fixed upon a stand about eight inches high, and upon this he rests the back of his head, whilst his luxuriant locks hang over it without any risk of being crushed. The short time left to me before the sun went down and darkness supervened was well taken up in watching the ever-changing shadows and shapes of objects that would be liable to deceive the sight in the absence of moonlight, and also in arranging a night-sight to my rifle. I find a strip of white paper fastened by elastic bands along the whole length of the barrel in a line with the sight answers the purpose better than a piece of card fitted round the barrels near the sight. During three hours' watching nothing was heard or seen to move near us excepting two hippos that came out of a pool above us, and having walked close past us quite leisurely they entered the river again at a lower point to pay a visit, probably, to their next-door neighbours. It being then too late to expect any elephants to do us a similar honour, my bed *à l'Arabe* looked too attractive to be longer resisted, and having warned Essafi not to disturb me on account of visitors, unless they were unpleasantly obtrusive, I was quickly lost to consciousness. Awaking at dawn I found Essafi had also retired to his couch during the night, so it was as well that no visitors did arrive. After sunrise our horses were brought out to us, as well as some hot breakfast, and the day was spent in the elephant woods. We found numerous very recent tracks, but it was evident that the herd had gone to retreats beyond the reach of a day's hunt. I might have had a shot at a small leopard in our path, but I did not wish to disturb the country by firing, so after looking savagely at us for a moment it sprang into the long grass and disappeared. Sometimes we ride through grass far above our heads, but as a rule it does not exceed three or four feet in height. During my absence last night from camp a few Arab guests arrived, and by special request a performance was given by Vivian and Albert with the galvanic battery, with a success as great as on the previous occasion.

April 3.—Vivian again on the track of the elephant, aided by Essafi. A new hunter volunteer from our Arab party, anxious to earn a few dollars, declared with great confidence that he could show me some lions, and to my cost I gave him a chance, for with the activity almost of a monkey he hunted along the high and low ground bordering the river here, following now and again the fresh tracks of lions until midday, when he had quite tired me out, and I was obliged to tell him that we must return home. On arriving there I found a note from Ranfurly, asking me to come to Coke's camp to see him, as he was lying ill there with dysentery. It did not take long getting ready to start on so important a mission, and having filled my haversack with sundry useful things, I mounted my horse and joined the bearer of this sad message, the young soldier Abdullah, who was accompanied by an Arab mounted like himself on a camel. Keeping on the high flat land away from the river, we were able to ride very rapidly, a proceeding rendered necessary by the lateness of the day, but the pace after three hours began to tell on my back, for whilst their camels were apparently trotting along leisurely my unfortunate horse had frequently to gallop to keep up with them. Thus for four hours we contiuued on our way with scarcely a halt until sunset, when we again approached the river, and after crossing this we were soon at our destination. Abdullah *en route* suddenly left us and galloped off to an Arab we saw to our right, and much to my surprise he seized hold of the terror-stricken man's spear and carried it off in triumph. This was evidently thought to be a capital joke by Abdullah and his companion, as they rode on side by side and examined the weapon, and it gave me the chance of seeing how thoroughly an Egyptian soldier appreciates the connection between might and right. On my arrival I found that my haversack with its treasures and toilet requisites for the night (a tooth-brush) had been jolted off the back pommel of my native saddle during some part of the journey.

Ranfurly has without doubt a sharp attack of dysentery, from which he has been suffering for a few days, but he has been very well looked after by Emanuel, in the same way as Cumming was on the Salaam, and we must hope that this attack also may neither prove a long nor very grave one. It was most probably produced in the first place by the air of their camp at Emhagga being poisoned by the decaying meat that their men had left lying about in the immediate neighbourhood for the vultures, and which had not been found out by them. Passing the camp at Emhagga one day I observed a very unpleasant odour from this source, and I pointed it out to Ranfurly. When first attacked, he was just beginning to have excellent sport, and in his anxiety to make up for all the lost time before his arrival on the Settite, he would not give in, and the two last days, before he was compelled to do so by prostration, he devoted to rhinoceros-shooting in the distant woods, and thus greatly over-fatigued himself by long exposure to the broiling sun. Yesterday, Arkwright brought him to this camp to place him under Emanuel's nursing, and it was then thought advisable to send for me without delay. He is very cheerful, and is now lying comfortably in his patent hammock near us, and joining in the general conversation; and Cumming has fortunately had an amusing story to tell us of his day's experiences with the rhinoceros under the leadership of the renowned 'Jali.'

'Jali,' like the rest of his people, singular as it may be, is not above a bribe, and by an offer from Cumming which almost amounted to promising whatever he chose to ask, besides half the spoil, he has agreed to remain with him as his hunter until his final departure from the country. With the assistance of the veteran to-day a rhinoceros was in course of time found, which patiently submitted to receive four or five balls from the twelve-bore rifle, and then falling down apparently dead they walked up to him. Rejoiced at his success, as it was his first rhino, Cumming sat on the body to contemplate his prize and examine the bullet-holes, until suddenly a convulsive movement passing through its huge frame, made him spring off his comfortable seat, and with Jali beat a speedy retreat. At the same moment the rhinoceros also sprang up, and to their mutual astonishment went off at a gallop, and on being again found required another shot before he finally succumbed. Arkwright and Ranfurly had wonderfully good sport during their stay at Emhagga. The former killed a lioness on four successive days, and finding them all asleep had no trouble in despatching them. His previous experience of that portion of the river was probably the chief cause of his success, for he knew where to look for them. Ranfurly has been equally lucky with rhinoceros, killing two in one day, and another at night when watching for them by the river's side.

Though I could not see Vivian before my hasty departure yesterday, I expect to find him to-morrow evening at our old camp near here, Hel-Egheeme, as we had decided upon returning to-morrow, owing to the total absence of game lower down the river.

April 4.—A slight improvement is apparent in the condition of Ranfurly. Men were out to-day searching for my valuables, and though they have not found them they will be sure to do so to-morrow, with their marvellous powers of tracking, stimulated by backsheesh, and, if necessary, they will go the whole distance. The loss

I most regret is that of my thermometer, but, even if found, the maximum one for registering the temperature in the sun will soon be of no use, as this has now reached 153°, and mine is only graduated to 160°. Vivian has arrived, and I returned with him this evening to Hel-Egheeme, but Hadji Basheer has been left behind at Emberaga to wait for the return of some of our men from the Hamran village.

April 5.—Paid Ranfurly two visits, and feel satisfied that there is a diminution of the grave symptoms of his disease, and find him very willing to carry out all the orders he receives.

It is certainly very pleasant to return to this part of the river, as the country is so much more open on each side; and whenever there is a breeze, and this is by no means infrequent now, we get the full benefit of it. Between Emberaga and El Effaara the river, for a short distance, flows rapidly through a very narrow channel between high and precipitous cliffs of a dark-coloured stone, producing even now a fine effect, and when it is at its greatest height this must be much increased. There is one animal we frequently see near the Settite, to which as yet I have made no reference. It is the wart-hog. The body is like that of a small wild boar, but the head, which is most hideous, has several big nodules on it, from which it derives its name, and it has projecting tusks from the upper and lower jaw. It is comparatively tame, and we have not troubled the species much, as it is too mangy-looking to add it to our dinner list: the Arabs will eat it, however, readily enough, and Albert says they get over the difficulty in connection with their religion by saying that if they have the Koran in one hand and no pig in the other they may not eat it, but if they have some pig and no Koran they may eat it. (N.B. I have not seen Albert read ' Baker.')

CHAPTER XVI.

April 6.—To-day a great change has taken place in the arrangement of our several parties. Though Ranfurly's dysentery is becoming arrested, he is so prostrated by it that its effects are not likely to pass off immediately, and it is necessary that he should remain under my immediate observation. He has been therefore brought down quietly on horseback the short distance to our camp this morning, to remain with us until he is strong enough to rejoin Arkwright, or until our arrival at Kassala, where a general *réunion* is to take place about April 23 or 24.

The three others have gone some hours' journey together up the river to see what game is to be found there. Step by step we have gradually ascended the river in spite of the opposition and fear of our men, and as we have found more game the higher we have gone there is every reason to expect that the latest arrivals will meet with great success in their new ground. Hadji Basheer tells us the rather annoying news that during the night after Vivian's departure from Emberaga elephants passed close by the site of our camp on their way to drink, and that some also paid El Effaara a visit the night after we left there, and one was caught in an Arab trap. This trap is a very simple contrivance, though it must take some time making, for it consists of a pit which is dug in one of the main approaches to the river specially favoured by elephants, and then very carefully covered in with sticks, straw, and the surrounding soil. The mouth is much bigger than the bottom of the pit, so when an elephant falls into it his legs become cramped up and he is powerless to move, and as he is within reach of their spears the Arabs can kill him by inches at their leisure. The Hamrans are making the most of our presence, and of their consequent protection from the Basé in this neutral territory, by driving their immense herds of cattle all over the country. More than two thousand drank at the river to-day, almost opposite to our camp, and Albert took it upon himself in our absence to frighten the drovers away with the discharge of a few cartridges, and by telling them that the next time they came near us they would be fired upon with more effect. I went out for a stroll along the river this afternoon with Essafi, chiefly to find something for the larder; but my thoughts were soon turned in a different direction by Essafi pointing me out a lion sitting close to the water's edge, quietly gazing on the mangled remains of a hippo which had been drawn yesterday into a shallow part by the Arabs. From a high bank under shelter of some trees, about fifty yards from the lion, I was able to take a steady quiet shot at him without being observed; and as he was half facing me with his side (the right) only partially exposed, I calculated that the most fatal spot would be the lower part of the neck on that side, hoping that from my elevation the bullet would take an oblique course into the chest and reach the heart. My anatomical calculations bore no practical fruit, for with a loud roar the lion sprang up, and in a moment disappeared up the bank as if he had not been touched. The old business now commenced, but though tracking a lion in the low valleys is a very easy matter, it is quite the reverse on some of the stony hills bordering them here, where the pad leaves no mark, and when the blood-track ceases to be found. So it happened in this instance, and after great perseverance Essafi was obliged to give it up. We were ascending a hill at the time, and no sooner had he said the word 'mafeesh' than our lost friend, giving a low growl, sprang out of a big bush just over the crest of the hill, and had quite disappeared when we reached the top. He had been resting in an old haunt, and a patch of blood showed that he was wounded. It was now time to return home, and Essafi gave me the usual comforting information of our hunters that the lion would be found 'bookra' (to-morrow). We have become almost too careless about night visitors in doing away with tents and camp-fires, considering the proximity of the lion's roar and the cry of the hyæna, which is almost equally loud; and consequently, both last night and the previous one, two lions took advantage of our kindness and paid us a visit whilst we slept, but they did not approach nearer than thirteen yards from Ranfurly's bed, so far as we could see by their tracks. Vivian has found nothing to-day, and of late our game-list has had no important additions made to it, so it is more to be regretted that my lion was not bagged. Whether we have driven them away, or whether there were originally very few lions on the Settite, we cannot say; but certain it is that we hear them roar much less frequently at night, and seldom see their tracks now. Ranfurly and Arkwright between them diminished their number by one near Emhagga, which some Arabs assisted them to find, by telling them that it was prowling about near a herd of their cattle.

Ranfurly still improves in one respect, but the heat is most trying to him, and he feels very disinclined to take any nourishment. He has unfortunately an especial aversion to rice in any form, and to milk either in the fresh state or prepared in any way. Still in our 'invalid' box we have plenty of arrowroot, 'Liebig's Extract,' and brandy if required, and Mohamed makes him excellent soup from fresh meat, which is always carefully strained; and last, though not least, the medicine-chest contains all that is required from it. His favourite drink is rice-water, which is freshly made every day, and kept very cool in bottles suspended under trees and wrapped up in wet cloths. The oppressive state of the atmosphere is his great enemy, for there is no movement of air; and though he lies all day under a big tree, and has waterproof sheets fastened to the branches over his head, it is very difficult to keep off the sun entirely, and the tents are unbearable. Vivian and myself find that we can now keep cooler whilst walking about under the scorching midday sun than if we remain quiet in the shade. Our heads are well guarded by helmets, and as a protection to the spine I always wear over it under my coat a long pad made up of numerous folds of white muslin.

April 7.—To-day has been an eventful one to me, and long will it be impressed on my memory. After spending an hour or two with Ranfurly, reading a portion of my diary to him, I went off with Essafi in search of yesterday's wounded lion; and, to make our success more certain, Essafi obtained the assistance of the best tracker amongst our Arabs, who was promised a dollar if we found our friend, and we adjourned at once to the place where we last saw him. The track from this point could only be followed for a few yards owing to the stony ground, and having decided that it was useless to attempt to follow it up, they began a regular hunt in wide circles around the hill. For two hours they laboured on up and down the adjacent hills, sometimes finding the track, but almost instantly losing it again, until their patience became worn out, and they had to give up the hunt in despair. Returning home we walked in line at intervals of thirty to forty yards, and thankful I was that, lion or no lion, the day's work was drawing to a close; for even my two followers, like myself, were quite done up with the oppressive heat, and perhaps even more by the reflected heat from the hard ground than by the direct sun's rays. We had not gone far in this way, one man being on each side of me, when suddenly I heard a loud roar on my left, and on looking in that direction I saw Essafi to my intense astonishment running like a hare towards me down some sloping ground, and a lion bounding over the low bushes in full chase after him and every moment gaining upon him. Essafi almost touched me as he passed on; and before this time he was so exactly in my line that I could not fire. Now was my chance however, and as the lion came to the ground after his next spring, and when only ten yards from me, I fired at him with the express; and it is hardly needful to say how great was my relief when I saw him make a feeble attempt to turn and then fall dead before me. It was a grand sight to see him advance with a continuous half-roar, and making a succession of long springs; and when I stood over his dead body I felt very thankful that he had been the victim and not one of us. The bullet I hit him with yesterday had managed to glance round under the skin of the neck, and was found lying quite superficially near the left shoulder. The last bullet entered the left side of the chest obliquely through the back of the shoulder, and split the heart into two pieces; and it is therefore a good instance of the value of express rifles with expanding bullets in lion-shooting, and in this we are all agreed. I was too much done up at the time to take any measurement of him, and I am now very sorry not to have done so; for since the head and skin have been brought home I have measured the latter when laid out, and find it is ten feet nine inches from nose to tip of tail, and it must therefore have been larger than my last one, whilst equally deficient in mane. Ibrahim, who says he thoroughly understands how to prepare skins, only takes off all the fat carefully; and then having washed them and given them a good rubbing in with the wood ashes, he hangs them up so that they may have the full benefit of the sun to dry them. No wonder we felt the heat of to-day, for the maximum thermometer registers 150° in the sun, and I feel this evening, for the first time, decided ill effects from it.

April 8, 9, 10, 11, 12.—'Mafeesh.'

April 13.—The morning following my lion adventure I awoke only to realise that at last the sun had mastered me, and, suffering from an intense headache, to know that I must pay the penalty of exposure to it. From that time to the present I have been completely prostrated by sunstroke, suffering almost night and day very great pain in the back of the head with great throbbing, and with general nausea; and, to add to my troubles, there has been much painful swelling of the glands of the neck. The temporary relief obtained by having water poured from a height over the back of my head and neck enabled me to attend to the wants of my sick friends, now two in number, for Hadji Basheer has been attacked with dysentery, and in so grave a form that it is a very doubtful matter if he will ever see Kassala again; and the rest of the day I have been compelled to lie perfectly quiet under a tree, with my head enveloped in wet cloths, and unable to read or even to write up my diary. From the commencement of my attack I felt sure that relief might be obtained by a loss of blood. But who was to bleed me? And as day after day passed without any diminution of the bursting sensation in my head, I began to be anxious about the future, until yesterday afternoon, when the happy thought 'Why not bleed yourself?' became too strongly impressed on my mind to be resisted, and I set to work to carry it into effect. In Vivian's absence, Albert became chief assistant; whilst Mohamed the cook and

Ibrahim stood near, to have a finger in the pie, if chance offered. Now bleeding yourself in the arm is a very much slower performance than when the victim is some one else, and when I had succeeded in making the necessary puncture in my left arm, it was cruelly disappointing to find that the result was *nil*. Still there was the right one to be experimented upon, so after bandaging up the left the performance was reversed, and this time my efforts at self-relief met with the success, I think it may be said, they deserved. After losing eight ounces of blood I felt very faint, and asked Albert for some water; but no response came from him, and after repeating my request without effect I looked up and saw him as white as a sheet, and the next moment he fainted away. This had quite as good an effect upon me as water, and arm No. 2 having been tied up after a fashion, the *séance* was closed and I retired feeling decidedly relieved, and to-day the improvement continues. Ranfurly's attack is quite arrested, but it has left him so very weak that I fear he will be unable to resume shooting again, unless it be near the camp.

One day last week Vivian paid a visit to the island below Emhagga to look for a lion, and after hunting amongst the bushes for some time the sharp eye of Mohamed discovered one lying asleep under the branches of a very overhanging mimosa. More than a minute elapsed before Vivian could make it out, and it was only by lying down that he could get a shot at it, when he fired at its side without knowing the direction of the head. On being hit the lion sprang up and disappeared, and though they hunted for it for some hours they could not find it again. The search, however, gave them the valuable information that the lion had not left that part of the island, as no fresh tracks could be seen in the sand surrounding it, and the next day they resumed the hunt. Again the surrounding sand was free from the track of a lion, so a diligent search was commenced, and every bush in turn examined, but owing to their great thickness it was quite impossible to do this thoroughly, and at last, failing to find the lion, they were obliged to adopt the expedient of setting fire to the grass. The result was so far satisfactory that it soon brought the lion into view, dead, but the fire had so singed the skin that it was quite spoilt. This is particularly vexing, as it is the only one either of us has shot with any pretence to a mane. From the remnants brought home, it must have been a very fine fellow, both in size and mane.

Comparing the skull with that of my last lion, there is a very marked difference in the shape of them, and whilst Vivian's has a greater length, mine has a greater breadth. Coupling this fact with the absence of mane in one, and its presence in the other, are they, it may be asked, distinct species? During my recent attack the temperature charts have not been neglected. The heat has continued very oppressive, and the thermometer registers to-day 102° in the shade and 155° in the sun, and there has not been a breath of air. Albert, however, persists in ignoring the sun, and, though strongly and repeatedly warned of his folly, will wear nothing on his shaven head beyond a white skull-cap.

April 14.—To-day we have without doubt commenced the homeward journey, which we intend to continue by easy stages, and this evening finds us encamped on a very small island, now dry on one side, a few miles below Emhagga, named 'Amaretakari.' Before our departure Albert complained of a very severe headache, and when he arrived with the camels we found him looking more dead than alive, with all the symptoms of sunstroke. Our camp has therefore become a very sick one, but the other invalids are improving; and though the old soldier required to use his utmost strength to reach here on horseback he is very plucky, and as if he were determined to pull through his attack. The infusion of ipecacuanha-root has had a very beneficial effect upon him. The elephant-hunters who visited us at the Royan when on their way to Abyssinia have had great success, killing so many as forty elephants in this short space of time. Their proper chief is Essafi, and he therefore regrets that he has lost so good a chance of gaining honour and glory, though the dollars would not have been so plentiful as in his present enterprise. He says that the Abyssinians are afraid of the elephants, and won't hunt them alone. If they find, however, a herd with some young ones they will give them chase, and catching up with the small fry think themselves very clever if they hamstring one. According to their calculations, a man who kills an elephant, without any limit being made as to size, is equal to twenty men, whilst he who kills a lion is only equal to five men; and there is a rule among the married women never to wear their bracelets, ear or nose rings, until their husbands have killed an elephant. Here, as along the rest of the river, it is hopeless to look for antelope, for the country has been so disturbed by huge droves of cattle; and Vivian will soon find it a difficult matter to get even an ariel or gazelle for the larder. I tried one shot to-day, and do not intend to repeat the performance for the present, as it caused such painfu vibration in my head. News has been brought this evening that an Arab fired at a lion the other day near the Hamran village, and hit it in the shoulder, and that the animal instantly turned upon him and with one blow with his paw on the back of the neck struck him down dead. Perhaps this will be a useful warning to the rising Hamran generation not to attempt lion shooting with single-barrel rifles, or they will find to their cost that the new weapon they are gradually becoming familiar with is more liable to lead them into danger than the one by which their ancestors made themselves so celebrated as hunters. Sheik Aghill is not yet turned out of office, and that we may be kept aware of the fact he has sent us a present of some onions.

April 15.—Albert has to pay the penalty of his folly in ignoring the sun, and is now very ill, suffering intensely in his head, and in a state to cause some anxiety for the future. Even our dark-skinned friends begin to find the heat tell upon them, and at their special request I went through the performance to-day of bleeding Mohamed the cook from the arm, and of cupping Essafi.

These Arabs bear innumerable marks over their bodies where incisions have been made to draw blood, as it is a very favourite practice amongst them. Both Ranfurly and myself find it a difficult matter to shake off our weakness, and feel in the sun a common enemy. The moon is also a source of great annoyance to us, for, being in the second quarter, the light is so strong that sleep is rendered almost an impossibility without first paying a visit to the medicine-chest, for that most invaluable of medicines to us, 'chloral.' I have a great advantage over Ranfurly in being able to eat my food, whilst he cares for nothing beyond soup and arrowroot. He is looking forward to our arrival at Kassala to get at our stores of Lehman's captains' biscuits, for which he has a great fancy, and they certainly are an improvement upon the more common kind left in our present supplies, though these are quite good enough for all practical purposes. Our supply of rice holds out well, and the goats show but a slight falling off.

This evening some heavy thunder-clouds passed over our heads from the east, and there was a slight shower of rain (the first we have had here), followed by a short but sharp hurricane, which required the united efforts of some of our party to save our tent from being carried away bodily. Now that it has passed over, we derive some advantage from our unwelcome guest, for it has made the air feel less oppressive.

April 17.—Owing to the illness of Albert, we were obliged to postpone our departure for Emberaga until to-day, and he has stood the journey better than we might have expected. I hope now that he will soon rally, but he seems to have so completely lost all power of rousing himself that I fear he will not shake off the effects of this attack for a long time after our separation at Cairo. Essafi, after a great chase *en route*, caught a young baboon, and all his time has been taken up this afternoon watching him, koorbatch in hand, to prevent him biting through the rope by which he was half strangulated. We remedied this defect by having the rope fastened round his loins, and he was then tied to a tree and left to his own resources. His chief amusement now appeared to be to try how many times he could turn round a branch until he became suspended in mid-air, though he frequently almost succeeded in committing suicide involuntarily before he could be untwisted. At last he laid down exhausted and fell asleep—a sound sleep, for he never awoke, and rumour has it that too much koorbatch was administered after he was caught. London society has thus lost a valuable addition, for already a most noble career had been marked out for our young friend, if not relative.

The temperature to-day has been the highest yet recorded by us—viz., 156° Fah. in sun, and 110° in shade.

CHAPTER XVII.

April 18.—We arrived at the Hamran village Gwayha before midday, and were received by Sheik Aghill, who placed at our disposal a mansion consisting of strips of matting stretched over some poles, and furnished with two angareps, and soon afterwards a dish of meat, cut into small pieces and stewed, was presented to us. It had quite a pleasant taste, but this was rather marred by the idea that it was probably a bit of an old cow that had died from disease or old age.

We have taken for Ranfurly a very snug straw house, in shape like a beehive, and quite new; but it is so valuable in the eyes of its fortunate owner, that nothing will induce him to leave it. Two extra doors added to it by knocking parts of the circular wall down have made it comparatively cool and habitable during the day. Albert we have deposited in another place, and Hadji Basheer has rolled himself up comfortably under a tree by our baggage. Albert's illness renders him quite incapable of giving us any assistance, not even as an interpreter, for we can hardly get him to open his mouth, and he is quite indifferent to what is passing around him. Our position is therefore becoming complicated, having to communicate our wants through Ibrahim by the means of the little French he knows, and through Mohamed the cook, with his few words of English or ours of Arabic. Though Ranfurly has been quite free for a week from all evidence of dysentery, it is but too apparent that he is almost hourly losing strength—now probably from being unable to eat any of the food our reduced supplies can afford him, excepting Liebig's Extract, nor will he hardly taste some chicken we have obtained here for him. In this respect we have no difficulty with Albert.

Sheik Aghill has tried his little game of robbery again, but has been on this occasion completely beaten. In fact it is quite evident that, though nominally Sheik, he has lost all power; for when we refused to pay his demand of four dollars per camel to Kassala, an Arab from a neighbouring village offered, to supply us at one and a half dollars per camel, and finally we engaged our own camel-men with some others at this rate, without Aghill having anything to do with the arrangement. So a great change must have come over the spirit of his dream since our previous visit to him.

April 19.—Last night we had our first experience of a thunderstorm breaking over our heads, and a very disagreeable one it was. The lightning had been, as usual, forked and very vivid, and sometimes travelled in zigzags to a great distance from one point to another, but from past experience we attached no importance to it. The mansion of matting was found much too stuffy to remain in, and we therefore had the tent pitched just outside the village, and Ranfurly having joined us before sunset, he and I took possession of the tent for the night to avoid the moonlight, whilst Vivian preferred remaining outside. He was soon disturbed from a peaceful slumber by some large drops of rain falling on his face, when he sought protection under the common roof from the coming storm. It rapidly burst upon us with all its force, and just as we began to feel uncomfortable about the safety of our tent, the question was settled for us by a sudden squall which started the few pegs, and down it came upon our heads. Assistance was soon at hand, and no one was the worse for the disaster, and it was repitched before the rain did much harm. Most fortunately also no damage was done to our weapons, though they were suspended from hooks round the pole, and consequently came down with a crash. Ranfurly is doing his best to keep up his pluck, notwithstanding his failing strength, and indeed he is now so weak that he requires the support of an arm to enable him to move about. Albert, on the other hand, is continually groaning, and by his despondency he makes his prospect of recovery a poor one. Hadji Basheer is now convalescent, and his rapid recovery has been a source of astonish-

CALIFORNIA

ment to us all. Vivian and myself have been well occupied in sorting the horns and skins, which have gradually increased here into a most imposing pile, and deciding which we will leave behind; afterwards in cleaning and packing up all weapons no longer required, and in distributing amongst the people the remaining collection of small presents, the Sheik receiving the lion's share. My labours were added to not only by our own sick, but by constant arrivals from the village, and their confidence in my powers was evidently unbounded, for they brought a camel to me with a huge tumour over the left hind-knee, for which an ounce of lead in the right place was the only treatment I could suggest, though it would entail the death of the sufferer. Then came the final partings, first with the Sheik, who at the last moment tried to sell us a donkey, and then with some of the men we leave behind, including the faithful Essafi. Saying good-bye to such a constant companion of one's daily rambles brought the fact more definitely home to our minds than anything else that we were really turning our backs, and probably for ever, on the country inhabited by the splendid race of Arabs of which he is such a good representative; and in the expression of his face on the last shaking of hands with us all, there could be read something more than sorrow for the departure of the well-known dollar-bags. The other hunter, Mohamed Fagerole, remains with us at present, as his home is near Kassala. As we left Gwayha several of the inhabitants turned out, and for reasons best known to themselves showed a very laudable anxiety to have the last shake of hands. It was then just after sunset, and as there was fortunately a moon we were able to continue our journey for five hours, chiefly through a mimosa wood, and then halt at an uninhabited village of straw huts. All the invalids were mounted on horseback, and Ranfurly has borne the journey fairly well, and the prospect of reaching Kassala forms a splendid stimulus to help him on his way. Albert has arrived here, and that is something to say, for three times he would dismount and lie down for ten minutes or more. I remained behind with him, and on the last occasion the Arab guide and myself had the greatest difficulty to get him on his legs and remount him. Somehow or other on he must come if possible to Kassala, for to have left him at Gwayha would have been to seal his doom. At Kassala he has friends, and will have every care taken of him if we can only get him there, but his utter want of pluck makes this far from certain.

No anxiety about fresh meat for to-morrow, for we have just killed a kid we brought from Gwayha, besides some chickens. As nothing will keep in the present heat more than twenty-four hours, we may find some difficulty in this respect as we proceed.

April 20.—On the march again yesterday soon after

7 A.M., and halted at 10 A.M. under some shady mimosas, where we remained till 4 P.M. to avoid the great midday heat. Ranfurly has exchanged his horse for a camel, as he has a very comfortable saddle for the latter; and from long practice he experiences no fatigue from the swinging motion. The baggage camels were given an hour's start in the afternoon, and the chief Arab was told to halt earlier than the previous night. It was with great difficulty that Albert was induced to leave his resting-place and remount; and anticipating much trouble again with him, Vivian agreed to remain behind with me to make sure that his Arab guide did not leave him to the hyænas. Ranfurly found it better to keep steadily on, and was very soon within sight of the advance party, and never pulled up until 3.15 A.M. when they voluntarily came to a halt.

Were we to live for a hundred years, the weary and anxious hours passed by Vivian and myself during that night's journey would remain vividly impressed on our memory. After a few hours' progress, Albert, as we expected, dismounted and laid down. When we came up to him we compelled him to remount and go on, and then tried our best to cheer him; but directly we dropped back a little the performance was immediately repeated. We then kept close behind to prevent a further repetition, but he signally defeated us; for his horse starting at something by the way, poor Albert was shot off him; and having fallen to the ground without making the slightest effort to save himself, lay stretched out like a dead man. In fact, for the first moment we thought he was dead, for he made no attempt to move or speak; but on finding that he had a good pulse and that no bones were broken, we made him drink some whisky-and-water and lifted him into his saddle; then as before, with one man leading his horse, and another by his side to hold him up and to supply him with water, which he kept on drinking, we effected another start. Now our anxiety began to be great, and our eyes could scarcely be taken off the grey steed in front of us, so much did we dread another halt. The fall, however, appeared to rouse him, and he made his horse walk at so good a pace that he soon distanced our camels, and reached a huge plain some time before us. Possibly it was the prospect of not being able to cross this apparently endless expanse as seen by the light of a full moon that made him give in again, for directly we came to it we could see the horse standing still, and a few moments more brought us to Albert lying on the ground and looking almost dead. He now implored us to leave him there for the night; but as to comply with his wishes was to leave him to die, we were compelled to remount him and force him to move on. But where were the rest of our party? Before us lay the unmistakable vast plain we remembered to have once before crossed, and if they had not already halted we felt sure that they would not do so until they reached the other side of it; and then the anxious question came, how would Ranfurly bear the fatigue? Albert again soon distanced us when once *en route*, and though we frequently strained our eyes in looking for the horse, we never saw it again until on arriving at a wood some hours afterwards, we found it tied to a tree, and close to the rest of our party. Ranfurly, though much exhausted, was very thankful to have accomplished so much of the journey; and, after a little food, both he and Albert quickly fell into a sound sleep. Vivian and myself were not long in following their example, and only awoke when the sun, by shining directly on our heads, aroused us to the fact that he was up for the day, and that the sooner we sought shelter from him the better. Much as we have had cause to grumble at mimosa-thorns, we now found them most useful in supporting blankets that we stretched between the trees as a means of obtaining the shade which the trees themselves were too small to yield. Ibrahim says that the camel-men would not halt till they arrived here, and it certainly was better to do this than stop in the middle of the plain. With two such serious cases of illness, and the great difficulties we have experienced through the incapacity of Albert, we could not well afford to add to our troubles; but an unlucky cloud is hanging over our heads, for Mohamed the cook, having fallen off his camel, has so injured his foot that he can scarcely walk, and one horse has a large swelling on each side and is unfit for further use. Ibrahim is now the only man we have to do everything for us. He certainly does his best to get through his multifarious duties, but we have almost come to a dead-lock.

April 22.—At 5 P.M. yesterday our invalids were much refreshed by their long rest, and were quite ready for a start, and the sight of the Kassala mountains, though very distant, gave them a fresh stimulus. To my surprise Albert only halted once to lie down before we terminated the night's march at 2 A.M. On arriving at the village near Kassala, where we spent the first night after our departure from that town, my wish was to remain there until the afternoon, but both Ranfurly and Albert begged to be allowed to push on at sunrise. Ranfurly, after three hours' rest, was the first to be up and ready to proceed, and at 6 A.M. we were again mounted and off. When within one hour of Kassala, Albert utterly collapsed, and, stretched at full-length on the ground, declared that he must die to-day, and then crying like a child implored me to let him stay there. The sun, however, was rapidly rising, and it being therefore of importance that not a moment should be wasted, it became necessary to remount him and to use a little force to overcome his feeble powers of resistance, to which he added the free use of his koorbatch; and at

10 A.M. I was indeed thankful to be able to seat him in a chair under some trees in Kassala in front of the shop of a Greek friend. Here he was made as comfortable as possible, cool refreshing drinks were given him, and douches of vinegar and water applied to the head. Shortly Ranfurly and Vivian arrived at the shop, the former looking almost as exhausted as Albert, and every attention was paid to him. He was taken into a dark quiet room, where he remained till sunset, excellent soup was brought to him, and his head and hands were bathed with vinegar and water, whilst a little black boy continuously fanned him. During this time our old house was rendered habitable, and after the rest and kind treatment of our Greek friends, Ranfurly felt so refreshed that he walked 'home' with us, only supported by an arm.

Munsinger Pasha is away, much to our disappointment, but his representative, the Vakeel, appears anxious to attend to all our wants. Mr. Cohen is also very ready to help us through any difficulties, and as he speaks English he will probably not lack the opportunity.

April 23.—Ranfurly shows decided signs of increasing exhaustion, and he is losing flesh rapidly. The journey from the Hamran village was a hard trial of strength for him, but it could not be otherwise than a forced march, owing to the total absence of water, and now we feel we have completed by far the worst part of the desert journey. Our reserve stores were found in good order and have been duly appreciated, and Ranfurly has enjoyed this morning a basin of bread and milk. (Lehman's biscuits with cow's milk.) Our difficult position was improved last evening by the arrival of Arkwright's and Ranfurly's dragoman 'Lorenzo,' with their heavy baggage, for he will remain with us and take Albert's place. The rest of our party arrived this evening, and they have settled down in another house near us. About two hundred and sixty camels laden with ammunition left Kassala to-day for Darfour, in charge of numerous soldiers, and it is calculated that they will not reach their destination under two months. The Egyptian Government is making such demands upon the camels here for the present expedition, under Colonel Gordon, that it is only with very great difficulty they can be obtained for private individuals. This morning there was but little hope of our getting any, but fortunately some arrived to-day from Souakim with goods for the Greeks, and the Vakeel has promised to let us have the best of them, so that we may start to-morrow. It is very important that we should not lose a day, as we have now ample time to go by easy stages to Souakim, for the steamer of May 9 or 10; and Ranfurly thinks he will get on better in the fresh air of the desert than in this confined atmosphere. We have talked over the question of his remaining here a little while longer for the following steamer of May 30, but it is the universal opinion both of ourselves and the European inhabitants that it would be better for him not to risk exposure to the rapidly approaching rains, when the climate becomes very unhealthy. Arkwright was caught by them last May a few days before reaching Souakim, and was in a great plight for even that short time.

M. Voight, the chief of the telegraph-office, has announced to us the victory of Oxford over Cambridge, on the Thames, and he has lent us three 'Illustrated London News' of March; so, thanks to that invaluable paper to the traveller, we shall be able to learn most of the home news of that month.

Albert asked for a looking-glass to-day, and after carefully inspecting his dreadfully altered face and bloodshot eyes, all he said was, 'My poor teeth, my poor teeth quite spoilt!' So whilst his remark brought to light a vanity, it also gave some proof of his being more hopeful of recovery. His condition is rather curious, and though he is undoubtedly very weak, he looks as if he might rouse himself a little if he would only be less despondent, and the more notice there is taken of him the worse he is. I actually succeeded in making him laugh by telling him that the best treatment for him would be a good dose of koorbatch on the back.

April 24.—The night has come, and still we are in

Kassala; but all is bustle and confusion in our courtyard, for the new men could not be collected until the evening, and they are now busily arranging and cording up our goods by candle-light, to enable them to load their camels rapidly in the morning. The delay to-day was owing to some hitch in the payment of their wages for the last journey. We would have been only too glad to keep our own men, but the Hamran Arabs cannot safely travel through the Hadendowa country, and we are compelled therefore to return to the latter troublesome tribe. The new camels are the most miserable creatures we have yet seen, and look as if half of them would die in the desert. Coke, Cumming, and Arkwright give a most satisfactory report of their visit to the junction of a stream with the Settite, named Hor Méhétepe, about four hours' journey beyond their last encampment near us, and five elephants, three rhinoceros, two giraffes, and one lion were numbered amongst the killed. Arkwright one night knocked over two elephants with a right-and-left, and they laid on the ground near him for an hour trumpeting; but the place was so dark that he could not venture to approach them until morning, when he found one dead and the other decamped. He killed also on that night a giraffe. Another day he fired three shots at an elephant, which then turned upon him and made him escape for his life; afterwards, when riding home without any ammunition, he found himself amongst a herd of elephants, and one of them gave him chase for some time, until his horse managed to distance his pursuer. Both Coke and Cumming also shot elephants, and the former on one occasion rode close to a herd of from one hundred and fifty to two hundred, and succeeded in bagging one of them. Several lions were seen, but Coke only was fortunate enough to kill one. They all agree in saying that far more game is to be found near the Hor Méhétepe than lower down the Settite. They found the Hor dry for three miles above its junction with the Settite, but then they came to a pool which proved to be a very favourite haunt of the elephant and rhinoceros. Cumming almost walked on to two sleeping rhinoceros, and dropped one after another with a right-and-left, and one day he killed three elephants.

We have again paid a visit to Mr. Cohen's live stock, and saw several new additions. Amongst these are two young lions, which played about the yard like kittens, and were more friendly, for they did not attempt to scratch or otherwise show their disapproval of being handled by strangers.

Mr. Cohen is now only waiting until he can collect fifty or sixty camels to take a large portion of his zoological collection to Souakim, *en route* for Europe, and after landing at Hamburg he will visit many of the capitals, and he thinks that in two or three days at latest he will be able to effect a start from here.

Night at Kassala is certainly not favourable to the sleep of the sick man, owing to the never-ceasing noise from sunset to sunrise. No wonder that the dogs keep up a continual barking, for the cry of the hyænas as they prowl round the town is quite enough to keep them on the alert; but it is none the less disagreeable, and especially when combined with the discordant screeching of women and the braying of donkeys.

CHAPTER XVIII.

April 25.—5.30 A.M. actually found us outside the Kassala gates and commencing our last desert journey, accompanied by two soldiers whom we have taken to keep our Hadendowa Arabs in order, remembering the trouble we had with them on a previous occasion. Hadji Basheer, Mohamed Fagerole, and Albert are numbered amongst the absent ones. Albert's prostrate condition compelled us to leave him behind in the house we occupied, but we have given him all the stores we could afford, and have made every other possible arrangement for his comfort, besides engaging a man to look after him. Now that he is left a good deal to his own resources, it is probable that he will see the necessity of rousing himself, and we hope that he will be able to accompany Mr. Cohen to Cairo.[1] Lorenzo has under his charge seven baggage-camels, and these with ours make a total of twenty-four. We have now no horses, for

---

[1] Albert arrived in Cairo about the middle of June with Mr. Cohen, but he was in a very weak state, and he had the misfortune of being robbed by Arabs in the desert of all his things.

Ibrahim was given the best, Jali's hunter, which he has temporarily exchanged for a donkey with an officer of his old corps. After our departure from Souakim he is to have it again, and he says he will make a fortune with it selling water there. Hadji Basheer was presented with the next best horse, and the other two collapsed before arriving at Kassala. The goats have trotted along by the side of the camels very contentedly to-day, and look as if they meant to complete the journey with us. So far this has been very successful, for, travelling faster than our baggage-camels, we arrived at a good shady halting-place at 10.15 A.M., had a comfortable luncheon cooked by Ibrahim, and did not leave again till 5 P.M., when we had allowed them an hour's start, and finally joined them at 9 P.M. as they halted for the night at a regular camping-ground within a few miles of water. The other division of our party will leave Kassala to-morrow or next day, if they can get camels by that time, and join us *en route*. Ranfurly has not felt the day's journey at all fatiguing. Several men were at work yesterday making a species of ambulance for him with palm-leaves, but he so much preferred having his own saddle that it was not completed.

April 26.—Having encamped last night near a minute village consisting of six or seven mat huts, we had the full benefit of the barking of their dogs, and one of them, with a keen eye to business, paid us a visit and eat up a basin of bread and milk which had been placed by Ranfurly's bedside. Awaking at 4 A.M., I roused up our staff, and then looked round the camp for the Arabs, but neither man nor camel could be seen, so it was supposed that they had remained at the water last night and that they would return at sunrise, and we all laid down again. Soon afterwards I saw one Arab quietly arrive, and I told the soldier. He at once jumped up and seized hold of the man, but could obtain no information from him with regard to his companions. The soldier then, as a useful precaution, tied him up hand and foot to a tree, and a native of the village was sent to the water to look for the others. He returned with the bad news that they were not there, and then it became only too apparent that they had gone off with their camels and had left us stranded in the desert. Our prisoner then became more communicative, and said that his comrades had gone on to Souakim or to some village two or three days from here, because their camels were so tired after their journey from Souakim to Kassala that they felt sure they could not return to Souakim laden. They have carried off two water-barrels and some skins, but have left most of their saddles and ropes with us, and when we caught the Arab it is supposed he was about to take away some of the ropes when he imagined we were asleep. Ibrahim's donkey has now become a useful friend to us, for we have been able to despatch a soldier upon it to Kassala with all speed, the distance being about twenty-five miles, as the bearer of a letter to the Vakeel explaining our position, and begging him to send us more camels without a moment's delay. Now as I write we are sitting patiently under a tree to await his return, whenever that may be, but probably another morning will dawn upon us before our minds can be put at rest.

April 27.—A careful watch was kept last night over our prisoner and property, as it was feared that our deserters might not be far off, and that they might take advantage of the darkness to pay us a visit and carry off their property; but no one came, and the morning did dawn upon us without our receiving news from Kassala. When we returned after an early breakfast to our shady tree our position was not altogether bright, and we felt quite helpless to take any further steps to improve it. We had at least to thank the Arabs for not postponing their departure one more day, for had they done so, and thus left us several miles from water, our position would have been critical. Now provided that the soldier did not follow suit, we knew that we should only suffer from loss of time, though this was serious enough so far as Ranfurly was concerned. He, however, took the matter very quietly, and joined Vivian and myself in trying to kill time by watching the domestic occupations of the women and children in the huts close to us. The latter had no impediments to freedom of movement in the way of clothes, but their mothers were so enveloped in a huge dirty brown sheet that half their time was taken up in keeping it wrapped round them. One family was on the move to-day, and the mansion was packed up before our eyes by the simple process of pulling down three strips of matting, rolling them up, and then collecting the wooden supports over which they were stretched. At 11 A.M. our imprisonment terminated, for there arrived three mounted soldiers, with our own soldier on the donkey, and seventeen camels. It was indeed a joyful sight, though the number was far too limited for our wants; and now with no future *contretemps* we shall still be able to reach Souakim by the 9th, without any forced marches. M. Voight writes that great regret was felt for our misfortune, and that the Vakeel at once put into prison all the relations of our deserters who could be found, and had handed over their wages to our new men. At 6 P.M. we renewed our journey, but with great difficulty, for our new camels are so weak that some of them could not rise from the ground when laden, and were obliged to have their burdens lessened and rearranged. The deficiency of seven camels compelled us to leave a great portion of our baggage in the desert in charge of one of the soldiers, with the understanding that two of the others should return to Kassala for more camels, and that on their return they were to pick it up and join us on or before our arrival at Souakim; and we stimulated them to extra exertion by the promise of good backsheesh. Owing to the slipping first of one camel and then of another our progress was so ridiculously slow that in two hours we could barely have accomplished so many miles; then a camel playfully shook off the whole of his load, which fell with an ominous crash to the ground, two or three more immediately laid down, and the confusion, at last, became so complete in the total darkness that we were compelled to call a halt for the night. At this rate our prospect of reaching the coast has again become poor indeed. The prisoner was taken back to Kassala by the soldiers; and as he had to keep up with them on foot, whilst being dragged along by a rope fastened round his neck, he is not likely to have on the whole a pleasant journey. Our present feeling is that we wish his friends could be similarly treated; for, so far as they were concerned, we might have died where they left us. The country is so open here that we have little chance of killing game, and we therefore bought a respectable-sized sheep at the village to-day as a temporary measure. Ranfurly has added to our live stock two young black ostriches, as well as two paroquets which he exchanged for some cartridges with Mr. Cohen. The ostriches when sitting look much more like porcupines, and they are only about the size of hens. The aviary is a large deal box, closed in on one side only by wire network, and it is carried on top of a camel-load, much to the apparent discomfort of its inmates. Lorenzo is their guardian, and he thinks he will be able to bring them with us to Cairo.

April 28.—Leaving the baggage party to follow us so that we might make the most of the early morning, we were able to start at 5.30 A.M., halt from 10.30 A.M. to 4 P.M. under the shade of some mimosas assisted by blankets, have luncheon and a nap in the interval, and then go on again until 7.30 P.M. Ibrahim, who accompanied us on his donkey, gave us good proof of his powers of usefulness. He first caught some goats and milked them for our especial benefit; and even Ranfurly was able to enjoy the refreshing draught, having quite got over his objection to it, though rice unfortunately is as repugnant to him as ever. Further on, he snatched up a sheep from a flock wandering about unguarded; and having carried it in his arms to his donkey he hoisted it upon the saddle-bags, and then mounting himself behind he trotted up to us looking very proud of his performance. In a country where food is so scarce, it is just as well not to be too particular how it is obtained, so we congratulated him accordingly.

After a separation of several miles from the flock, Ibrahim thought that his prize might carry itself, so after tying a rope round one leg he let it down, but falling with a jerk the rope broke, and away went the sheep with all our happy calculations of stolen cutlets. Ibrahim was not to be so easily defeated, so gave it chase, and after the lapse of half an hour we found him resting under a tree holding his recent companion by the leg. Another escape, a little later, though cleverly planned, was even less successful, for having made a bolt to another flock the shepherd at once caught it and gave it up, as he supposed, to its rightful owners. At midday the baggage-camels passed us, and finding that Mohamed had also added a sheep to our live stock by some means or other we sent ours on with him as it appeared resigned at last to its fate of marching on till otherwise wanted. When about two hours from our night halting-ground we saw one of our Arabs resting under a tree with both sheep and goats. He implored us to give him some water, as he said he was dying from thirst; and as he looked in great distress from this cause we gave him a good draught, and he then promised to follow us immediately to the next camp.

The goats preferred joining our party, and so thirsty were the poor brutes that they would scarcely allow the Arab to drink from his bowl; and after he had had his fill we were still able to spare our faithful friends a little from our nearly empty skins.

Throughout our journey we shall be obliged to be very sparing of the water, owing to the loss of half of our barrels and skins through the desertion of the Arabs when they went off for the presumed purpose of filling them. If the Arabs ever return to the place where they left us, they will have the pleasure of seeing a pile of ashes to indicate what we did with their property to ensure their not having it again. Unfortunately they can replace their ropes and simply made saddles far more easily than we can our water-barrels.

Lorenzo tells us this evening the bad news that the camels are so weak they constantly come down with their loads, and that he does not believe they can reach Souakim. He therefore suggests that we seize any camels we meet, and compel the owners to make an exchange.

A cattle-drover reports that our other division was here yesterday, so it must have passed our camp in the darkness of the previous night.

April 29.—5.30 A.M. sees us again *en route*, but no thanks to any of our men, Lorenzo and Ibrahim included, for they sleep like pigs. In this respect more almost than in any other we miss Emanuel in the desert journey, for he was always up before sunrise; now I have to go round every morning and shake the men till they wake up, in which performance our solitary soldier gives a willing hand, and sometimes foot, if I can only find him out first; but they coil themselves up so much amongst the baggage that it is difficult very often to distinguish sacks from human beings. Arrived at a well at 7.30 A.M., where we were able to enjoy the luxury of washing hands and faces. Soon afterwards we met some Arabs with unladen camels returning from Souakim, and they agreed to let us have seven of them at the six-dollar rate we paid at Kassala.

Vivian then remained behind with them to wait for the arrival of our baggage party to complete the arrangements, and Ranfurly and myself pushed on. Thanks to a fresh breeze every morning from the south-east, the heat before 11 A.M. is far from being oppressive, and it is therefore very favourable for Ranfurly, who begins to show signs of some improvement in strength, and quite enjoys his morning rides. Towards evening the wind generally goes round to the north-west, and becomes so light that the heat is felt proportionately greater. At 11 A.M. we halted at the dry bed of a river, and found excellent shade under a clump of dome-palms. Here a general halt took place later, as there were good wells, and green trees for the camels to feed upon, and we did not move on again till 6 P.M. The time was not altogether lost upon us, for we were able to indulge in a bath, to the apparent amusement of some natives who looked on from a respectful distance; then drink milk to our hearts' content, and buy a sheep. The Arab with our two sheep did not come into camp last night, so that we must hope that he, at least, found his way to some cattle-drovers, whatever became of our doubtful property. At 10 P.M. we encamped for the night, and therefore so far we are dividing the day's work into easy stages. This unfortunately cannot depend upon our will, but on the nature of the ground, for where there is water or food for the camels there we must break the journey.

April 30.—The Hadendowa Arabs are at their old games again. Though they were called at 4 A.M. no camels were ready before 9 A.M., and the oft-repeated story that their camels had strayed and could not be found was all that we could obtain from them as a reason for the delay. There was certainly some truth in it this morning, for one camel could not be found, and the unfortunate owner on his return to camp after a long unsuccessful search received a good thrashing from the soldier with a koorbatch, possibly as a warning to the others to be more careful in future. The man appeared to accept without a murmur the justice of his sentence, for he laid himself down on his face very quietly and bore the severe punishment without flinching. We have gained a great acquisition in the Arab who joined us yesterday as chief in charge of the additional seven camels, for he is very industrious, and though he won't assist the others much he gets his camels ready in good time. To encourage him, we have promised him three extra dollars if he will bring us into Souakim on the 7th. His great anxiety is to arrive there in the evening, so that he may be off again before daybreak, for if he is seen by any officials he expects to be forced into the Government service to carry ammunition to Kassala. The rest of our men sent from Kassala are under orders to report themselves on their arrival at Souakim for this duty, and we therefore intend to keep a sharp look-out after them when near Souakim, fearing that they also may leave us stranded in the desert.

So far we have not come upon our original camel track, and believe we are more to the east and more amongst the mountain ranges. Desolation on all sides is even more complete than before, excepting in the occasional small valleys where dry river-beds are seen, and on each side dome-palms and other signs of vegetation. In some of these hollows, where water can be obtained by sinking wells, Arabs are generally found surrounded by their flocks and herds. It is fortunate for us that such is the case, for ariel and gazelle are very rarely seen, and our fresh meat supply depends upon what sheep we can buy, or otherwise obtain. Our walking dairy is daily diminishing its supply, but we have a good substitute in our reserve store of Anglo-Swiss milk, which remains quite unaffected by the heat; and a tin of Australian meat is even found a pleasant change to a chop from the desert. Ranfurly still gains ground, and is able to eat some solid food now.

May 1.—A strong wind to-day from the north-east, and therefore in our faces, has made camel-riding very fatiguing, and especially as in many parts of the desert it blew up clouds of sand. We divided the journey as usual, and Vivian having shot a dik-dik, we had it roasted whole *à l'Arabe* for luncheon. Since our arrival in camp at sunset Ranfurly has complained of great pain in the right side and shortness of breath. It is a most unfortunate night for him, as there is quite a hurricane blowing, but he is tolerably well protected from it by having his angarep placed against a big mimosa, and we have managed to dine in a way, whilst lying on a rug, by the light of the kitchen fire.

May 2, 6 A.M.—The gale continued all night, and rendered sleep almost impossible. No tent could have withstood it, and in the more exposed position of Vivian and myself we had to keep a very firm hold of our bedclothes to prevent their being whisked off to Kassala. Ranfurly has more pain in the side, and there is distinct evidence of his being attacked with pleurisy. This is indeed a serious complication, weakened as he is already by disease. The young ostriches died in the night, but as the men had left the open side of the cage exposed to the wind, it is only surprising that the paroquets retained any life in them.

9 A.M.—The day's journey has again been well divided, and a halt was made for the night soon after sunset at our first telegraph station. Our midday rest, from 11.15 A.M. to 3.45 P.M., was under a very fine clump of dome-palms. Vivian and myself were making some bread and milk there for Ranfurly, and stooping down at the time, when a dome-nut, blown off by the wind from the top of a high tree, whizzed past my ear and struck Vivian directly on the spine. So severe was the shock that it made him almost faint away, and he had to lie down for a time to recover himself, and throughout the afternoon he has felt much pain in the injured part. The gale has continued with almost increasing force all day, and the Arabs had such great difficulty in making the baggage-camels face it, that their progress was consequently very slow. The afternoon's ride has been a most trying one for Ranfurly from the same cause, and this evening, with an increase of pain in the right side, the breathing has become very short. The medicine-chest is fortunately at hand, and contains some useful appliances besides drugs, from which he is able to ob-

tain some relief. Whilst the camels were feeding during the midday halt, we now learn that one Arab took advantage of the opportunity to decamp with two of them. This, however, is not of much consequence, as our camels are very lightly laden, and we hear that we shall arrive to-morrow at a telegraph station where we can replace them by others. According to the statement of our Arab chief we are now more than half-way to Souakim, and ought to reach it easily in five days.

May 3.—The gale greatly abated last night, and Ranfurly preferred the shelter of a tree to a hut that the soldiers of the station placed at our disposal, and as the minimum night temperature is now as high as 62° there could be no objection to his wish being carried out. During the night he became so much worse that, had not a slight improvement taken place towards morning, it seemed hardly possible that he could reach the coast; and though a decided change for the better can now again be seen, his condition has become the source of the greatest anxiety.

Our calculations about the desertion of the Arabs have already proved but too true, for during the night two of them went off with four camels. No one, of course, had seen them depart, not even the soldiers of the station; but these came forward very readily to assist us to obtain other camels from the local Arabs. At 8.30 A.M., however, none had been found, and as the morning was rapidly advancing, Ranfurly and myself thought it advisable to make a start with all the available camels, whilst Vivian preferred remaining behind to assist Lorenzo in guarding the baggage left for the future arrivals. It was with no small difficulty that even we two were able to be off, for when we told our paragon of a camel-man that we required two of his camels to ride, he looked dreadfully distressed, and, what was more to the point, he decidedly objected to our proposal. After much labour we discovered that he did not like being separated from any of his camels, and when he found that he might follow us with his portion of our baggage as soon as he liked, he was quite willing to give them up to us. After two hours' ride, accompanied by our soldier, besides Ibrahim and a guide, we arrived at a great feeding ground for camels, and found several there. Ibrahim instantly seized one, and having tied up one leg to keep it quiet he went after others, and then came upon a small boy who was watching him. This individual began screaming most lustily, and quickly brought to his side a youth somewhat older than himself. A long parley ensued, and ended in five more being led up to us and taken back to our station by the soldier. We then resumed our journey, and halted at 1.45 P.M. under some mimosas; at 3 P.M. our advance baggage party passed us, and after giving them an hour's start we purposed following them to the next telegraph station. Having timed our camels to walk at over three miles, and the baggage-camels at two and a half miles per hour, we calculated upon catching up with them before sunset, but when darkness set in they were not within hail. As time went on we began to think that our guide must have lost his way, and our fears of this increased proportionately as he changed his course constantly from side to side, until the barking of several dogs far in the distance to our left proved that they had been well founded, for he at once turned off in that direction, and at last, to our great relief, we caught up with the others when wending their way up a hill. On the summit of this hill we found the telegraph station, where all understood we should pass the night. It is a great comfort that Ranfurly finds camel-riding so little fatiguing, and on his arrival here after six hours in the saddle he was certainly less exhausted than myself. The soldiers stationed here have been most willing to lend us any aid, and wanted us to sleep in a straw hut, but we find that placing our angareps outside one is more conducive to comfort and to obtaining air. Coke and party only left here at midday, owing to the weak condition of their camels, and as we found a camel lying in our path which had recently died it probably belonged to them. A few thunderstorms have passed over the desert lately, which have made a great change in the appearance of the mimosas since we last saw them, for

Y

most of them are budding, and in sheltered nooks are quite green, affording a very pleasant contrast to the general desolation surrounding them. The rain must have been heavy, and must have rendered the ground very slippery for camels, judging by the sliding marks made by their hoofs at the time.

May 4.—Another dilemma has arisen, for Vivian's party did not arrive during the night, and as they must have had time to do so by sunrise, it is supposed that they missed the station in the darkness and waited in the neighbourhood for daylight. Ranfurly passed a very restless night, owing to his difficulty of breathing making it necessary for him to sit up very often, but he was so anxious not to lose the morning that I decided at 8 A.M. to comply with his wishes and continue on our way. Before doing so I gave an order to Ibrahim to put sundry requisites into the donkey's saddle-bags for our luncheon, dinner, and breakfast to-morrow, and told Mohamed, whom I left in charge of our stores, that he was to wait till midday at the station, and then, whether or not the others had arrived, he was to follow us to the next station, a ten hours' journey for the baggage-camels.

For two or three hours our course lay in a valley, and we were thus protected from the strong and rapidly rising wind, but after this time we entered upon a vast stony plain, over which it blew in such hot blasts in our faces, as if it had come direct from a furnace and would dry up our very blood, that poor Ranfurly could not endure it, and we were compelled to seek the shelter of a very small mimosa, aided by a bank under which it grew and by a waterproof sheet fastened under its branches. Before arriving here I shot a gazelle, and so supplied our small party with a good luncheon and some strong soup for Ranfurly, and then carefully preserved the rest against future emergencies. At 4 P.M. the wind, though still amounting to a gale from the north-east, was much cooler, and having resumed our journey we progressed very well for a time ; but then a new trial came upon us, almost greater that the last, for we suddenly found ourselves in the midst of a sand-storm which made every thing invisible beyond the radius of a few yards, and rendered it almost impossible to keep the eyes open a moment. Now there was no chance of escape from the blinding storm, not even a stunted mimosa to give us partial protection from it, so on and on we went over the desolate plain, hoping constantly that we might reach some place of shelter, until, after two hours had elapsed, we partially escaped it by entering upon more rocky ground. I had a pair of gauze spectacles and a green veil for Ranfurly, which were a great protection to his face, and, holding on to the pommels of our saddles to prevent being blown off, we continued silently on our way. The wind showed no signs of abatement at sunset, and our camels had so much difficulty in making any way against it that we did not arrive at our station till 9.30 P.M., and we were both then almost equally fatigued. Fortunately we have a little water left in our skins, for the soldiers here declare they have none and cannot get any before the morning, as the mountain where it is found is some distance off, and is frequented by robbers, who would steal the camels if they went there at night. Having had the best dinner our supplies will admit of, we intend sleeping on the waterproof sheet under the protection of a hut, and as we have two pillows and three blankets we ought to manage pretty well. No chance of Mohamed's party arriving to-night, but I hope by to-morrow morning we shall all be together again, for the non-appearance of Vivian this morning has added much to my anxiety.

CHAPTER XIX.

May 5.—Ranfurly has passed a very bad night, and spent a great portion of it sitting on a camel-saddle with his head resting on pillows placed against the hut wall. Towards morning the breathing improved, and he was able to lie down and have a short sleep, which so refreshed him that he wanted to lose no time before being in the saddle again. A necessary delay, however, occurred to get our water-skins filled, and in the meantime I trusted that our party would arrive. At 8.30 A.M. they were not even in sight, and if it was difficult for me to decide how to act for the best yesterday, it became doubly so now, for further delay would mean the loss of a day and of our steamer, whilst going on implied saying good-bye to our baggage and depending upon the few stores we have with us for three or four days. On examination of these stores I found we had the following :—One and a half half-pint tins of Anglo-Swiss condensed milk, two tins of cocoa milk, two small pots of 'Liebig,' one small tin of arrowroot, one box of sardines, one pound of rice, eight 'hard-bake' biscuits, a few dates and figs, a handful of tea, and half a pint of whisky in our old friend the 'telescope' barrel. Two pint saucepans, with spoons, knives, forks, and cups completed the list, excepting the important items of two water-skins and a leathern water-bottle. In fact it amounted to this, that there would be about enough food for Ranfurly, a limited supply of rice for the two men and myself, and that for our meat we must trust to the rifle; and as we had saved half yesterday's gazelle, there was something to start upon. Taking therefore into consideration the very great importance of not losing a day, I decided upon carrying out Ranfurly's wishes, and at the hour named we again turned our steps homewards. Ranfurly is now fully aware of the grave character of his illness, but we say little about it, for all our thoughts are centred in the hope that we may reach Souakim, and this makes him keep up his pluck wonderfully. Frequently I turned round yesterday to look at him, expecting each moment that he would tell me he could no longer face the storm, but the never-failing smile of patient endurance was his silent response. No sand of importance blown up this morning, but the wind has been almost as violent as yesterday, and it was so fatiguing to face it continuously that we were obliged to call a halt after four hours. Gazelle soup and half a pint of 'bread and milk' flavoured with whisky made a good luncheon for Ranfurly, whilst the soup-meat with some rice supplied my wants, and toasted gazelle Ibrahim's; but what was to be done for the Arab, for he refused to eat meat, as it gave him a pain in the stomach? We could not let him starve, so a little rice and a biscuit had to be given him from our precious stores, and with the promise that we would buy some dhurra for him on arrival at the station he fell asleep quite contentedly. But his weak digestion has rather complicated our position, for when we did arrive at our destination the soldiers declared that they had not an atom of dhurra, and that they were entirely dependent upon what they could seize from passing caravans. About sunset we stopped for half an hour to let Ranfurly rest and have a cup of chocolate, and then went on again till 11.30 P.M. The same difficulty again about water as at last station, but we had enough to cook our dinners, and afterwards Ranfurly laid down on an angarep inside a hut. Our guide to-day begged us to try to save his two camels from being taken by the soldiers at Souakim, and his alarm for their safety was probably much increased by our passing a large caravan laden with ammunition, and under a very strong escort. Whatever may be in store for him or them, one thing is certain—viz., that they *shall* go to Souakim, and to prevent any chance of escape I make him stay close to me during the midday halt whilst Ranfurly sleeps, and whilst I occupy my spare time in writing up my diary, and watching the fettered camels as they feed; and at night he remains at my side, and his camels are kept fettered within the enclosure. No gazelle seen to-day, and, should this high wind continue, it would be almost impossible to hold a rifle steady, much less aim straight with eyes blinded by sand.

May 6.—Whatever advantage there may be in halting at telegraph stations, the distance they are from water is one great drawback. Early this morning I sent off the Arab on a camel with some soldiers, and he did not return for five hours. In the meantime, some Arabs arrived and told us that Vivian (by their description) with the baggage was not far behind, so our minds are now relieved from anxiety about him. Shortly afterwards an Arab came to ask for the assistance of the soldiers to bury a man who was lying dead close by, having been robbed and murdered by some Arabs during the night. Ibrahim accompanied them, and told us afterwards that he remembered our passing this man mounted on a camel just before we arrived at the station. Ranfurly had a bad night, being unable to lie down, but towards morning his breathing became again relieved, and he was able to sleep. On the return of our camel-man with the water we were off without further delay, rested from 2 P.M. to 4 P.M., and after a short halt at 7 P.M. we arrived at our station at 10.30 P.M.

The violent gale must have driven the gazelle to the

mountains for protection, for again none have been seen; but as it has gradually abated, I live in hope that the larder may be replenished to-morrow. 'Tis time it should be so, for our remnant of gazelle would not keep over yesterday; our men have therefore been on very short commons. Having bought a fowl in the morning from an old woman before starting, Ranfurly has been able to have some soup without touching our store of Liebig, and the pickings came in very well for me. An excellent lot of soldiers are at this station, and they are very ready to help us, bringing us at once water from a well close by, fire-wood and an angarep, but to our request for dhurra we have only received the same reply as before, adding that they have received no rations for two months, and were entirely dependent all this time upon passers-by.

Our thoughts are now so much taken up with looking forward to the much-desired arrival at Souakim that the fine desert mountain ranges and glorious sunsets are almost passed unnoticed. Not so the moon, however, for with her coming began our troubles; she remained with us throughout them, and as I have watched her career I have tried to be superstitious enough to hope that with her present decline a brighter era might commence for us.

Dream on as we may, the fact of our crossing the desert is ever forced upon our attention by the constantly recurring skeletons or bodies of camels in our path, to some of which we have to give a very wide berth. Though we may not enter Souakim to-morrow night, our journey will then be to all intents and purposes over, for we shall encamp so close to the town that we shall be able to get there early the following morning; and this will be the better plan, for if we arrived there at night we could not cross to the Governor's house on the island, and should be obliged to encamp on our previous most insanitary ground.

May 7.—Before our departure we bought a stout water-skin from an Arab to ensure a sufficient supply, and Ibrahim received orders that this was not to be touched till night. No poultry at this station. Ranfurly had his usual breakfast of bread and milk and cocoa-milk, and just before starting a cup of arrowroot; the Arab and I divided the remnant rice, and Ibrahim was content to wait, as he was sure I should shoot a gazelle for luncheon. At 7 A.M. we were off, and for a time passed over some very rough irregular ground.

Determined not to miss a chance of a shot I would not mount my camel, but kept well ahead of my party. At last in the distance I could see what I supposed was an ariel just disappearing over the crest of a hill without having observed us, so I ran as fast as possible to this point, hoping then to get within shot of it. Unfortunately I miscalculated its movements, for it had not gone on, and as breathless I reached the top of the hill I saw it scampering off from a point close to me ; and, to add to my annoyance, I found that instead of its being an ariel it was the first ibex seen by any of our party. Three hours passed, and still nothing for the pot, and I was almost beginning to despair of finding any gazelle when the Arab pointed some out to me about two hundred yards off, and then by a lucky shot, having to allow for a strong wind, I knocked one over. Seldom have men enjoyed a luncheon more than we did ours on this gazelle, and even Ranfurly found himself equal to eating a good portion of the 'roasted' liver whilst his soup was undergoing a slower process of cooking. The Arab had quite forgotten his objections, but from the quantity he consumed he ought to have every reason to remember them again.

Still it is not to the quantity of gazelle he chooses to eat that we have any objection, but to the amount of water he drinks, for if he gets his mouth to the neck of a full skin he nearly empties it unless compelled to give it up ; and if a careful watch had not been kept over our skins, he would have soon exhausted our daily supply. Four hours' rest during the heat of the day, which of late, owing to the wind, has not been at all oppressive, and another of half an hour before sunset, enabled Ranfurly to proceed without experiencing much fatigue until 10.30 P.M., when, finding a moderately good tree to protect us from any wind that might arise in the night, we settled down to cook and eat our last desert dinner, and to rejoice over the news that when there would be sufficient light we should be able to see Souakim. A dreadful blow then occurred to our happiness and to our prospect of dinner on Ibrahim telling us that the new water-skin which was slung from Ranfurly's saddle had been burst by a blow in the darkness, and was quite empty. Collecting then the remnant of the other skins, it only amounted to a pint and a half. With a portion of this Ranfurly was able to have a cup of chocolate and some arrowroot, and myself some of the latter, whilst our men had to content themselves with the prospect of arriving early in the morning at Souakim. A cup of bread and milk was then placed by Ranfurly's side for the night, and he soon fell into a sound sleep. He finds one great comfort in an excellent pillow belonging to Vivian, and it is his constant companion by night and by day. The stores have lasted very well, for though Ranfurly has always had some light food five or six times in the twenty-four hours there still remains a little which would be quickly consumed now but for the want of water, and for the same reason the gazelle is left unroasted.

May 8.—The desert journey is over, Souakim is reached, and our long-desired goal is won, and not an hour too soon; for beyond a cup of chocolate for

Ranfurly, no fluid could pass our lips before leaving our resting-place at 6 A.M., and when we reached our haven of rest soon after 8 A.M. the sun was becoming unpleasantly felt by men who had been so many hours without water. As we entered the town several soldiers followed us to the pier, to carry off our two wretched camels so soon as we should dismount. Our Arab besought us to protect him from them, and they promised not to take possession of his camels until after we had seen the Governor concerning them.

Directly after we landed on the island we met Coke and Cumming on their way to a boat to be taken on board the mail steamer, as she had arrived a day sooner than was expected, and was then starting for Suez. As another, now in harbour, had been advertised to leave to-morrow, Arkwright preferred postponing his departure that he might if possible rejoin his old companion Ranfurly; and I was very glad to hear them all say that they thought he was looking better than when we left them at Kassala. Arkwright introduced us to his friend Ali Effendi, the Steam Packet Company's agent, who had kept open house for the first arrivals since yesterday, and now wished to extend his hospitality to us. Words cannot fully express how thankful we were to find ourselves, after our long and anxious desert journey, lying on comfortable Persian carpets and cushions in a cool and airy room; and it seemed now as if our troubles had really terminated, and that we might rest mind and body, and look forward with more hope to the future. The day had not far advanced, however, before Ranfurly began to wish himself in the saddle again; for though we had a constant relay of boys to fan off the flies, they were a source of great annoyance to him, and his breathing was more oppressed than usual. When the wind was moderate, he always had said that he preferred the swinging motion of the camel to sitting still, as it somehow appeared to assist his breathing.

At 6 P.M. Vivian arrived, and he was in such an exhausted state that he could barely walk the few yards distance from the boat to our house without support, and he then threw himself down on an angerep and almost fainted away. When he had been allowed a little time to recover himself, he declared he had never felt so done in his life; and that had his day's journey required another hour to accomplish it, he must have spent another night in the desert. On arriving at the second telegraph station from Souakim, he heard that we were just in front of him; and at once pushed on, hoping to catch us up and add something to our supplies, which Mohamed reported to be most limited; and at the last station he left the baggage, and rode on with an Arab guide expecting momentarily all day to see us. We had been more fortunate in our riding camels, and had latterly exceeded our ordinary three-mile rate per hour, whereas his own had to be changed twice; and on one occasion they so completely broke down that he was compelled, on meeting a mounted native, to force him to make an exchange of animals. Ali Effendi gave us an excellent dinner at sunset, besides having sent us some good soup and boiled chicken during the day; and Ranfurly was able to sit at the table for a short time, and have soup, omelettes, and 'mishmish,' all of which he appeared to enjoy.

May 9.—When I laid down last night near Ranfurly I looked forward to our both having a few hours' sound sleep; but my hopes were destined to be soon disappointed, for hardly had he closed his eyes before he showed a tendency to delirium. Towards midnight he dozed off quietly, and being myself very weary I, also, fell asleep. Suddenly I woke up with a start, and found him seated up in bed and praying aloud. Almost breathless, I listened, fearing to disturb his thoughts; until having repeated slowly, and with intense earnestness, the Lord's Prayer, he became silent. I then went to his side, and after a few moments' conversation with him he leant his head on my shoulder and fell into a deep sleep. This morning there was such a manifest improvement in his breathing, and he has felt so much better all day, that we have become far more hopeful about him. There has been much to arrange. First of all, Ali Effendi positively refused to allow us to go on board the steamer till the passage-money was paid, which could not be done till the arrival of our baggage. We therefore had to pay a visit to the Governor to ask him to give an order to that effect, and we at the same time reported the infamous conduct of the Hadendowa Arabs, the delay of our baggage, and our desire consequently that the departure of the steamer might be delayed a few hours so that we might take it with us. As the Governor could speak no other language than Arabic, we were obliged to take as our interpreter Ibrahim, upon whose slight knowledge of French we have had so long to depend; but he got so drunk last night with Arkwright's cook that he continues in a most muddled state, and when he was brought into the august presence of the Governor he could not speak from fright, and we had to turn him out. It so happened that at the time of our visit a Maltese was present, who speaks English and Arabic equally fluently, and he very kindly acted as our interpreter.

The Governor, whom we reminded of the original firman from the Khedive presented by us to his representative on our arrival here, promised all the assistance in his power. He gave us an order for the payment of our passage, if necessary, after our arrival at Suez, and at once despatched a soldier on a fast dromedary to meet our baggage, and then to come back as quickly as possible and report the probable time of its arrival. Our Maltese interpreter, Emanuel Chassaro, is the captain of a small Egyptian gunboat stationed here. He served for some years in the English navy, and, amongst other men-of-war, on board the 'Agamemnon' when commanded by Captain, now Admiral, Sir Thomas Symonds, of whom he has evidently the happiest recollections; and when he found that we knew his late master he became doubly anxious to serve us.

The next proceeding was to lay in a good stock of provisions for the sea voyage, having, as before, to find our own supplies on board.

The chief Greek stores are on the island, and after obtaining there nearly all that we required, we crossed over to the mainland and inspected the small shops on each side of the chief thoroughfare without being able to add anything beyond some very good-tasting bread and a few eggs, for Mohamed had the commission to buy our live stock of sheep and poultry there. The bazaar was well thronged with people in very varied costumes. Some men were very gorgeously attired after Eastern fashion, and though most of them had their splendid heads of hair coated with a white layer of fat, a few had it dyed a bright red colour.

All the women were unveiled and enveloped more or less in a white robe, and, besides numerous bracelets of silver, wore the usual ornament of a ring in the right nostril. Some of the young girls whom we saw squatting round their small stores of seed had features that, minus the colour of their skin, many a European girl might with good cause envy. But of all hideous forms of living humanity, it is impossible to imagine anything could exceed that of the almost naked old woman water-carrier, as she toils along bent nearly double to support the well-filled skin she carries on her back. On our return to Ali Effendi's house we received a visit from a most sickly-looking Greek, who tried to be on very familiar terms with us, but when he began to give a minute account of his illness to Ranfurly we gave him more than a hint to be off, and then we discovered that the purport of his visit was to ask for money to pay for his passage by our steamer. Considering the state of our finances his trouble was clearly to no purpose, but he was not at all disposed to believe that our position was exactly similar to his own, so far as want of cash was concerned. The Vakeel, or Under-governor, who first received us, is still alive and well, notwithstanding our liberal present of medicine, and he even asked for more. This time we gave him in addition six bottles of whisky in return for his kindness in taking charge of the stores we left here, consisting of, amongst other things, champagne, claret, and soda-water, and with these no one feels disposed to find fault now. Besides constant relays of coffee, our host Ali Effendi has given us two excellent feeds per diem. In the centre of the table round which we all sat was placed a large metal tray laden with sundry dishes, whilst others were laid on the floor under the charge of a domestic, whose time was fully occupied in whisking off the thousands of flies and keeping several cats at a distance. Our late habits of life made it easy for us to fall in with those of our host and dip our spoons into the common bowl of soup, and afterwards to practically accept the doctrine that fingers were made before knives and forks by diving into the several plates of mutton, beef, and poultry cut into small pieces, and free from an excess of 'butter,' garlic, or other horrible addition. Besides these, we had rice, mishmish, olives, bread soaked in 'butter,' and bread dry, bread new, and bread old, but the *pièce de résistance* to all was a pile of pancakes, very heavy and rather cold, which began and ended each repast, and, though sufficiently palatable to attract more than a passing notice, it was not, we found afterwards to our cost, the *most* digestible food we had eaten for some months. Ali Effendi is almost turned out of his house by our large party, but he does not appear to mind it. About sunset yesterday, and again early this morning, twenty to thirty poor people collected near his house, to each of whom he gave one or two small loaves of bread from a basket which a small boy carried on his head in front of his master as he walked amongst them, and whatever motive may influence him in this system of charity, it was evidently not got up for our special observation. Another kind act he does for the poor is to have a large tank outside his house well filled with water, where they can always drink or fill their jars; but somehow the man's expression belies his acts, and gives the impression, however false it may be, that they have something beyond charity for their basis. Still he does good in his generation, and probably few other men here follow his example. The heat has been oppressive to-day, owing to the absence of any wind, so Ranfurly remained in a darkened room until near sunset, when we took him on board the steamer 'Coffeet' lying at anchor in the harbour just outside the town. We had previously chosen a comfortable cabin for him, and he went directly into it, and appeared much pleased with the change, as a pleasant breeze rising at the time made it cool and airy. The first engineer, named Bock, is an Englishman, and he is very anxious to serve us; and if neither our baggage nor servants arrive before our departure to-morrow, he will be a valuable acquisition, and especially as the whole crew from the captain downwards are Egyptians, excepting the second engineer, who is also an Englishman.

CHAPTER XX.

May 10 (*noon*).—Ranfurly has passed a very restless night, but now and again he fell into a sound sleep, especially towards morning, when he awoke feeling much refreshed, and after having had some chocolate and soup he came on deck, and is now lying on a sofa in Mr. Bock's cabin.

The departure of the steamer has been put off from hour to hour by Ali Effendi, but he is puzzled to know how to act for the best without involving himself in any risk. The main portion of our baggage arrived late last night, but as Lorenzo, a little way behind it, is still absent with Ranfurly's baggage, and as he is particularly wanted for Ranfurly now that Ibrahim has left us, Ali Effendi has at last yielded the point, and to allay his fears Arkwright has given him an explanatory letter to the Admiral of the Port.

Night.—Ranfurly is dead, and it is well therefore that the departure of the 'Coffeet' was postponed, for now can be performed on land the last sad office for his remains, which may be a source of some small comfort to the relatives who have to mourn his loss. Throughout the day he suffered from the most profuse perspiration, but he was able to hold a long conversation with Mr. Bock, and spoke to him hopefully of the future. In the afternoon I took him by his request to his cabin, when, complaining of feeling very weak, he laid down. In a few minutes he dozed off, but wandered very much at times until the evening, when on being raised by his wish to have some food he instantly turned deadly faint, and after being laid down again at once he was with difficulty revived by stimulants and by rubbing the extremities. Lorenzo arrived just at this time, and Ranfurly became sufficiently conscious to be able to give him a look of recognition, though he did not attempt to speak; and then so gradually and tranquilly did he fall into his last sleep, that it was impossible to fix by some moments the exact time about sunset when the dread words had to be said that all was over for him whom we had so much loved.

Vivian shortly went on shore to make arrangements with the Governor for the funeral to take place early to-morrow morning, and received from him the promise that men should be kept at work all night. Our first idea was to bring poor Ranfurly's remains to England, but we found that this was impossible from the means not being at hand; and we have therefore consented to their being laid in some ground on an island near the ship's anchorage, which has been set apart for the burial of Europeans, of whom a few already rest there.

May 11.—The coffin was brought at sunrise, and very soon all preparations were completed and the mournful ceremony commenced. The Governor of Souakim, Alli Addeen Bey, and all the other officials were present and joined the procession, which included, besides Vivian and Arkwright, Mr. Bock, who has rendered us some special service, the second engineer, and the two engineers of the Egyptian steamer, 'Samanood' (a troop-ship waiting in harbour for the arrival of the young Prince of Darfour), these being the only Englishmen here, and upon me fell the painful duty of performing the last office for the dead, whilst the crew were formed up in line on either side of us.

Our utmost thanks are due to Alli Addeen Bey for the promptitude with which he has come to our aid. He has taken all the necessary arrangements for the burial entirely into his own hands, and by having about fifty men at work all night a grave was dug out of a bed of chalk, and walled in by this morning. In fact, though a perfect stranger to us, he has not only given us every assistance in his official capacity, but has also made us feel that his heart, as that of a true friend, has been in the work, and from which he never rested until, after heading the procession to the grave and remaining there till the service was completed, he shook hands with us and bade s farewell, whilst we attempted as best we could to thank him for all he had done for us. Ranfurly's head rests on his favourite pillow, which is covered with black satin, and the tomb is situated next to one bearing the name of Dr. Simpson on a stone slab, and as a temporary measure a stone cross will be placed over it.

It is a curious coincidence that it was on this small island that Ranfurly first set foot on arriving in this country. How little could he have thought that over the ground upon which he then stood his lifeless body would so soon be carried!

The Governor has telegraphed to the Khedive, and we have done so to General Stanton, as we cannot send a message farther than Cairo by the only available route —viz., viâ Kassala.

The 'Coffeet' left harbour about 11 A.M., and this evening finds us far away from Souakim, now so painfully associated in our minds with the events of the last two days.

The 'Coffeet' is an old English screw steamer, the 'Sydney,' which for many years ran between England and Australia. There are no passengers excepting ourselves and the sickly Greek youth, who we find is just recovering from a fever. His passage was paid for by a general subscription. Our Maltese friend at Souakim, Captain Chassaro, says that a consul is sadly wanted there to represent the chief nationalities, for from one hundred and fifty to two hundred Europeans arrive there annually, and many are much in need of assistance, pecuniary or otherwise. A fresh breeze directly ahead of us, though very pleasant as yet, promises, according to the Egyptian captain, a rough passage to Suez.

May 12.—The wind has greatly increased, and the sea has been running so high all day that we have spent the greater part of it on our backs. Thanks, however, to the Greek, we have had something to interest us, for he told Arkwright this morning that he had seen one of the crew stealing the claws from the package of our lions' skins. This is a very old grievance, and one that we have always done our best to guard against, knowing what great value the natives attach to both nails and whiskers as charms. Arkwright at once wrote to the captain to complain of the theft, adding that if they were not returned the matter should be reported to the Viceroy, and Mr. Bock translated the note to him. This so frightened him that he set to work with a will to find out the culprit, whom unfortunately the Greek could not recognise, and failing to do so he adopted the following plan to obtain the lost property—viz., to muster the crew, and tell them that basins containing sawdust would be placed on each deck, so that the claws might be dropped into them at night without the thief being observed; and if they were found there in the morning nothing more would be said, but if not found every man would be flogged in turn until they were given up. Mr. Bock says that the captain is very anxious about this matter, for on a recent occasion of a somewhat similar kind the Viceroy summarily dismissed every man from the ship, not excluding the captain.

Vivian some time ago found some claws in a curious way. The paws of his burnt lion had been left by the river's side to be cleaned, and they disappeared. It was naturally supposed that our Arabs had stolen them, but they threw the blame on the Marabou storks, and as one was near at the time it was shot, and upon opening the throat two claws were found inside it. Now that it is too late we regret we did not kill a few more of these birds, and collect the beautiful feathers that are under their tails.

May 13.—After breakfast the captain came to Arkwright with a grave face, and presented him with some minute objects which he said had been found in the basins, and asked him if they were the lost property, though they were only the points of the claw of a very small crab or other shell-fish, and required a close inspection of the palm of his hand to see them at all. The night's experiment having therefore signally failed, the crew were assembled and the flogging process commenced.

It had not proceeded far before Mr. Bock reported it

to us and begged us to stop it, for he declared that the captain would go right through the crew if necessary, so we then made him promise to postpone the operation until to-morrow, and give the crew another chance by a repetition of last night's experiment. The mode of flogging was to make the victim lie down on his face with his hands crossed behind him, when one man sat on his shoulders, and another on his legs, whilst the boatswain vigorously applied a knotted rope-end to that part of the body which nature has so well adapted to this purpose.

It has been blowing a gale nearly all day from the north-west, and our speed not having been more than two knots an hour, the captain wanted to anchor and wait for better weather, but the engineers' advice to struggle on against it prevailed with him.

In the afternoon a sudden crash startled us all very much, and nearly frightened the Greek out of his life. It was caused by the rudder-chain breaking, and the result was general confusion amongst the crew, in which shouts of 'Stop! stop!' as they rushed about were heard in every direction. The engines having been at last stopped, the steamer for a few moments became motionless, and then in swinging round she caught the full force of the wind and sea against her side and heaved over, first on one side and then on the other, to such an extent that it was only by holding on with all our might to anything within reach that we escaped from being hurt by a little too rapid travelling over the deck, whilst the general breakage of everything movable was the inevitable result. Mr. Bock told me in the morning that he thought the chain would break owing to the great pitching of the steamer from her having no cargo beyond two or three hundred tons of gum and hides. A priest (?) came this evening to tell us that he had had a dream, and had discovered by it that two men were implicated in the theft of lions' claws and that he could give their names. Upon further questioning him, he declared them to be two of Mr. Bock's best men who were on duty at the time, and therefore could not have been absent. It was, however, a happy dream, for Mr. Bock would certainly not have quietly allowed these men to be flogged, so by the general wish the matter was allowed to drop.

May 16.—The 'Coffeet' has arrived at Suez, and as there is a mail train starting immediately with Indian passengers for Alexandria, I have decided upon accepting this chance of travelling with all speed to England, as the bearer of our sad news, whilst Arkwright and Vivian remain behind to look after the baggage. Our goats are still with us, and Mohamed has been given one, and an engineer the other.

May 17.—I have joined Coke and Cumming on board the P. and O. steamer 'Malta.' Captain Hyde, who is in command of her, has been most kind in making all the arrangements he can for my comfort on deck, as there is no berth vacant; and a lady on board has given me the most useful present of a felt hat to replace my completely worn-out helmet. Our telegram from Souakim reached Cairo in three days, and now we are already far away from the land where we have left a valued friend to pay the penalty of our rash venture in 'Life with the Hamran Arabs.'

APPENDIX.

WEATHER REPORT.

Date	Locality	Weather Report	Min.	Max. in Shade	Max. in Sun	Temp. two to three hours after sunset
			°F.	°F.	°F.	°F.
1874						
Dec. 13	Cairo	— —	44			
14	,,	— —	41			
15	,,	— —	42			
16	,,	— —	42			
17	,,	— —	41			
20	,,	— —	43			
21	,, to Suez	— —	47			
22	Suez to Souakim	Cloudy—fresh breeze S.E.	57			
23	Red Sea	,, light ,,	69	82		
24	,,	Cloudless ,, ,,	75			
25	,,	Cloudy ,, ,,	76	84		
26	,,	,, ,, ,,	78	86		
27	Souakim	,, ,, ,,	76	89		
28	,,	Cloudless ,, ,,	76	90		
29	,,	—				
30	Souakim to Kassala	Cloudy—heavy dew	66			
31	,,	,, two slight showers at night	70			
1875						
Jan. 1	,,	Cloudy—wind N.E.	67			
2	,,	,, ,,	68			
3	,,	,, ,,	65			
4	,,	,, ,,	65			
5	,,	Cloudless ,,	65			
6	,,	,, ,,	55			
7	,,	,, ,,	55			
8	,,	,, ,,	57			
9	,,	,, ,, heavy dew	44			
10	,,	,, wind W.	53			

WEATHER REPORT—continued.

Date	Locality	Weather Report	Temperature			
			Min.	Max. in Shade	Max. in Sun	Temp. two to four hours, after sunset
			°F.	°F.	°F.	°F.
1875 Jan. 11	Souakim to Kassala	Light clouds—wind N.W.	47			
12	,,	,, ,, N.E.	44			
13	,, (arr.)	,, ,, N.E.	54			
14	Kassala	Cloudless ,, N.W.	51	81	115	
15	,,	,, ,, N.W.	53	80		
16	Kassala to Hamran village	,, ,, N.W.	55	81		
17	,,	Light clouds ,, N.E.	49	85		
18	,,	,, ,, N.E.	51			
19	,, (arr.)	,, ,, N.W.	51			
20	Hamran village	,, ,, N.E.	49	81		
21	Hamran village to Zahani	,, ,, N.E.	43	83		
22	Zahani to Gadamur	Cloudless—wind N.E., very light	51			
23	Gadamur	,, ,, N.W. ,,	45	85		
24	,,	,, ,, N.W. ,,	33	81		
25	,,	,, ,, N.E. ,,	53	83		
26	Gadamur to Emberaga	,, ,, N.W. ,,	47			
27	Emberaga	,, ,, N.W. ,,	35			
28	Emberaga to El Effaara	,, ,, N.W. ,,	47			
29	El Effaara	,, ,, N.W. ,,	55	89	127	
30	,,	,, ,, N.W. ,,	50	91	118	76
31	,,	,, ,, N. ,,	54	92	130	78
Feb. 1	El Effaara to Emhagga	,, ,, N.W. to E.	48			
2	Emhagga	,, ,, N.W., very light	50			
3	,,	,, ,, N.E. ,,	52	91	131	80
4	,,	Light clouds ,, variable ,,	55	95	133	80
5	,,	Cloudless ,, N.W. ,,	52	94	135	80
6	,,	,, ,, N.W. ,,	49	90	134	78
7	,,	,, ,, N.W. ,,	47	93	135	79
8	,,	,, ,, N.W. ,,	49	94	137	79
9	,,	,, ,, N.W. ,,	47	94	145	82
10	,,	,, ,, N.W. ,,	50	93	139	80
11	,,	,, ,, N.E. ,,	51	91	137	75
12	,,	,, ,, N.E. to S.E. ,,	51	97	142	83

WEATHER REPORT—continued.

Date	Locality	Weather Report	Temperature			
			Min.	Max. in Shade	Max. in Sun	Temp. two to three hours after sunset
			°F.	°F.	°F.	°F.
1875 Feb. 13	Emhagga	Cloudless—wind N.E., hot blasts	50	96	137	75
14	,,	Cloudy in ,, S.E. ,, evening	47	93	131	73
15	,,	Light clouds ,, S.W. ,,	50	92	130	73
16	,,	Mist—wind S. to S.E. ,,	60	87	122	73
17	,,	Occasional clouds—wind N. to N.E., gusty	40	89	115	78
18	,,	Very cloudy morning—wind N. to N.E., gusty	52	91	117	75
19	Emhagga to Henna	Cloudless—wind N.E.	43	—	—	78
20	Henna to Berket Johda (Royan)	,, ,, S.S.E. to S.	47	—	133	
21	Berket Johda	,, , S.E.	48	—	125	
22	,,	,, ,, S.W.	48			
23	Berket Johda to Immam	,, ,, S.	47			
24	Immam	,, ,, S.W.	47	95		
25	Immam to Berket Johda	,, ,, N.W.	49			
26	Berket Johda to El-la-Mab	,, ,, N.E.	48			
27	El-la-Mab	,, ,, N.	48			
28	,,	,, ,, N.W.	43	90	130	
Mar. 1	,,	,, ,, S.W.	39	90	130	
2	,,	,, ,, N.E.	44	91	130	
3	El-la-Mab to Eddebabeha	,, ,, N.	47	91	132	
4	Eddebabeha (Settite)	,, ,, E.S.E.	50	93	130	
5	,,	,, ,, E.S.E.	55	93	130	
6	,,	Thunderstorm over Abyssinia—wind N.E.	59	94	125	
7	,,	Cloudless—wind N., strong breeze	60	93	120	
8	,,	,, ,, N.W. ,, at night	60	90	115	
9	,,	,, ,, N.W.	60	90	118	
10	,,	,, ,, N.W.	62	90	120	
11	,,	,, ,, N.W.	60	92	125	
12	,,	,, ,, N.W.	59	92	128	

A A

WEATHER REPORT—*continued*.

Date	Locality	Weather Report	Temperature			
			Min.	Max. in Shade	Max. in Sun	Temp. two to three hours after sunset
1875			°F.	°F.	°F.	°F.
Mar. 13	Eddebabeha (Settite)	Cloudless—wind N.W.	65	93	135	
14	,,	,, ,, N.W.	66	95	130	
15	,,	—	—	—		
16	,,	Cloudy ,, N.W.	65	97	135	
17	Eddebabeha to Hel-Egheeme	—	65			
18	Hel-Egheeme	Thunderstorm over Abyssinia—wind N.W.	63	—	145	
19	,,	Cloudy ,, N.E.	65	—	140	
20	,,	Thunderstorm on all sides—wind N.E. to S.W.	65	100	145	
21	,,	Cloudless —	67	100	148	
22	,,	Light clouds—wind N.W.	62	100	143	
23	,,	,, ,, S.W.	62	102	147	
24	,,	,, ,, S.W.	65	105	152	
25	,,	,, ,, S.W.	62	105	153	
26	,,	,, ,, N.W.	60	105	152	
27	,,	,, ,, N.W. misty morning	60	100	140	
28	Hel-Egheeme to El-Effaara	Mist all day—wind N.W.	62			
29	El-Effaara	Light clouds ,,	48	95	128	
30	,,	,, ,,	52	101	134	
31	El-Effaara to Emberaga	,, ,,	60			
Apr. 1	Emberaga	,, ,,	70	105	140	
2	,,	,, ,,	—	105	140	
3	,,	,, ,,	66	108	140	
4	,,	Cloudless —				
5	Emberaga to Hel-Egheeme	,, —	60			
6	Hel-Egheeme	,, —	58	97	150	
7	,,	,, —	45	99	150	
8	,,	,, —	58	100	150	
9	,,	,, —	60	100	148	
10	,,	,, —	55	100	140	
11	,,	,, —	52	100	150	
12	,,	,, —	55	99	148	
13	,,	,, —	52	102	155	
14	He'-Egheeme to Amaretakari	,, —	58			

APPENDIX. 355

WEATHER REPORT—continued.

Date	Locality	Weather Report		Temperature			
				Min.	Max. in Shade	Max. in Sun	Temp. two to three hours after sunset
1875				°F.	°F.	°F.	°F.
Apr. 15	Amaretakari	Cloudless	—	—	105	148	
16	,,	,,	—	65	108	150	
17	Amaretakari to Emberaga	,,	—	68	110	156	
18	Emberaga to Hamran village	,,	Heavy fall of rain with thunder at night	68			
19	Hamran village to Kassala	,,	—				
20	,,	,,	—	74			
21	,,	,,	—				
22	,,	,,	—	—	102	125	
23	Kassala	,,	—	—	100	125	
24	,,	,,	—	65	100	130	
25	Kassala to Souakim	,,	—	62	100	125	
26	,,	,,	—	58	98	125	
27	,,	,,	—	62			
28	,,	,,	wind S.E. to N.W.	58			
29	,,	,,	,,	55	100	130	
30	,,	,,	,, S.E. to N.E.	52	98	132	
May 1	,,	,,	,, N.N.E. to S.E.	50	98	125	
2	,,	,,	,, E. to N., a gale	62	92	117	
3	,,	,,	,, E. to N., gale stronger	62			
4	,,	,,	,, E. to N., gale	63			
5	,,	,,	,, N. to N.E. ,,	68			
6	,,	,,	,, N.E., strong gale	62	92	118	
7	,,	,,	,, N.E., fresh	56	92	125	
8	,,	,,	,, N., slight	62			
9	Souakim	,,	—	—	89		

SMITH, ELDER, & CO.'S NEW BOOKS.

LIFE WITH THE HAMRAN ARABS: a Sporting Tour of some Officers of the Guards in the Soudan during the Winter of 1874–75. By ARTHUR B. R. MYERS, Surgeon, Coldstream Guards. With Photographic Illustrations. Crown 8vo. 12s.

STUDIES OF GREEK POETS. SECOND SERIES. By JOHN ADDINGTON SYMONDS, M.A. Crown 8vo. 10s. 6d.

ETRUSCAN BOLOGNA. By Captain R. F. BURTON. With numerous Illustrations. [*Nearly ready.*]

HUMAN NATURE: a Mosaic of Sayings, Maxims, Opinions, and Reflections on Life and Character. Selected and Arranged by DAVID W. MITCHELL, Author of 'Ten Years in the United States.' Fcp. 8vo. 5s.

INTOLERANCE AMONG CHRISTIANS. By the Hon. ALBERT S. G. CANNING. Crown 8vo. 5s.

FRENCH PICTURES IN ENGLISH CHALK. By the Author of 'The Member for Paris' &c. &c. Crown 8vo. 7s. 6d.

HOURS IN A LIBRARY. Second Series. By LESLIE STEPHEN. Crown 8vo. 9s.

THE SHORES OF LAKE ARAL. By HERBERT WOOD, Major, Royal Engineers. With Maps. 14s.

THE LIFE OF GOETHE. By GEORGE HENRY LEWES. Third Edition. Revised according to the Latest Documents. Demy 8vo. with Portrait, 16s.

EVOLUTION OF THE HUMAN RACE FROM APES a Doctrine Unsanctioned by Science. By THOMAS WHARTON JONES, F.R.S. Demy 8vo. 4s.

Second Edition. Now ready.

A LIFE OF THE EARL OF MAYO, Fourth Viceroy of India. With a Narrative of his Indian Administration. By W. W. HUNTER, B.A. LL.D. 2 vols. demy 8vo. 24s.

'A work of literary art and rare excellence. A most valuable and profoundly interesting work.'—HOME NEWS.

'A most artistic and graphic portraiture.'—DAILY TELEGRAPH.

'Nothing could exceed the completeness with which Dr. Hunter has told the story of a noble life and of a great career, and he has done it in a manner that may fairly be described as masterly.'—HOUR.

ESSAYS ON THE EXTERNAL POLICY OF INDIA. By the late J. W. S. WYLLIE, M.A. C.S.I. of H.M. Indian Civil Service, sometime Acting Foreign Secretary to the Government of India. Edited, with a Memoir and Notes, by W. W. HUNTER, B.A. LL.D. 8vo. with Portrait, 14s.

London: SMITH, ELDER, & CO., 15 Waterloo Place.

SMITH, ELDER, & CO.'S NEW BOOKS—*continued*.

STRAY PAPERS. By JOHN ORMSBY, Author of 'Autumn Rambles in North Africa.' Crown 8vo. 7s. 6d.

'A charming book of essays.'—PICTORIAL WORLD.
'Mr. Ormsby is a keen observer, has a very happy knack of description, and a humour at once rich and abundant.'—SCOTSMAN.

ESSAYS ON SOCIAL SUBJECTS. By 'JACOB OMNIUM.' With a Memoir by Sir WILLIAM STIRLING MAXWELL, Bart., M.P. Crown 8vo. with Two Portraits, 9s.

'A very amusing and interesting book.'—SATURDAY REVIEW.

AS LIFE ITSELF. By the Author of 'Clare Peyce's Diary.' Fcp. 8vo. 4s.

'A little volume of charming verse, which fully entitles the authoress to a name and place amongst the poets of the present generation. A touching story in excellent verse.'
COURT JOURNAL.

THE SOLDIER OF FORTUNE: a Tragedy in Five Acts. By J. LEICESTER WARREN, M.A., Author of 'Philoctetes.' Fcp. 8vo. 9s.

'It is almost impossible to open a page without coming across some idea or expression, probably a score of ideas and expressions, of striking and original beauty.'—ACADEMY.

THE KING'S SACRIFICE, and other Poems. Fcp. 8vo. 9s.

NEW NOVELS.

Two vols, demy 8vo. 21s.

THE HAND OF ETHELBERTA.
By THOMAS HARDY,
AUTHOR OF 'FAR FROM THE MADDING CROWD.'
With 11 Illustrations by George du Maurier.

LOLA: a Tale of the Rock. By ARTHUR GRIFFITHS, Author of 'The Queen's Shilling,' 'Memorials of Millbank,' &c. &c. 3 vols.

A MADRIGAL, and other Stories. By the Author of 'The Rose Garden.'

PARLEY MAGNA. By EDWARD WHITAKER, Author of 'Lucy Fitzadam.' 2 vols.

'Mr. Whitaker's book is clean and wholesome, as well as exceedingly clever.'—STANDARD.
'A story possessing an indescribable charm; it is thoroughly original in its conception, and its genuine humour is altogether free from coarseness or vulgarity.'—COURT JOURNAL.

A VERY WOMAN. By M. F. O'MALLEY. 3 vols.

'One of the freshest novels that it has been our fate to read for some time.'
COURT CIRCULAR.
'A clever and well-written novel, with much grace, spirit, and imaginative power, as well as skill in the delineation of character.'—SCOTSMAN.

London: SMITH, ELDER, & CO., 15 Waterloo Place.

www.ingramcontent.com/pod-product-compliance
Lightning Source LLC
Chambersburg PA
CBHW022334230426
43664CB00040B/545